The New School of Information Security

The New School of Information Security

Adam Shostack and Andrew Stewart

Addison-Wesley

Upper Saddle River, NJ • Boston • Indianapolis • San Francisco
New York • Toronto • Montreal • London • Munich • Paris • Madrid
Cape Town • Sydney • Tokyo • Singapore • Mexico City

U.S. Corporate and Government Sales
800-382-3419
corpsales@pearsontechgroup.com

For sales outside the United States, please contact:

International Sales
international@pearson.com

Visit us on the Web at informit.com/aw.

Editor-in-Chief
Karen Gettman

Acquisitions Editor
Jessica Goldstein

Managing Editor
Gina Kanouse

Project Editor
Anne Goebel

Copy Editor
Gayle Johnson

Indexer
Cheryl Lenser

Publishing Coordinator
Andrea Bledsoe

Cover Designer
Adam Shostack
Andrew Stewart

Composition
Jake McFarland

Library of Congress Cataloging-in-Publication Data:

Shostack, Adam.
The new school of information security / Adam Shostack and Andrew Stewart.
p. cm.
Includes bibliographical references.
ISBN 0-321-50278-7 (hardback : alk. paper) 1. Information technology—Security measures. 2. Computer security. 3. Computer security equipment industry. 4. Business—Data processing—Security measures. I. Stewart, Andrew, 1975- II. Title.

HD30.2.S563 2008
658.4'78—dc22

2007052580

Pearson Education, Inc
Rights and Contracts Department
501 Boylston Street, Suite 900
Boston, MA 02116
Fax: (617) 671 3447

ISBN-13: 978-0-321-50278-0
ISBN-10: 0-321-50278-7

Text printed in the United States on recycled paper at RR Donnelly in Crawfordsville, Indiana.
First printing March 2008

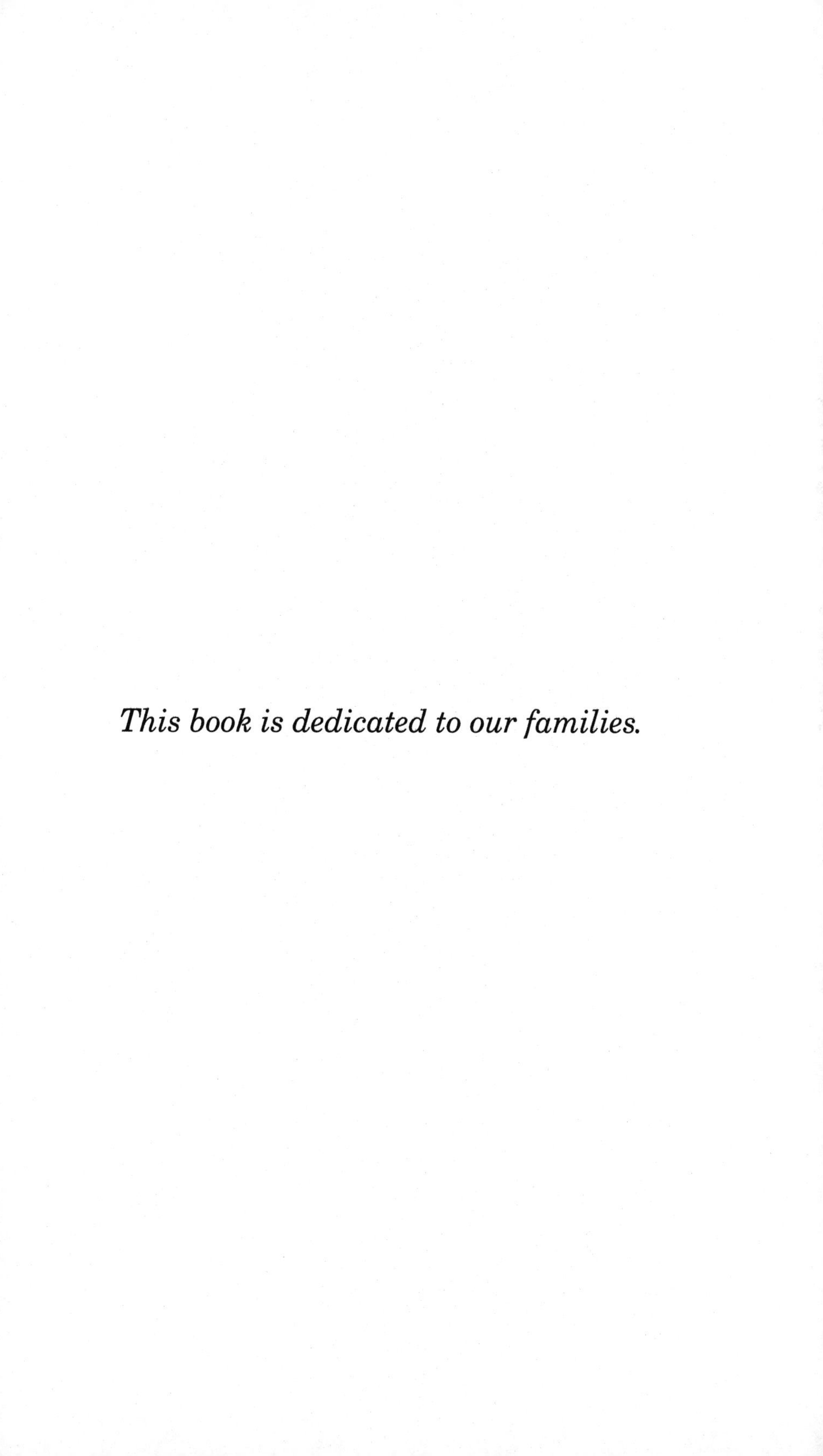

This book is dedicated to our families.

Contents

OBSERVING THE WORLD AND ASKING WHY	Spam, and Other Problems with Email	4
	Hostile Code	7
	Security Breaches	9
	Identity and the Theft of Identity	11
	Should We Just Start Over?	14
	The Need for a New School	15
THE SECURITY INDUSTRY	Where the Security Industry Comes From	19
	Orientations and Framing	25
	What Does the Security Industry Sell?	27
	How Security Is Sold	33
ON EVIDENCE	The Trouble with Surveys	46
	The Trade Press	50
	Vulnerabilities	52
	Instrumentation on the Internet	54
	Organizations and Companies with Data	55
THE RISE OF THE SECURITY BREACH	How Do Companies Lose Data?	64
	Disclose Breaches	68
	Possible Criticisms of Breach Data	70
	Moving from Art to Science	74
	Get Involved	76
AMATEURS STUDY CRYPTOGRAPHY; PROFESSIONALS STUDY ECONOMICS	The Economics of Information Security	82
	Psychology	95
	Sociology	99

SPENDING

Reasons to Spend on Security Today	106
Non-Reasons to Spend on Security	110
Emerging Reasons to Spend	112
How Much Should a Business Spend on Security?	116
The Psychology of Spending	122
On What to Spend	126

LIFE IN THE NEW SCHOOL

People Are People	132
Breach Data Is Not Actuarial Data	136
Powerful Externalities	137
The Human Computer Interface and Risk Compensation	139
The Use and Abuse of Language	142
Skills Shortages, Organizational Structure, and Collaboration	144

A CALL TO ACTION

Join the New School	149
Embrace the New School	153
Make Money from the New School	157
Final Words	159

ENDNOTES 161

BIBLIOGRAPHY 213

INDEX 229

Preface

"I didn't have time to write you a short letter, so I wrote a long one."

—Mark Twain

We've taken the time to write a short book, and hope you find it enjoyable and thought-provoking. We aim to reorient security practitioners and those around them to a New School that has been taking shape within information security. This New School is about looking for evidence and analyzing it with approaches from a wide set of disciplines. We'd like to introduce this approach to a wider audience, so we've tried to write this book in a way that anyone can understand what we have to say.

This isn't a book about firewalls, cryptography, or any particular security technology. Rather, it's about how technology interacts with the broader world. This perspective has already provided powerful insights into where security succeeds and fails. There are many people investing time and effort in this, and they are doing a good deal of interesting research. We make no attempt to survey that research in the academic sense. We do provide a view of the landscape where the research is ongoing. In the same spirit, we sometimes skim past some important complexities because they distract from the main flow of our argument. We don't expect the resolution of any of those will change our argument substantially. We include endnotes to discuss some of these topics, provide references, and offer side commentary that you might enjoy. Following the lead of books such as *Engines of Creation* and *The Ghost Map*, we don't include endnote numbers in the text. We find those numbers distracting, and we hope you won't need them.

Some of the topics we discuss in this book are fast-moving. This isn't a book about the news. Books are a poor place for the news, but we hope that after reading *The New School*, you'll look at the news differently.

Over the course of writing this book, we've probably written three times more words than you hold in your hands. The book started life as *Security Decisions*, which would have been a book for managers about managing information security. We were inspired by Joan Magretta's lovely little book, *What Management Is*, which in about 200 pages lays out why people form organizations and hire managers to manage them. But security isn't just about organizations or managers. It's a broad subject that needed a broader book, speaking to a wider range of audiences.

As we've experimented with our text, on occasion removing ideas from it, there are a few fascinating books which influenced us and ended up getting no mention—not even in the endnotes. We've tried to include them all in the bibliography.

In the course of writing this book, we talked to a tremendous number of people. This book is better for their advice, and our mentions are to thank them, not to imply that they are to blame for blemishes that might remain. If we've forgotten anyone, we're sorry.

Simson Garfinkel and Bruce Schneier both helped with the proposal, without which we'd never have made it here. We'd both like to thank Andy Steingruebl, Jean Camp, Michael Howard, Chris Walsh, Michael Farnum, Steve Lipner, and Cat Okita for detailed commentary on the first-draft text. But for their feedback, the book would be less clear and full of more awkward constructs. Against the advice of reviewers, we've chosen to use classic examples of problems. One reviewer went so far as to call them "shopworn." There is a small audience for whom that's true, but a larger one might be exposed to these ideas for the first time. We've stuck with the classics because they are classic for a reason: they work. Jon Pincus introduced us to the work of Scott Page. We'd like to apologize to Dan Geer for reasons that are either obvious or irrelevant. Lorrie Cranor provided timely and much appreciated help in the academic literature around security and usability. Justin Mason helped correct some of the sections on spam. Steven Landsburg helped us with some economic questions. We would like to thank Adam's mom and Andrew's wife.

We'd also like to thank the entire community contributing to the Workshop on Economics and Information Security for their work in showing how to apply another science in broad and deep ways to the challenges that face us all in security.

It's tempting in a first book to thank everyone you've ever worked with. This is doubly the case when the book is about the approaches we bring to the world. Our coworkers, managers, and the people we have worked with have taught us each tremendous amounts, and those lessons have been distilled into this book.

Adam would like to thank (in roughly chronological order) cypherpunks Eric Hughes, Steve Bellovin, Ian Goldberg, and others too numerous to name, for fascinating discussions over the years, Ron Kikinis, coworkers at Fidelity, Netect (Marc Camm, David Chaloner, Scott Blake, and Paul Blondin), Zero-Knowledge Systems (Austin and Hamnett Hill, Adam Back, Stefan Brands, and the entire Evil Genius team), my partners at Reflective, and the Security Engineering and Community team at Microsoft, especially Eric Bidstrup and Steve Lipner. In addition, everyone who I've written papers with for publication has taught me a lot: Michael J. Freedman, Joan Feigenbaum, Tomas Sander, Bruce Schneier, Ian Goldberg, Austin Hill, Crispin Cowan, and Steve Beattie. Lastly, I would like to thank my co-bloggers at the Emergent Chaos Jazz Combo blog, for regularly surprising me and occasionally even playing in tune, as well as the readers who've commented and challenged us.

Andrew would like to thank Neil Todd and Phil Venables for their help and guidance at the beginning of my career. I would also like to thank Jerry Brady, Rob Webb, Mike Ackerman, George Sherman, and Brent Potter. Please note that my mentioning these people does not mean that they endorse (or even agree with) the ideas in this book.

Finally, we'd both like to acknowledge Jessica Goldstein, who took a chance on the book; Romny French; our copy editor, Gayle Johnson, and our project editor, Anne Goebel.

About the Authors

Adam Shostack is part of Microsoft's Security Development Lifecycle strategy team, where he is responsible for security design analysis techniques. Before Microsoft, Adam was involved in a number of successful start-ups focused on vulnerability scanning, privacy, and program analysis. He helped found the CVE, International Financial Cryptography association, and the Privacy Enhancing Technologies workshop. He has been a technical advisor to companies including Counterpane Internet Security and Debix.

Andrew Stewart is a Vice President at a US-based investment bank. His work on information security topics has been published in journals such as *Computers & Security* and *Information Security Bulletin*. His homepage is homepage.mac.com/andrew_j_stewart.

The New School of Information Security is:

- Learning from other professions, such as economics and psychology, to unlock the problems that stymie the security field. The way forward cannot be found solely in mathematics or technology.
- Sharing objective data and analysis widely. A fetish for secrecy has held us back.
- The embrace of the scientific method for solving important security problems. Analyzing real-world outcomes is the best way for information security to become a mature discipline.

Chapter 1

Observing the World and Asking Why

In December 2006, Turkish authorities announced the arrest of Ali Y'nin and nine accomplices for bank fraud. They accused Y'nin of leading a gang that sent millions of virus-laden emails. About 11,000 of the recipients opened the email message and unknowingly infected their computers. Then when the victims used online banking services, the gang captured the passwords for those bank accounts and drained them using false identification, fake ATM cards, and Western Union money transfers.

How have we found ourselves in a world in which a small Turkish gang can drain bank accounts on such a massive scale? The police state that Y'nin and his accomplices sent 3.4 million emails and compromised about 11,000 bank accounts. That is a success rate of only 0.3%, but it is hard to imagine that Y'nin was disappointed at being able to access the bank accounts of "only" 11,000 people.

Part of the answer is that because the interconnected world of computers and the internet provides many advantages to criminals, they are drawn to electronic crime. Attacks can be automated and carried out in large numbers. Imagine Y'nin attempting to perform the same fraud, but in person at bank branches. If each member of his gang tried to walk into the same bank branch claiming to be a different person each time, even a bored security guard would catch on after a while. If the gang spent all day traveling to different banks and spent one hour per account, they would be doing nothing but going from bank to bank eight hours a day for over six months. The internet makes everyone more efficient, even criminals. Perhaps especially criminals.

Although Y'nin and his gang were eventually caught, it is much harder to catch an electronic thief than a robber in the physical world. Investigating a burglary might take the police an hour or perhaps a day. An electronic break-in executed across international borders might require months or years of investigation. Only a few national police agencies take on cases that require such an investment of time and effort, whereas anyone connected to the internet can now attack computers around the world. In some of these countries, laws about electronic crimes might not be clear, or there may be no effective local law enforcement to make an arrest. Is it illegal to send email spam from China? What happens if an attacker launders his attack through a computer in Nigeria? Some large companies are dedicating resources to helping police forces investigate attacks that matter to them, but it is not clear if this strategy is a good investment. Another challenge for law enforcement is that the skills required to investigate computer crime quickly go out of date because of the rapid advance of technology. If an officer learned to develop latent fingerprints thirty years ago, that knowledge is still valuable in investigating crimes. In contrast, the ability to perform a forensic investigation of a computer that runs Windows 95 is of little use today.

Because attackers can carry out attacks in a highly automated way and because they are unlikely to ever be caught, online crime is attractive to criminals not just in Turkey, but everywhere. American brokerage houses have found themselves losing millions of dollars to schemes in which criminals use other people's money to "pump and dump" the stock market. The scheme starts when a thief buys some thinly-traded penny stock. The thief then breaks into the victim's bank account and uses the person's money to buy up that stock. The stock rises in price, and the thief then sells his holdings in the now-inflated stock, leaving him much richer and the victim much poorer. (If the thief is clever, he might even set up automated sale orders. The link between the thief and the automated selling of the stock is hard to prove, as is the fact that someone gained illegal access to the victim's account.)

When confronted with computer crime, it is hard to shake the impression that information security is failing. It can seem that these failures are everywhere, filling our electronic world with spam, computer viruses, and identity theft. Even worse, these problems seem to increase even as we spend more time and money on security. We might expect that a rise in electronic crime is a natural result of the world's becoming increasingly electronic. As money and influence move online, so do crime and vandalism. But as crime and vandalism move online, so must security. Ideally, security shows up first and allows us to preempt problems, but that seems to be a rare occurrence. It is often easier to experiment with and build software without security features, so they tend to get added later or not at all. The design of security measures can also cause frustration by getting in the way of the wrong things, so people seek to minimize such features.

But information security matters; it *is* important. It matters to companies and their shareholders. It is of great importance to the general public, whose personal data is stored by the companies and organizations with which they interact (and by some with which they don't). We all hope our private files and email correspondence remain secure. The security industry and security professionals are the guardians of that personal information. They seek to frustrate bad guys such as Y'nin and his ilk by employing standard ways of working and by deploying security technologies. Unfortunately, these efforts have not always been successful.

This chapter delves into some of the most apparent failures of information security. These topics often have a nuanced history. By discussing them in detail, we lay the groundwork for the first half of this book, in which we analyze the myriad factors that have allowed such failings in information security to occur. In the second half, we build on the sum of these observations to reveal what we believe must happen to improve the state of information security in the world, how those changes can be made, and who is in a position to make them. Everyone will benefit from these changes, from multinational corporations to individual consumers.

Many books about information security focus on an idealistic notion of what security *should* be, or they approach security problems from a purely mathematical or technological perspective. Our approach is to begin by looking at the state of the world and trying to understand why it is the way it is. We believe that only through a balanced, well-rounded understanding of the nature of problems can we begin to design solutions that are both effective and efficient. We begin our discussion with a widely visible failure of information security.

Spam, and Other Problems with Email

The flood of unsolicited email flowing into our mailboxes seems to get worse each year, despite more antispam software, more laws, and more email lost to spam filters. In 1994, a law firm decided that the internet would be an ideal way to advertise its legal services. The firm sent a message to thousands of discussion groups, advertising its services. This was widely seen as having opened the floodgates to today's deluge of spam.

Sending an email message is so inexpensive that it makes sense to send one to every email address that can be found, rather than trying to pick specific recipients. Imagine if companies didn't have to pay anything to deliver paper catalogs.

Everyone's mailbox would be stuffed full of catalogs from every company in the world! After all, they can't make money unless people know about their revolutionary product. The United States today doesn't have a general-purpose privacy law that forbids the secret harvesting or sale of most types of personal information, so email addresses are not protected. Privacy laws in other countries vary, but strong privacy laws don't seem to inhibit spam.

There are two types of spammers. The first are companies you did business with once, which then send you emails forever. Even if you ask them to stop, the mail keeps coming. Consumers see this as spam. However, these companies have real products to sell. They're not outright fraudsters. The second type are criminal spammers who send spam about things such as sex pills, stocks, or quick fixes to your credit. These criminals often break into computers and use them, along with their network connections, to send spam.

As spam was rising, so was a new problem—*adware*. Adware companies called themselves "affiliate marketers." They claimed that people *chose* to install software that displays pop-up ads to the user. Sometimes this was and even still is true, but often the adware is embedded in other software and installs itself without the meaningful consent of the PC's owner. (By meaningful consent, we mean that the person installing the software understands what he is getting into.) Adware can also piggyback on a program that a user wants. Sometimes this is done with the cooperation of the author of the desirable program, who takes part of the revenue and earns a living by giving away his software. Other times, this is done as an unauthorized repackaging of innocent software. The adware industry has been creative in devising new ways for its software to surreptitiously install on people's computers. Adware uses innovative means to ooze into the obscure corners of a computer so that it can't easily be removed. Today, some experts say it can be more cost-effective to reinstall a computer than to remove a bad adware infection.

Another attack that uses email is *phishing*. Phishing is the art of sending fraudulent emails designed to look like they are from a company such as a bank. The phisher's goal is to lure people into visiting a web site that *looks* like their bank's real web site. The phisher (or an associate) then uses the fake but authentic-looking web site to convince people to provide personal information such as usernames, passwords, or mother's maiden name. The attacker then takes that information and uses it to access the victim's real bank account. Unpleasantness ensues.

At its root, phishing is a fraud that exists because of the difficulty of authentication—verifying that an entity is who it claims to be. It can be hard to identify the real sender of an email. It can be hard to tell whether a web site really belongs to a given bank. Banks and other institutions that conduct business online have the same problem in reverse. They can find it difficult to identify their customers when someone shows up at their web site to log in. As with spam, the ability to perform phishing attacks is facilitated by the global, largely anonymous nature of the internet. In January 2006, more than six billion emails were recorded as part of 15,000 different phishing scams.

Criminals use phishing attacks because they work. In a test of people's ability to distinguish real email from fake, only 6% got all the answers right, and only half of real emails were recognized as being real. Even so, many companies that do business online have not yet adopted some simple measures that would help protect their customers. Phishing attacks use fake web sites to harvest the personal information of victims, so companies that do business online should advise their customers to never click a hyperlink in an email. Companies should also never send their customers links in an email. Customers should be told that whenever they want to visit the company online, they should use a bookmarked web address, and that web address should ideally be delivered using traditional postal mail. (This advice is intended for those companies that have ongoing relationships with their customers, and who send them occasional alerts.) Rather than take these measures, many companies have instead made things more difficult for their customers by registering new web addresses, using confusing web addresses, and using certain technologies in their web pages that make it easier for fraudsters to camouflage their actions.

To be fair, some companies have sought to address the problem of phishing by implementing a new breed of authentication technologies. In theory, these products help the customers identify when they are at a real web site rather than a fake. In practice, they don't seem to work. For example, in a 2007 study, one of the market-leading products in this space was shown to be ineffective 92% of the time.

As we depend on email more and more, its security weaknesses become ever more apparent.

Hostile Code

Viruses continue to plague our computers. The first viruses were created in the early 1980s. Early viruses were handcrafted, and their creators had some degree of skill. Virus creation became much easier with the introduction of powerful virus-creation toolkits. This has led to a dramatic upswing in the number of viruses. This problem with viruses is not unique to any one vendor of computer software. Viruses affect a wide variety of systems, from mobile phones to mainframes.

For the last twenty years, the majority of anti-virus (AV) products have relied on explicit knowledge about every virus that exists in the world. That knowledge is codified within a *signature*. When a piece of AV software can match the bits in a file to a signature in its library, it blocks or deletes what it presumes to be a virus. This approach is effective close to 100% of the time when the AV software has a signature for the particular virus that happens to be attacking the computer. When it doesn't, this approach doesn't help. The value of an AV product therefore hinges on two things: the AV product vendor must identify new viruses and create signatures for them, and those signatures must reach the end user's computer as quickly as possible. Most AV products are updated daily or weekly with new signatures, but this is a never-ending race between the virus writers and the AV product vendors. Even if you run AV software, your computer might become infected by a virus before a signature is installed. The dramatic changes in virus creation over the past quarter century contrast with the rather tepid evolution of AV products.

Commercial AV products have typically been signature-based. Vendors have periodically brought products to market that use heuristics, such as analyzing behavior, to try to identify viruses. The idea is to remove the dependency on signatures by learning how viruses tend to act. But this technology can struggle with distinguishing between hostile and benign actions, and it can have an error rate of 50% or more. We certainly have fewer problems with computer viruses due to the degree of protection that AV software can provide. But we have only treated the symptoms. Viruses continue to be created at a very high rate. We haven't solved the problem with existing technology, and millions of people continue to be affected. With no cure in sight, it seems that viruses will be with us for some time.

Specialists refer to self-propagating network viruses as worms. On November 2, 1988, Robert Morris, Jr., a student at Cornell University, released the first internet worm. Morris claimed that his intention was not to create damage, but to attempt to determine the size of the internet at the time. It had a bug that caused it to infect machines too quickly.

The Morris Worm, as it became known, pre-dated a raft of damaging internet worms that took root on the internet and within enterprise networks from 2001 onward. There was no fundamental difference between the methodology or techniques used by those modern incarnations of worms and the original Morris Worm. (The Morris Worm targeted the most popular operating systems on the internet, just as subsequent worms have done.) A decade passed between the Morris Worm and those later incarnations.

Viruses, worms, adware, and other hostile code are now lumped together under the generic term *malware*, meaning software that no one wants around. We have gained more knowledge of malware, and the defensive technologies we can employ have become more robust. But modernity is little consolation if we continue to fall victim to the same problems.

Security Breaches

In mid-2006, the *New York Times* and the Associated Press revealed that a laptop containing the personal information of 26.5 million U.S. veterans had been stolen. This is about 9% of the U.S. population. The 26.5 million individuals who were affected were all living veterans who had been discharged since 1976. When the data breach was announced, much uproar occurred in the press and among veterans. The question most often asked was, how could this happen? The reality was that many other organizations of all sorts and sizes have suffered similar breaches in their information security. The organizations affected by these security breaches range from government departments to nonprofit organizations and multinational corporations. Only some states require companies to publicly disclose breaches. Reports are most prominent (or at least most visible) in the English-speaking world, so we are most able to discuss breaches that affect Americans.

TJX is an example of a company that announced a breach. TJX owns well-known brands in the U.S. such as T.J. Maxx and Marshalls, and it has retail stores in Canada and Europe. TJX announced on January 17, 2007 that its computer systems had been hacked. The personal data that was compromised included customer information related to purchases and returns, and it contained credit and debit card numbers. The number of credit and debit card numbers compromised by the attackers is unknown, but estimates (and opinions) range from about 45 million to as many as 200 million cards. According to a TJX press release, TJX believes that its systems were intruded upon from as early as July 2005 until January 2007. Eighteen months was enough time for the attackers to thoroughly ransack the TJX computer network.

Some of the data that was stolen from TJX was used to commit crimes. Police in Florida arrested six people suspected of a fraud scheme that used the stolen credit card data. Unfortunately for TJX, one of the victims was Massachusetts Attorney General Martha Coakley, whose information was used to fraudulently purchase a Dell computer. That probably contributed to the early momentum of the investigation.

Over half of all Americans have been sent notices that their personal data may have been compromised in one of the many breaches that have been disclosed. This number seems low given the vast number of databases containing personal information, the rates of reported laptop theft, and how personal information is bought, sold, and traded. One effect of these "breach notices" is that the sorry state of information security has become more visible, and people want to know why things are so bad.

Chapter 4 is devoted to breaches, so we won't dwell on that topic here. Suffice it to say that security breaches can cause real pain to individuals whose personal data has been compromised, and one of the major causes of concern with such incidents is the threat of identity theft.

Identity and the Theft of Identity

Imitation is the sincerest form of flattery, but no one is flattered by having their good name and credit used for fraud. Such frauds include emptying your bank account, applying for credit, or getting medical care in your name. Personally identifying information such as your full name, national identity number, bank account details, and so on are valuable precisely because they can be used by someone else to impersonate you.

The desire to commit fraud is an important part of the rapidly growing and widely misunderstood crime known as identify theft. Before we can discuss it, we need to describe identification, authentication, and authorization. These three concepts are often confused. *Identification* concerns the labels we provide for things. Much like *The New School of Information Security* identifies a book, "John Wilson" identifies a person. We use other identifiers to identify people, such as "Dad." Dad is not a *unique* identifier, but most people are pretty sure whom they mean when they say it. A bank with eight customers named John Wilson needs to be able to differentiate between them. Anyone can claim to be John Wilson, so how can we tell if he really is? The answer lies in *authentication* to figure out which John Wilson is *authorized* to take money from account number 1234.

You may plan to have coffee with John, and he might tell you that he is tall, bald, and is wearing a green shirt today. Those are authenticators. They help you recognize John at the coffee shop. But if you're a bank, you want to make sure that John is authorized to withdraw money, so you might check his signature, password, or PIN. Identification and authorization are tricky. Too many organizations believe that anyone who knows your social security number (SSN) is you.

The same information about us is stored repeatedly, by different organizations and in different places. Tremendous duplication occurs, and many organizations continue to design processes that depend on these little pieces of data. The problem is that many of these identifying fragments were never designed for the ways in which they are being used. The SSN was not designed to be secret, and yet it is widely believed to be secret and often is treated as such. The result is that SSNs are used as both an identifier and an authenticator. We are told it is important not to hand out our SSN willy-nilly, but at the same time, everyone demands it.

If something is valuable, it should be protected, and we should give our personal information to only trustworthy organizations that really need it. Unfortunately, most organizations seem to think that they are trustworthy and that they must have our personal information. Landlords, utility and insurance companies, employers, hospitals, governments, and many others all profess to be completely trustworthy. It's likely that these organizations, storing the most personal information imaginable, will authorize hundreds of thousands of other completely "trustworthy" people at a variety of organizations to see it, increasing the possibility that it will become compromised.

Why do these approaches persist? The idea that we have a "core identity" that is truly "us" seems to be both strong and pervasive, as does people's desire to build on it. These drivers seem to be deep-seated, despite the practical problems. The willingness to build identity systems without testing our ideas mirrors and reinforces a willingness to build security systems on faith. The deep-seated desire to make identity-driven systems work is not only emotional, but also economic: the use of SSNs to identify us is inexpensive to the people designing the systems. Other systems might cost more to deploy, might be harder to use, or might be more intrusive on the surface.

One outgrowth of such faith is the fastest-growing crime in America today, identity theft. This term calls to mind the deep sense of violation that many of its victims feel, because we often believe that our identity is our "good name" and one of the most important things about us.

To get a credit card in the U.S., all you need is a date of birth and an SSN that match a record in a database. Criminals who obtain credit take on as much debt as they can and then disappear. The loan is reported to credit bureaus and collection agencies. Collection agencies attempt to track down the person identified, thinking that he is the person responsible for the debt, and a Kafka-esque nightmare ensues.

Credit fraud is not the only goal of identity fraudsters. They can obtain medical care under false names, leading to a risk that medical records will be unfortunately intertwined. They can obtain driver's licenses and passports under false names, leading to repeated arrests of innocent individuals. As more and more systems are based on the notion of identity, the value of identity fraud will grow. Some states have proposed "identity theft passports" to help victims of identity fraud. However, the more we tighten the security of identity systems, the less willing authorities will be to believe they can be compromised and defrauded. This will increase the value of compromising these systems and make victims' lives more difficult.

Addressing identity theft will likely involve some investment in technology, and perhaps more importantly, an understanding of the motivations of the various participants that make it such a problem. One of the themes of this book is using economic analysis to increase our understanding of systems and using that understanding to reach better outcomes. Looking at identity theft allows us to see that all the players behave rationally. That rational behavior imposes costs on everyone who touches the financial system.

Should We Just Start Over?

Describing the many failings of information security could easily take an entire book. We have described only some of the most visible problems. Given the nature of these issues, perhaps we should consider the radical step of rebuilding our information technologies from the ground up to address security problems more effectively.

The challenge is that building complex systems such as global computer networks and enterprise software is *hard*. There are valid comparisons to the traditional engineering disciplines in this respect. Consider the first bridge built across the Tacoma Narrows in Washington state. It swayed violently in light winds and ultimately collapsed because of a subtle design flaw. The space shuttle is an obvious example of a complex system within which minor problems have resulted in catastrophic outcomes. At the time this book was written, the Internet Archive project had 85 billion web objects in its database, taking up 1.5 million gigabytes of storage. During the 1990s, such statistics helped people understand or just be awed by the size of the internet, but the internet *is* undoubtedly one of the largest engineering projects ever undertaken. Replacing it would be challenging.

Even if we "just" tried to recreate the most popular pieces of computer software in a highly secure manner, how likely is it that no mistakes would creep in? It seems likely that errors in specification, design, and implementation would occur, all leading to security problems, just as with other software development projects. Those problems would be magnified by the scale of an effort to replace all the important internet software. So, after enormous expense, a new set of problems would probably exist, and there is no reason to expect any fewer than we have today, or that they would be any easier to deal with.

Much of the usefulness of the internet comes from its open-platform nature that allows new ideas to be developed and incubated. The ability of people to invent the world wide web, instant messaging, and internet telephony stems in part from limited (if any) restrictions on who can do what. Imagine if Internet Service Providers (ISPs) were required by law to collect and keep copies of passports from their customers, or if an official "internet certification board" had to approve new software. The rate at which individuals came online and at which new products were brought to market would be substantially slower. The internet's success depends to a large degree on an open philosophy, which in turn requires accepting a certain amount of insecurity.

In recognizing this reality—that security threats and vulnerabilities will always exist—the question becomes, how efficient and effective can we make our response to those security challenges? If we are not making good decisions today, why not? Creating balanced solutions requires that we understand the true nature of problems. We need good information with which to make the right decisions.

The Need for a New School

Criminals and thugs seek to take advantage of the increasingly electronic nature of our lives. Some crimes occur in the physical world, and others take place purely in the realm of computers. These problems can contribute to distrust of the internet as a medium for commerce and interaction. Problems such as data breaches and identity theft portend doom, but the mere fact of their existence raises important questions. Perhaps our approach to information security is flawed. If it is, a dollar spent on information security is unlikely to be spent well.

We wrote this book not because we are pessimists, but to help coalesce and accelerate the rise of a New School of Information Security. That New School is focused on putting our ideas and beliefs through tests designed to draw out their flaws and limitations. By testing our ideas, we can learn to do better than simply following our superstitions and ingrained beliefs. Such testing allows us to improve on the status quo. The New School is concerned with analyzing on what basis we make security decisions today and with seeking data to support rational decision-making. The New School also believes we can make better decisions by learning from other sciences, such as economics. If there were a single information security community, we could say that parts of the New School have been percolating through it for a while. We hope to help organize, add context to, and extend these ideas into a coherent whole.

Some might say that we are already doing enough, that our current approaches and existing levels of investment are sufficient. If we were to implement new approaches—new training, new technologies, and new processes—would their cost be justifiable? Our answer is that investing in new ways of thinking is inexpensive.

Some security practitioners are beginning to question the received wisdom of their profession. In parallel, the way in which businesses view their information security needs is changing. Organizations want to know how to protect themselves in this new world, but they also want to ensure that they are making security decisions that are both effective and fiscally responsible. A skeptical, pragmatic, and forward-thinking outlook is emerging and will become a new consensus. That consensus is the New School of Information Security.

A psychologist friend likes to say that there are three ways to deal with any problem: you can change it, you can accept it, or you can go nuts. This book is offered in the hopes that we can effectively change some things, accept others, and fail to go nuts.

Chapter 2

The Security Industry

Imagine that the police have arrested two people, Alice and Bob, for a crime. The police don't have enough evidence to convict either, so they hope to convince each to testify against the other. If Alice testifies against Bob, but he doesn't testify against her, he'll go to jail for ten years, and she'll go free. If they testify against each other, they'll both go to jail for five years. If they both remain silent, they'll each serve six months on a minor charge. The police offer Alice and Bob the same deal, but each must make his or her decision in a lonely cell. Each one's fate, and the fate of the other, lies in their hands.

Several factors might influence their decisions. For instance, they might be friends. Let's consider their dilemma from a purely rational point of view. If Bob stays silent, the best move Alice can make is to testify against Bob, because she will walk free. Even if Bob decides to testify against Alice, her best move is *still* to testify against him, because she would receive a shorter sentence than if she stayed silent. Because Bob is likely to use the same strategy, the end result for both Alice and Bob is worse than if they had cooperated and acted in their *collective* self-interest. This puzzle is known as the "prisoner's dilemma." It is considered a classic in the field of game theory—the study of incentives and decision-making that mixes mathematics with economics.

Can the prisoner's dilemma teach us anything about how we approach problems such as spam, viruses, data breaches, and identity theft? If the prisoner's dilemma is a good model of the security industry, then yes. (We may be oversimplifying, but it illustrates our point.)

An entire industry is made up of those trying to solve security problems. Most of the participants in the industry are trying to make money by doing the right thing—delivering better security to their customers. In many ways, the industry succeeds at delivering a set of products people want. No one has to write their own firewall anymore. Antivirus products are on the shelf of every computer store, priced at less than a good book on how to write such software. The market for security products is functional, but not optimal. Individual or organizational actions do not always lead to what's in the best interests of organizations, the general public, or the security field as a whole. Sometimes one person profits at the expense of another. This is particularly true in the area of security technologies, but many other examples exist.

A big part of the problem is in having enough information to make the right decisions. (Is it better for Alice to testify against Bob or to stay silent?) A lack of evidence to support decision-making allows vendors to sell anything, because customers can't distinguish useful products from useless ones. Salespeople refer to this as "throwing things at the wall to see what sticks." If we had a perfect market, and if consumers were fully informed and entirely rational, perhaps things would be better. As things stand, buyers of security products don't have a lot of good information to help them make decisions. This can result in effective security technologies or approaches being sidelined or overlooked in favor of the latest and greatest.

In support of observing the world and asking why, the purpose of this chapter is to examine how various parts of the security industry act. We will structure our analysis by describing what products and services are sold, how they are sold, and how effective they are. We will begin by examining the various groups that make up the security industry in order to understand their motives and how different groups might influence the development of ideas.

Where the Security Industry Comes From

One of the earliest influencers of security was the U.S. military, which influenced the development of the computer and information security industries in a number of ways. Military networks have always been targets, and of course the military has systems and information that it wants to keep secret. Information security has been around since information has been recorded. The computer security industry couldn't get started until computers existed, and many of the earliest computers and networks were built by the military. This led the U.S. military to fund early and influential research in computer security. In the 1980s, the Department of Defense wrote and published security standards and then required that the IT vendors the government did business with met those standards in their products. Because of the size of the deals involved, companies such as IBM, Honeywell, and DEC spent lots of money on security features demanded by their government customers. Most governments and militaries train personnel to operate and manage their information technologies, and many of those individuals eventually transition to the commercial sector, bringing their training, education, and culture with them. Because the military invests such a large amount in information technology, and because so many people flow through its organization, the military exerts broad influence.

Contrary to widespread belief, the military does not have access to any special data set that would enable it to make better decisions than, say, a large corporation. It may have data on the use (and abuse) of specialist platforms such as multilevel secure systems, but those findings do not have particular use in a traditional IT setting, where such technologies are rare.

On the other side of the fence (both figuratively and, well, physically) are *hackers* and *crackers*. We use the traditional meaning of the word hacker: someone who is adept at pushing a system beyond expected boundaries, and not usually with malicious intent. Hackers influence the security industry in two main ways. The first is their involvement as technologists in start-ups and established security companies, performing research and influencing product development. The second is as hobbyists, creating and releasing security tools, some of which have become widely adopted as alternatives to commercial offerings. Open-source projects founded by hackers have also inspired new lines of business in information security and IT. Crackers are people who break into computers, phone systems, ATMs—anything digital, ideally with a network connection. A broad spectrum of motivations exists, ranging from the desire for teenage bragging rights all the way up to espionage or mass fraud of the type carried out by Ali Y'nin and his accomplices. Web site defacement is often the electronic equivalent of teenage joyriding, but other motivations within this group include the promotion of political points of view, financial gain, or the pursuit of fun without regard for its impact. As we noted in Chapter 1, computers that have been compromised by crackers are often sold as spam relays.

The police are interested in crackers who break the law. The police are less concerned with preventive security measures than with investigative techniques. The science of digital forensics has progressed substantially, but it remains a niche specialty. Even for a large organization, the cost of training an employee in digital forensics is likely to exceed the number of occasions upon which that employee would have the opportunity to apply his or her new skills and therefore return that investment.

Some crimes are unearthed by accountants. Usually the crimes discovered by auditors are financial. It is unclear whether IT auditors are as successful at discovering computer crimes. Considering their visible role within businesses, auditors might be expected to exert a strong influence over the security industry, but in fact they do not. Auditors are concerned primarily with the timely delivery of audit data and its correctness, along with the controls that surround the business processes from which that auditing data originates. They are largely agnostic regarding the means used to deliver that information. It could be a paper process for all they care, as long as the data is readily available and the controls around the process are robust. Most audit work is performed by junior employees, who have relatively little technical skill and are less able to influence the selection of security products in use.

The security problems that exist in the world are a tempting opportunity for entrepreneurs. In general, the entrepreneurial approach brings many benefits. (Successful businesses make money because they offer customers something useful.) Security is a field wide open for entrepreneurship. Unlike, say, the pharmaceutical industry, information security is almost entirely unregulated. This makes it easy for parties to enter the market and provide products and services. To make lots of money in security, an entrepreneur must find a problem that customers can understand and that can be solved with technology. This can channel entrepreneurs and start-ups in security into a narrow market, focused on a small subset of the important problems. It may be that addressing the problems that exist outside that narrow market would provide more value in the long term. (We'll discuss this at greater length later in this chapter.)

Venture capitalists are in the business of investing in new ventures with potential for enormous returns. Some of the companies funded by venture capitalists become successful public companies. Others are acquired by larger companies, often looking to build more complete systems, and still others simply fail. The start-up business is speculative by definition, and many security start-ups seem to hit a plateau in their growth and then stagnate. There are plenty of reasons for this, but this isn't a book on start-ups or entrepreneurship. One theory is that such companies can survive for a while by selling their product to all the people they know within the industry, but that isn't sufficient to build a viable company in the long term. Another theory is that a finite set of large companies will buy new technologies simply to see if they work. Even smaller is the set of companies that will buy new security technologies.

Technological innovation also comes from hackers building tools to solve problems they're experiencing. Many of these hackers choose to give away the software they create under various open-source licenses. This is an important source of innovation, and many important security products have come from the open-source world. Some are at the center of companies, and others continue to operate as open-source projects. Companies that spring up around open-source projects often make money by selling ongoing support, such as intrusion detection rules for the latest attacks, or support and service.

As a market matures, there's a tendency toward vendors that offer "complete" systems. Most cars come with a stereo, and the market for replacement stereos is relatively small. However, many products now commonly available from the manufacturer start out as optional add-ons. Navigational systems are an example. Once expensive add-ons, they're now expensive factory or dealer options. The move toward complete systems tends to be a gradual one as the market figures out what a complete system entails, but it is often hard to compete with a systems vendor. Spelling and grammar checkers were once products separate from word processors, but no one needs to buy a spell checker today. Similarly, few organizations want to buy security as an "add-on"; they increasingly want security capabilities to exist by default. Most people don't want to invest the time to figure out what the best stereo is; they want to get a reasonably good one for their money. In the same way that it can be hard to compare stereos, it can be hard to compare the security of products. We'll return to this point later.

Another trend is for large IT vendors to use their market penetration and existing sales channels to shape parts of the security market. For example, when the market for products that protect computer desktops swelled as a result of internet worm infections, Cisco priced its product very inexpensively in comparison to competing vendors. It was a popular product, and Cisco is a major vendor, so why didn't Cisco charge a premium? One possible reason is that a widespread deployment of a certain technology within a business creates incentives for that business to employ additional technology from the same vendor (for interoperability, licensing, support, and many other reasons of efficiency). Another factor is that all vendors, regardless of their field, want the switching costs of their customers to be as high as possible. They understand that if their product is widely used within an organization, it can then become expensive for that organization to switch to a competing product. The more entrenched a product, the more power a vendor has to set prices for maintenance and licensing.

Industry analysts report on these practices and advise both public and private companies. Analysts are often given in-depth briefings by companies, and the quality of their analysis hinges on the rigor they place on gathering and interpreting data. (A brilliant analyst without data is a pundit.) A cynical view of the advice that research firms such as Gartner provide to business is that "no one ever gets fired for implementing Gartner recommendations." It *is* true that people often fail to hold analysts accountable for the advice they have given, and analysts rarely reveal the data that underlies their predictions.

The final group we will note within the security industry is academia. Researchers in academia investigate security topics, and their research is often a leading indicator of security technology trends. Much academic research in security is years or decades distant from the workplace, but academia is often the only place where a true picture of the strengths and weaknesses of security technologies can be found. This is most true for cryptography, but it's also true for technologies that are now considered everyday, such as intrusion detection systems. In a paper published in 1999, Stefan Axelsson, a researcher in Sweden, explained that the value of these products hinges not on their ability to detect attacks, but on their ability to suppress false alarms that drive up operational costs. This paper was one of the two most farsighted analyses of intrusion detection technology. Axelsson foresaw problems with these emergent systems long before most businesses had heard of them. (The other farsighted paper was Ptacek and Newsham's work describing how an attacker can evade the technology.)

Two favorite haunts of academics are conferences and standards bodies. Academics have a hierarchy of workshops, symposia, conferences, and journals in which they share their work and collaborate. These forums and the work they accept play an important role in shaping information security. The perceived importance of new work is influenced by where it is presented. Venture capitalists and the IT industry participate in some of these forums, so what is selected and presented influences what new technologies get attention outside academia. Standards bodies are one of the ways in which security protocols are developed. This work is typically done in an open and non-commercial fashion, but the desires of the commercial security industry can sometimes conflict with those ideals. For example, in 2002, a working group of the Internet Engineering Task Force published the draft description of a communication mechanism called the *Intrusion Detection Message Exchange*

Format that would allow security technologies to talk to general network management systems in a consistent way. This would allow businesses to connect such systems together. However, the business model of companies producing these products is to sell sensors and management consoles as a bundle. Implementing this new mechanism would mean that the customer was no longer locked in to using a suite of components from only one vendor, so none of the vendors implemented it. It could be argued that customers would benefit from being able to combine the output from multiple products to enable more effective security analysis to be performed. But this would not initially benefit each *individual* vendor, so we see the downward spiral of the prisoner's dilemma emerge.

Orientations and Framing

Our orientation is influenced by our cultural upbringing, education, training, and experiences. We're using the term *orientation* as defined by John Boyd in his Observe, Orient, Decide, Act (OODA) concept, often simplified and called a loop. In this sense, orientation is how people perceive and interact with the world. Orientation in IT is visible in the ongoing "UNIX versus Microsoft" divide. An example in the security realm is the palpable difference in orientation between a security practitioner with a policy and compliance background and someone with a technical or engineering background. To stereotype for a moment, the policy and compliance folks want to manage risks through process and controls, and the technical people want to build and deploy technology. These varying orientations manifest as different outlooks on and approaches to the world. If you want some excitement, gather a group of security professionals and ask them if it's a good idea to write down all your passwords and carry them in your wallet. There will be wide differences of opinion (and probably fireworks).

What we see as conventional wisdom is to a large degree shaped by our personal and social preferences, since what is convenient to believe is often greatly preferred. The phenomenon of "groupthink" is well known. It's easy to ignore reality when the people around you are all doing the same thing, and the act of challenging groupthink is usually highly unpopular. Like-minded people with a shared orientation tend to orient in similar ways. The most academically interesting topics within information security for Ph.D. students to study are those that their professors are interested in. A section of the hacker community focuses intensely on vulnerabilities and tends to believe that finding vulnerabilities in software is the most valuable skill for a security professional. Compliance practitioners within corporate security teams view security problems in terms of their possible effect on audit findings. They might dismiss a gaping security hole because they don't believe it will impact the bottom line.

Orientations often involve a complex bundle of opinions, experiences, and approaches. For example, a section of the hacker community refers to itself as "the underground." This self-labeled underground incorporates many ideas, including a love of investigation and learning, skepticism toward authority, respect for hard-to-acquire skills or knowledge, and a love of the forbidden. Every year in Las Vegas they hold Defcon, whose web site bills it as "the largest underground hacking convention in the world!" (The idea of a publicized event that is open to all comers being "underground" is an interesting contradiction.) At this convention, hackers get up on stage and explain how to break into things. Some include a caveat such as "Don't break the law."

Much of what happens at Defcon is perfectly above board. After all, hordes of law enforcement and military types are in attendance each year, and they don't go intending to break the law. However, they often misunderstand the motivations of hobbyists and computer scientists who attend Defcon, and culture clashes are common. Some of these clashes have involved the arrest of hackers for things they have presented on stage in front of a large audience. Prolific bank robber Willie Sutton never stood on stage talking about weaknesses in bank security systems, but hackers do so regularly. There are big differences in the orientations through which these groups see the world.

None of the orientations we have described are "wrong." In fact, they are often predictable, given the communities from which they originate. Unfortunately, making rational decisions in a microcosm does not necessarily satisfy goals that exist outside those relatively narrow views of the world. Those narrow views lead to inefficiencies and parochialism. Those inefficiencies manifest themselves in a variety of ways, but none more so than in the security products and services that are brought to market.

What Does the Security Industry Sell?

The face of information security seen by a Fortune 500 company or by an individual consumer is largely constructed by the marketing departments within the commercial security industry. The security industry advertises on buses, billboards, and taxicabs. It publishes trade magazines, runs conferences and award shows, operates security news and information portals on the web, provides training courses and professional certifications, creates security products, and delivers security services.

There's an elephant in the room. That elephant is the assumption that the security industry has evolved to solve the problems most in need of solving. For many industries, this is a reasonable assumption. Markets are powerful mechanisms for finding solutions to important problems, and problems that the market doesn't solve are often not worth solving. Markets fail in well-understood ways, and many of these seem to occur in the market for computer security. Do we focus on and "solve" the easy problems? Are we looking for our lost car keys under the streetlight only because it's dark everywhere else? Many of the products and services that the commercial security industry sells simply perpetuate an unsatisfactory status quo. They don't make the problem any worse—they certainly can help. But they often don't address the root cause of the problem.

A key observation that can be made about the evolution of security technologies is that new security products are often developed to compensate for the unintended side effects of prior security products. This suggests that the first set of products didn't tackle the problem at a deep enough level. The use of network firewalls to restrict the types of traffic that can flow into and out of private networks has led directly to the current situation in which every application developer simply makes all the traffic flow over port 80. They know that the web port will never be blocked, so they use it by default. Now businesses have to purchase *application* firewalls in addition to their normal firewalls. This type of incremental decision-making seems to be common in the evolution of security technologies. It is an example of individual participants within the security industry trying to make the right decisions and failing. Businesses and consumers look for products to improve their security, and the market responds. In doing so, the risks are often shuffled around, or attempts to address them are postponed.

As human beings, we are drawn to "new" products because in our minds "new" means "improved." ("It's new and improved!") This results in a fashion show of new security products every year or so, and sometimes, after several iterations, we end up back where we started. For example, vulnerability scanners found so many vulnerabilities within computer networks that companies began employing network-based intrusion detection systems so that they could focus only on attacks. Those technologies generated too many false alarms, so managed security service companies sprang up to allow companies to outsource that monitoring function. Some companies found that those outsourced companies were ineffective in their analysis because of the distance from the networks being monitored, so they took the security monitoring function back inside. To accomplish this, they began employing "vulnerability management" products. The circle is now complete, because essentially this new generation of products are glorified vulnerability scanners, albeit with a prettier executive dashboard.

As Kurt Vonnegut said, "So it goes." Security products often address only the symptoms, not the underlying problems. If the problem reappears in a slightly different way, a new product may well be needed. Lots of organizations have challenges within their environment with vulnerabilities, the uneven use of administrative software, network games, peer-to-peer and instant-message traffic, rogue servers, illegal software, and iPods connected to corporate workstations. Should an organization purchase a separate security product to address each risk? There is certainly at least one product for each. But almost all these risks could be addressed by a small number of fundamental activities: understanding the makeup of your IT environment, how it is configured, and how it changes over time. Today these activities are known as asset management, configuration management, and change management. If these fundamentals are correctly addressed, all these risks can be controlled, along with most predictable future permutations. The 80/20 rule, also known as the *Pareto Principle*, suggests that performance depends disproportionately on doing a few things really well. Does the current direction trumpeted by the commercial security industry represent the 80 or the 20? A company may well need to buy products to implement those processes, perhaps even specialist security products, but it is best to think through and understand the elemental nature of security problems and attack them at their root.

The majority of new security product development is carried out by security companies, and not by the other groups within the industry that we have described. Companies compete against each other within the market. Indeed, it is the nature of the IT industry to propel products onward and upward to ever-increasing levels of power and functionality. This unrelenting drive for new features can result in product functionality that overshoots the needs of the average customer. The rate of technological advancement within the security industry is ferocious. The result is that the average consumer might use only a small fraction of the functionality that exists in a given security product. It could be argued that whenever a vendor adds more functionality to its product, it increases the level of complexity. Bugs and misconfigurations arise from complexity, and a security bug is simply a bug with security implications. It is easier to make a simple system reliable, and it is also easier to make a simple system secure. As systems offer more powerful functionality, they often become more complex. Security practitioners often say that vendors should remove features. This is a seductive approach, but customers often need more functionality, and different customers often need different functionality. The result is large, complex pieces of security software, many of which have proven to have security vulnerabilities themselves.

Along with products, the information security industry sells services. Security services are no different from other IT services in that the quality of the work being performed varies greatly. Verifying that someone really has a specialist skill set can be expensive and difficult. One response has been the emergence of a market for security certifications, which now are available for many different specialties in the field. Organizations like to hire candidates who are certified because they see this as a diligent hiring practice. Because security has become an important business topic, this has led people to pursue security certifications in the hopes that they will become more marketable. This market for certifications has provided some benefit. Employers can validate that a prospective candidate has a certain baseline of knowledge in security. The downside is that a false economy exists within the job market, because many competent candidates who do not have a particular certification find their résumé hitting a glass ceiling. The result is that companies might not be hiring the best candidates.

When a company hires someone with a security certification, it knows that the candidate has passed a test. But does passing a test mean that the person will do a good job? The best-known security certification today—the Certified Information Systems Security Professional (CISSP)—employs a syllabus that is referred to as "*the* common body of knowledge." It amounts to a statement by the certification body of what a security professional should think about. Because of what is left out, it is also an implicit statement about what should *not* be thought about. With this approach comes a danger that people will feel cozy in their doctrinal view of what a security practitioner should know and perhaps reject the consideration of more novel perspectives. Organizations are unlikely to find a fresh perspective on their security challenges in someone who has just memorized 800 syllabus pages to pass a test. When the innovative British hairdresser Vidal Sassoon moved to New York in 1966, he refused to take the New York hairdressing exam. Local regulators had a formalized, rigid notion of how they thought a hairstylist should work. Sassoon thought it was absurd to have to prove his worth based on techniques and methods that he had learned and then abandoned. While no organization needs every employee to be a "rock star," few want all their employees to think the same way. Security certifications have a number of problems, and these criticisms can be leveled at certifications in other areas of IT as well. We are raising these issues because professional certifications have become a significant factor in the hiring of security personnel, and their perceived importance seems unlikely to fade in the near future.

In the same vein as professional certifications, "seal programs" are certifications for businesses. Online businesses care about security because some of their customers do. Companies want their prospective customers to trust the security of their web site so that those customers will use it. Some companies pay to enroll in seal programs in which a security "authority" evaluates the security of their web site according to some criteria, and then after some tests are passed, they can display a seal image on their site. The seal is supposed to signal to prospective customers that the site can be trusted. This is all good in theory, but less so in practice. As in the prisoner's dilemma, one party might choose to betray the other if she considers it to be in her best interest. Sites that are *not* trustworthy are drawn to such certifications as a way to help them dupe the public into thinking that they *are* trustworthy. Sites that *do* have good security do not feel the need to obtain the certification. This leads to "*adverse selection*," in which sites that seek and obtain trust certifications are in reality significantly *less* trustworthy than those without. This is perhaps not true of all seal programs, but a 2006 analysis of TRUSTe, a major seal vendor, showed that its seal participants were more likely to show up in a large database of malware distributors than their prevalence in the data set would lead one to expect.

The products and services that exist within the security marketplace are attempts to fulfill needs both real and imagined. Unfortunately, the security market isn't perfect. Organizations should keep in mind the subtle forces at work when considering the products and services that are available. We can learn a lot by examining how the security industry operates and what motivates the groups within it. By doing so, we can begin to identify situations in which acting in rational self-interest leads to both market inefficiencies and a failure to address underlying problems.

How Security Is Sold

Fear sells. We will hazard a guess that you do not know anyone who was attacked by the infamous "flesh-eating bacteria." So why would you know that flesh-eating bacteria even exists? The Centers for Disease Control recorded 600 cases of the bacteria in 1999 with a 25% fatality rate. So the risk of being killed by this bacteria or even coming into contact with it is infinitesimal. Even so, many newspapers around the world published headlines such as "Killer bug ate my face" and "Flesh-eating bug consumed my mother in 20 minutes." Why the disconnect with reality? The answer is that fear *sells*, and the results of fear can manifest in the marketplace with spectacular effect. Sales of duct tape spiked after the Department of Homeland Security announced that all Americans should include duct tape and plastic sheeting in "home disaster kits."

The security industry sometimes uses fear as a lever, either to sell products or advance an agenda. The worse a situation can be made to appear, the easier it becomes to convince someone to buy a particular product or undertake a particular piece of work. The security industry has, to a fairly significant extent, institutionalized the approach of using fear to sell security. It must be said that many security professionals have also taken up this approach and used it themselves. The industry has created a feeling of being under siege. The problem is that this can lead to decisions being made on the basis of emotional gut reactions—the antithesis of the ideal.

Taking advantage of people's fears and sense of being overwhelmed by security challenges, products are sometimes marketed as if they are the panacea for all security woes. One advertising campaign for a major security vendor was built around the phrase "security's silver bullet." Of course, it is naive to believe that all problems have fast, simple, and purely technological solutions. Advertising such as this does a disservice to the security field because it glosses over complex problems and presents the illusion of a reality in which a panacea exists. It makes you believe you can reach nirvana by using a particular service or installing a particular product.

Another marketing technique sometimes used by security product vendors is "proof by unclaimed reward." A vendor sets up its product on the internet and then invites attackers to attempt to break into it. When no one does, the company claims that its product "repels all hackers" or is "impossible to hack." The trick, of course, is that the vendor tries to set up its product or the surrounding environment in a way that makes it very difficult for an attacker to be successful. Also consider that just because the product was connected to the internet for a couple of weeks doesn't mean that anyone with skill will try to attack it. But sometimes they do. One vendor that ran five "hacker challenges" in the 1990s was hacked on the fifth. As of late 2007, the vendor had not paid the $50,000 "reward" it advertised. We're willing to bet that the vendor counted on the game being sufficiently rigged that they would never have to pay up.

One marketing tactic is to publicize that a product is used by this company or that government agency. Because they have such a reputation for security, the implication is that the product must be useful. That organization might well use a certain product, but perhaps for reasons that are not obvious to the rest of the world—partnerships, licensing agreements, experimental purposes, etc. The organization might also be augmenting the product with homegrown technologies or using it in a unique way. Lastly, note that just because someone buys a particular product doesn't mean that he will deploy it. It could be "shelfware," gathering dust.

A topic closely related to marketing and sales tactics is the relationship that industry magazines have with vendors. These magazines rely almost entirely on advertising from product vendors to support them. They offer free subscriptions to qualified subscribers, where "qualified" means everyone who can fill out the form. These magazines also perform product reviews. In an issue of one such magazine, the average rating for the twenty reviewed security products was four stars out of five. This result could be explained by the magazine's choosing to publish the results for only products that reached a certain rating (although one product scored only two stars in that same issue). They might really love those products. Another view is that the magazine relies on advertisements placed by vendors, so the magazine has an incentive to provide good reviews. In addition to that conflict of interest, a focus on products can create the idea that the problems "fixed" by products are the problems we should focus on. This is the path of Sisyphus, cursed to push a boulder up a hill for eternity.

Several industry conglomerates and organizations have established security checklists and certifications for businesses. The credit card associations have jointly established a set of criteria and checklists known as Payment Card Industry (PCI) standards, by which companies can be certified as having sufficient security to handle credit card payments. In a number of cases, companies that were certified to the PCI standard have suffered spectacular failures in their security. One of the most well known occurred in 2005, when CardSystems Solutions suffered a security breach in which attackers stole 40 million credit card numbers. Prior to the breach, CardSystems had hired a set of outside auditors to verify its security certification. "We followed the Visa rules to the letter, and the people who did the work are longtime security experts," the leader of the audit team was quoted as saying.

CardSystems had the required security certification, but its security was compromised, so where did things go wrong? Frameworks such as PCI are built around checklists. Checklists compress complex issues into a list of simple questions. Someone using a checklist therefore might think he has done the right thing, when in fact he has not addressed the problems in depth. For example, it is common to see checklists that require certain cryptographic algorithms, such as triple DES or AES 256-bit encryption. A good encryption algorithm is necessary, as is proper key management. Imagine if all instances of the product use the same key. Anyone who learns that key can read all the encrypted traffic. The checklist format allows such important issues to be glossed over.

Conventional wisdom presented in short checklists makes security look easy. A checklist implies that there is an authoritative list of the "right" things to do, even if no evidence of that simplicity exists. This in turn contributes to the notion that information security is a more mature discipline than it really is. Checklists, frameworks, and business certifications force companies to at least address the elements of security that each framework demands. ("A rising tide lifts all boats," perhaps.) On the other hand, all checklists are moot if we can't validate the value of their items. If we don't know which initiatives have value, companies are spending money very inefficiently, because insufficient evidence exists to determine the true value of controls.

In a similar fashion, the term "best practice" is a powerful lever for bringing someone around to your point of view. When you hear such a phrase, you might think that an official body vets and evaluates "best practices." Much like the U.S. Department of Agriculture (USDA) promulgates nutrition guidelines, there must be some equivalent, like a National Institute of Computer Security. There is not. "Best practices" are simply activities that are supposed to represent collective wisdom within a field. When a company doesn't have expertise in a certain problem domain or doesn't have the time or inclination to obtain it, it is very common for the company to simply adopt the "best practices" in that area. "Best practices" have proliferated within IT, and especially so within the security industry. Many security practitioners perceive the pursuit of "best practices" as defining a diligent security strategy. But we have to consider where "best practices" come from: they are dictated by consultants, vendors, and the security industry as a whole. Each of these groups has a vested interest in the security decisions that are made, and anyone can (and does) call their advice a "best practice." People find it difficult to argue against an authority or a perceived majority.

"Best practices" typically don't take into account differences between companies or, more generally, between industries. The security decisions at an oil firm are made in a very different context than in a clothing wholesaler, and yet we are told that "best practices" can apply to both. (Perhaps the same policies or actions do make sense for both. Declaring them "best practices" brings us no closer to figuring that out.) There is no good reason for a food packaging company to implement the security measures that a government agency might adopt. But the National Security Agency (NSA) guides for "securing" certain operating systems (which can be more than a thousand pages) are sometimes applied outside the government agencies for which they are intended. In reality, implementing such highly aggressive security measures is likely to lead to significant heartache and costs caused by trying to set the bar too high.

"Best practices" are designed to be vague enough to apply in the general case. Therefore, they are highly unlikely to match the specifics of any particular environment, and so they are inefficient by their very nature. For example, most law firms have not taken many steps to protect their core information asset: their document management system. Why? Perhaps because document management systems are somewhat of a niche technology, so they are not referred to in any generic "best practice" document! For a consulting firm, a "best practice" allows it to create a template for a piece of work so that it can easily be repeated, thereby increasing the firm's margin on similar engagements. As soon as a template and a script for performing a piece of work exist, an associate can do what would have previously required a senior manager or partner.

When *we* hear the phrase "best practice," we consider it a best practice to say: "Why? Prove that this 'best practice' really makes sense. Show me the evidence." Certainly, in some areas, standard ways of working have value. Some "hardening" practices can make an operating system more resistant to attack, such as turning off and removing unneeded functionality. It is also clear that some practices can help find the mathematical weaknesses in a cryptographic algorithm. Backing up data clearly has a lot of value. Software vendors have engineering insight into the systems they have built and can offer you useful advice on how best to operate them. We remain wary of "best practices" that are not grounded in mathematics, engineering, or science, because they are unlikely to ever be proven.

Consumer Reports is a publication that accepts no advertising. This arrangement allows it to focus unreservedly on the interests of its customers. Currently there are no "consumer reports" for security products and services, so it can be difficult to prove a product's worth. In the absence of empirical ways to do so, the security industry has historically used sales tactics such as appealing to fear. Perhaps this is not so different from other markets. It may also be that vendors truly believe that their product or service *is* a panacea or the ultimate solution—that the ends (better security) justifies the means. But even if they are right, the net result is not positive. Companies scared by security risks and led astray by vendor marketing are likely to spend very inefficiently. When acting as a consultant, one of the authors has on several occasions been told by companies that they have no time to document their environment, and then shortly thereafter been asked what brand of new security product they should buy. What would ultimately be more beneficial to those companies: understanding their IT environment, or adding the latest security technology to the mix? It could conceivably be the latter, but most companies would be better off having an accurate and up-to-date understanding of what they have built.

In Conclusion

We have reviewed some current thinking in the security field and have seen how current approaches have contributed to the malaise we described in Chapter 1. Almost no one in the security industry acts maliciously, but the decisions that we each make on an individual level don't always lead to the results that everyone wants. Ideas that are convenient to express can become the conventional wisdom, but even the relatively short analysis within this chapter has revealed large problems with that conventional wisdom. Buying products and "solutions" is easy, but the right thing to do is not always the easiest. The commercial security industry as it currently exists arranges itself to solve the problems that are in front of it and that it believes it can solve, so we shouldn't let it dictate priorities.

How then can we improve? One way is to look at other fields to see what we can learn. In 2003, Michael Lewis published *Moneyball*, a book about how the Oakland A's baseball team uses statistics to decide which players to buy or sell. In the book, Lewis describes how the general manager of the A's, Billy Beane, determined that the conventional wisdom for evaluating baseball players, such as focusing on batting average, was being used simply because it was easy to acquire. In the early 1970s, the Society for American Baseball Research created a more-detailed analysis that aims to measure the contribution of every player to the team's success. By being the first club to use that insight, the A's became competitive with teams that have far deeper pockets, such as the New York Yankees. *Moneyball* also describes a clash in orientations between the old and new ways of doing things.

Like Billy Beane and the Oakland A's, we in the security field must step back and examine the ways in which we make decisions, and see whether we can do better. It won't be a particular product or service that will drive that change. The answer lies in embracing objective data about successes and failures. Without proper use of objective data to test our ideas, we can't tell if we are mistaken or misguided in our judgment about what is important. Our particular orientations might lead us to believe that we alone can see the solution, and we might then turn it into a "best practice"! The answer to these challenges lies in gathering and using *evidence*, to which we now turn.

Chapter 3

On Evidence

In 1610, Galileo published his observations of Jupiter's moons. He used his findings to argue in favor of Copernicus' heliocentric model, in which the sun is the center of the solar system and not the Earth, as was widely believed at the time. Four years later, the Catholic Church formally denounced Galileo's work. In 1616, Cardinal Roberto Bellarmino committed Galileo to house arrest and instructed him not to further publicize Copernican astronomy. Galileo was punished because his findings undermined Church teachings. The Church was a tremendously powerful institution, with a bully pulpit that extended across Europe. It also had its own courts and police, and the power to excommunicate someone and damn a soul for eternity. In the end, history vindicated Galileo, because it is not power that counts, but reality.

Chapter 1 looked at some problems with information security. The subjects we touched on included organized computer crime, spam, viruses, data breaches, and identity theft. Chapter 2 discussed some structural issues within the security industry that, perversely, help these problems to persist. Some use highly visible failures such as viruses and spam to bolster their claim that information security is in radical decline. Others are equally resolute in their belief that we are either continuing to make steady gains or at least are not falling behind. Extremely skilled and experienced security practitioners can be found in both camps, but ultimately both positions should be tested to see if they can be disproved. If the position can't be tested, it's a belief—not science. This chapter examines *sources* of evidence and the value they might provide. In doing so, we can evaluate to what degree they can help us evaluate claims, large and small, and make the right security decisions.

Someone with no training in physics might think that heavier objects fall faster than lighter ones. But we know through scientific testing that all objects falling toward the Earth accelerate at the same rate (although they may be slowed by air resistance). It was Galileo who posed the hypothesis that everything falls at the same rate. He supposedly performed a test in which he simultaneously dropped two objects weighing different amounts from the Leaning Tower of Pisa.

The scientific orientation has been incredibly effective at increasing our understanding of the world. It includes formulating and testing hypotheses and sharing the methods of testing and results of those tests. A hypothesis is simply a testable suggestion. Tests never actually *prove* a hypothesis. Good tests fail to disprove the hypothesis being tested and thereby provide evidence in favor of the hypothesis. The difference is both subtle and important. For example, someone might hypothesize that the coelacanth fish is extinct, yet this was disproven in 1938 when a living specimen was caught. It's impossible to prove a negative, because there's always the possibility that a counter-example is out there somewhere. We might have other ideas we believe, but evidence to disprove them might be lurking right around the corner. The disproof of a hypothesis may or may not make it worthless. For example, Newton's laws of motion are still used in civil engineering, even though they are "wrong" and don't apply at very high speeds or at atomic scales.

The ideal way to test a hypothesis is by experiment. Good experimental design changes one variable at a time and sees what else changes, or pits two hypotheses against each other.

In the real world, constraints often make it difficult to create such a controlled experiment. Ethics, cost, and matters of practicality all impose limits. We can't move planets from their orbits to see if interesting side effects come about. Doctors don't believe they can really control, or even get accurate reports about, how much exercise people do over long periods of time. These constraints have led to a great deal of insight about how we can study the world without controlled experiments. Researchers have developed methodologies such as the double-blind study, in which neither the patients nor the doctors know who gets a placebo and who gets real medicine. This prevents expectations from having as much impact on the study. More generally, statisticians have developed sophisticated methods for extracting information from large studies, and the advent of cheap computers makes those methods ever more powerful. These methods aren't used much in security, because we lack data to which we could apply them.

There are fundamental questions we'd like to be able to answer. How *effective* are we as security practitioners? Are we pulling ahead of the bad guys or fighting a losing battle? If we are not improving, what's broken? In the absence of good testing and evidence, we can't answer these questions. Without the answers, talking points that claim either an improvement or a radical decline in security are unsubstantiated at best and self-serving at worst.

The act of seeking evidence is valuable. It is valuable when making decisions and when examining past strategy. The "state of the art" in information security is continuously moving forward, with new tools and techniques being developed all the time. But, in the real world, a student cannot graduate simply for having perfect attendance. The best intentions cannot be substituted for a passing score on the final exam. We should look for evidence of our success or failure to see if we are really making progress or if we are losing ground.

You might think that evidence abounds. It can feel like every technology magazine contains the results of a new survey about some aspect of security. The details of new security vulnerabilities are publicized far and wide. A cornucopia of "factoids" and articles in the security press and on security and IT web sites discuss vulnerabilities, hacking incidents, and so on. But are these data points useful? Do they enable us to make better security decisions, or is their purpose simply to entertain or distract? Do they allow us to formulate and test hypotheses? Do we have context for the data? Do we understand where biases might have crept in (or been introduced)? We can apply these tests to data to evaluate its value. In this chapter, we apply them to many of the sources of information that people rely on to make their security decisions.

It can be tricky to find objective data about information security. For many security initiatives, the more successful they become, the fewer bad things that happen. For example, suppose fewer security incidents happen. Then the difficulty is proving a negative—that a security incident *didn't* happen as a result of those actions. Was the initiative really a success, or was the outcome just luck? Perhaps an incident wouldn't have occurred even if the security measures were not in place. The absence of something can be hard to quantify, other than the recognition that it does not exist. We often only know how a security measure can fail after failure occurs. The majority of stories about information security in the popular press today describe incidents in which security has failed. Success is often silent, invisible, or boring. It doesn't make for a good story.

Continuing this thought about the nature of success and failure in information security, telecommunications companies offer service-level contracts to provide 99%, 99.995%, or some other level of availability for which they then engineer their systems. Telecommunications managers have learned to measure uptime, and they consider what each level of improvement costs. Moving from "three nines" (99.9%) to "six nines" (99.9999%) of uptime is usually exceptionally expensive, so people make choices about the appropriate level of investment in reliability. (To put "six nines of uptime" into perspective, it equates to only about 30 seconds per year of downtime.)

For telecommunications companies, data about the uptime of their systems is relatively easy to gather. Measuring security is much trickier. The first hurdle in measuring security is the question of what should be measured. What *is* "security"? The broadest answer is that security is a concept, much like happiness or intelligence. With intelligence, we've distilled some of that concept into properties that can then be measured, such as with an IQ test. There is nothing wrong with taking a high-level concept and deconstructing it into more palatable pieces; in fact, this is a useful scientific technique. We must do likewise with security, because if security can't be measured, it continues to be impossible to say whether we have more of it today than we did yesterday. Some of that analysis likely involves concepts from disciplines such as psychology, engineering, and operations. Security might be defined in terms of an absence of fear or the ability to resist attacks. It could also be defined as the level of assurance we have that engineering delivers what we hope it will deliver, even in the presence of clever adversaries. Any definition of security we propose is likely to be controversial. Where it enhances our argument, we'll be precise either in the text or in an endnote. Otherwise, we'll try to avoid a semantic war over definitions.

Philosophy aside, in the real world it is easy to find out precisely how many people died in car accidents last year. Data from independent tests is available regarding how likely occupants are to survive an accident in any particular make and model of car. But how long can a computer resist an attack? Is security better this year than last? Is there overspending or underspending on security? How does the level of security at any one company compare with its peers? Does the information that is available today allow us to answer these questions in an objective manner? Let's look at the potential sources of evidence that are available today, and we shall see.

The Trouble with Surveys

One of the most straightforward ways to try to understand a problem is to conduct a survey and see what everyone thinks. A logical place to begin looking for evidence is therefore in security surveys. Lots of people have done many surveys about various aspects of information security, but doing any survey in a scientifically defensible manner is hard. The first challenge is designing a set of questions that don't betray bias. Writing good survey questions is difficult, because the way in which a question is asked influences the answer. If someone is asked whether he thinks it is acceptable for an endangered species to become extinct, he will probably answer differently than if he is asked if the protection of a certain species of insect is more important than educating children.

The next challenge is finding a suitable set of respondents. For security surveys this can be tricky, because organizations hate talking about security failures. It is next to impossible to force any particular set of companies to reveal their history of security failures. A great many security surveys are simply published, and then anyone is allowed to respond. The difficulty here is that because anyone can answer the survey, the survey sample becomes self-selected. The people who answer the survey are unlikely to be representative of the larger world. This problem of self-selection is well known in surveying.

Security brings a unique set of challenges to surveying. Psychologists talk about the "valence effect," which is people's tendency to overestimate the likelihood of good things happening rather than bad things. Security professionals who are "in the trenches" will likely experience a *reverse* valence effect: believing that things are worse than they really are. This is because our recollection of painful events is highly influenced by the degree to which we were personally affected. Cops on the beat become cynical because they see bad things happen every day. Many security surveys today are answered by people who work directly in security, and these are the people fighting viruses and attacks.

One of the best-known surveys in computer security is the annual survey performed by the Computer Security Institute (CSI). In the 2004 edition of the survey, respondents were asked to rate the degree to which they agreed with the statement "My organization invests the appropriate amount in security awareness." The majority felt that their organization did not invest enough. But most respondents had the word "security" in their job title, so we have to consider the effect that selection bias might have had on this result. If the CFOs of those organizations were asked the same question, would their combined answer have been the same? No security survey targets only people outside the field. This leads to a selection bias effect. An anonymous telephone survey conducted of the authors of this book showed that 100% felt that this effect was "huge."

It is also clear that the organizations at which the respondents to security surveys are employed are not representative of average companies. The 2004 edition of the CSI survey had 486 respondents. For the organizations in which those respondents worked, 66% had more than 500 employees, and 81% had more than 100 employees. More than half of the companies (57%) had $100 million or more in annual revenues. We might reasonably expect that large companies experience more security activity than smaller companies. (Larger companies have more personnel and a larger internet presence. In short, they have more of everything—security activity included.) We also have no way of knowing within the companies surveyed whether wide variations exist in the degree of dependence on IT, corporate culture as it relates to propensity for risk-taking, and opinion as to the need (or not) for security measures.

A further impediment to the accuracy of surveys is that the vocabulary used in the security field is imprecise. Different people interpret terms such as "attack," "threat," "risk," and "intrusion" in subtly different ways. The concepts of a "vulnerability" and a "threat" are often confused, as is the difference between a "threat" and a "risk." Some businesses might perceive "port scanning" (the electronic equivalent of rattling a doorknob) as a hostile action, and others might consider it relatively harmless. Without a survey methodology that defines such terms, it is impossible to know what the respondents really meant.

Two professors at George Washington University analyzed the fourteen security surveys that were the most widely publicized from 1995 to 2000. They found that those surveys were replete with design errors in the areas of sample selection, the form of questions asked, and underlying methodologies. Unsurprisingly, the survey findings were wildly divergent. Seven of the fourteen surveys asked if the organization for which the respondents worked had a security policy. The results ranged from 19% in one survey to 83.4% in another. Eight surveys asked whether there had been unauthorized access to systems. The results ranged from 4% in one survey to 58% in another.

Today's security surveys have too many flaws to be useful as sources of evidence. Survey data does have *some* value, because it engenders the idea that data sharing will improve our collective understanding of security. But data from the security surveys that predominate today merely captures the feelings and perceptions of the respondents. This can be interesting if that is what you have set out to discover, but it doesn't help you make better decisions. Unfortunately, such surveys are often portrayed as authoritative. Bad data is often used to bolster the claim for the need to purchase new security products or services, either by vendors, consultants, or the security staff within companies. The U.S. Government Accountability Office (GAO) has presented the flawed data from security surveys to the U.S. Congress, possibly influencing government policy. Similarly, data from surveys has also been presented to the House of Lords in the United Kingdom, and probably elsewhere. (Refreshingly, the Lords were skeptical of the value of such surveys.)

Sometimes "statistics" take on a life of their own and become woven into the conventional wisdom. A prime example in information security is the claim that 70% of all incidents are caused by insiders. A well-known technology research and advisory firm has written that "70% of security incidents ... involve insiders." The report went on to state that "This finding should surprise no one." The report based that claim on only two incidents. In our research for this book, we were unable to find *any* credible evidence in support of the claim that 70% of all incidents are caused by insiders. A commonly quoted source was a survey carried out by the Association of Certified Fraud Examiners, but its focus is fraud and white-collar crime; the document does not even contain the word "security." Insiders certainly cause security incidents; we have seen and responded to them. Unless we know how many security incidents occur, we have no way of figuring out how many are caused by insiders. Examining security controls from the perspective of an insider is probably worthwhile. But let us not allow our analysis of the larger problem domain be swayed by catchy memes or "movie plot" stories. That is the path to misguided, inefficient spending that is ultimately driven by emotion and not evidence.

The Trade Press

Information security is now a large enough field to support several monthly magazines. These include publications targeted at practitioners, managers, and researchers. We refer to these as "the trade press" and exclude hacker magazines and academic journals that publish peer-reviewed articles.

The trade press provides several functions, including the broad dissemination of ideas, giving people a common frame of reference, and advertising new products and services. The trade press can be a good medium for publishing information that is not time-critical, such as stories and experiences. Early stories in the media introduced and popularized new attacks. An example was the "salami attack," in which a rogue programmer took rounding errors from thousands of accounts and put those fractional amounts into his own account. "Secrets of the Little Blue Box" was a 1973 article in *Esquire* magazine that explained how to manipulate the phone network. More recently, books such as *The Cuckoo's Egg* have told the story of East German spies breaking into U.S. defense department networks over the nascent internet, using a university astronomy department as a jumping-off point. These stories are great for what they are, but what makes them interesting is that they are unique. Stories typically need to say something new for them to be considered publication-worthy. This means that the more extravagant a story, the more likely it is to be published. The trade press leans toward stories that have entertainment value rather than instructional value. But entertainment is a poor source of evidence.

Magazines are ill-suited for publishing time-critical data. Some information security magazines dedicate several pages of each issue to presenting data about new security vulnerabilities and the prevalence and quantity of different types of attacks. This information is tracked month to month. One of the major data graphics used by one magazine is a map of the world showing the number of attacks that originated from each continent. A number of magazines track a top ten list of internet attacks.

If the intent of presenting such data is to empower and impel action, we must ask: *what* action? The types or quantities of attacks that occur on the internet as a whole do not have particular significance to any one organization—they are background noise. You might enjoy reading about them, but this shouldn't influence your day-to-day security decisions. Whether the general trend is up or down might be interesting, but it generally isn't useful. By the time a magazine goes to market, the information is almost certainly not useful. Perhaps the intent of publishing information about the number of attacks is to suggest that security is failing, or that the world is becoming a generally more dangerous place. We might expect, however, that as the internet grows and there are more participants, the number of attackers will also rise. Those attackers will look to automate attacks that they only previously carried out manually, increasing the number of attacks observed. But fewer attacks detected might *also* mean that things are getting worse, because it might mean that attacks are becoming more stealthy or successful and therefore are not detected. Therefore, no particular conclusion can be drawn from an increase or decrease in the number of attacks.

The internet is a far more suitable medium than books or magazines for delivering time-critical information such as the details of new attacks. Since 2001, the Internet Storm Center has acted as a clearinghouse for data about vulnerabilities and attacks that occur on a wide scale on the internet. The benefit of such sites is that they provide a window into activity that exists outside any one organization's environment. In theory, this then helps the organization determine whether it is being targeted or whether large swaths of the internet are also being attacked. These information-sharing efforts have value where they are carried out in an open and collaborative fashion.

Vulnerabilities

A *vulnerability* is a flaw in software that can be exploited. (The term isn't always defined this way, but it is what we use in this book.) Vulnerabilities are often discovered by researchers, who variously use them, sell them, or disclose them to various parties, including the vendor affected or the broader research community. How to maximize the value of vulnerability disclosure while minimizing the harm remains a controversial question. Here, we will focus on vulnerabilities as a possible source of evidence.

The task of researching and finding vulnerabilities in software can be time-consuming, complex, and can require highly specialized skills. However, the process of capturing and categorizing the quantity and types of vulnerabilities that researchers have found and published has become fairly robust. A number of databases freely available on the internet provide data about many years of vulnerabilities found in major software packages, including operating systems. But even though a large quantity of data about vulnerabilities exists, opinions vary as to whether the data signifies an overall improvement in security or a decline. It is difficult to apply the scientific method, because a number of variables are changing at the same time. Software houses add functionality to attract and retain customers. But as discussed in Chapter 2, the larger a piece of software becomes, the more opportunity there is for that code to have bugs—some of which will probably result in security vulnerabilities. The ability of software houses to find vulnerabilities in their products depends on the quality of their staff and tools. Public vulnerability counts depend on both the number of researchers and their skills. The side with the most people and the best tools will be most successful in the long run.

Software vendors have started trying to differentiate themselves from their competitors on the basis of the security of their products. Oracle has advertised some of its products as "unbreakable," even going so far as to claim that unauthorized users "can't break it" and "can't break in." Those claims were met at the time with incredulity from security researchers. In fact, an increasing number of vulnerabilities have continued to be found in Oracle products. Oracle has since backed away from the "unbreakable" claim, suggesting that the term actually refers to a "commitment to a secure product lifecycle."

Today it is not possible to write a computer program of any meaningful size in such a way that it can be proven that it does not have bugs, even when perfection is the goal. The space shuttle has been held up as a paragon of software-development virtue, but even its code has bugs. There have been cases where a vulnerability has been found in a piece of code that was written ten or twenty years earlier and reviewed many times. Tracking the number of vulnerabilities found in a particular IT platform or software product might be more indicative of how aggressively the code is being investigated for vulnerabilities, rather than the base rate of vulnerabilities that exists. Old code can also be found to be vulnerable to new categories of vulnerabilities as they are discovered.

As an aside, security vulnerabilities have been found in both commercial and open-source products built and sold by most of the major producers of information security software. In 2004, an internet worm used a single vulnerability in a security product line to compromise approximately 12,000 computers. The worm accomplished this feat in about 90 minutes and it also carried an intentionally destructive payload. This raises an important point: vendors of security products are no different from any other software vendor in terms of the internal and external forces that push on them. They want to sell products, and the sooner the better. Bugs and vulnerabilities are a natural consequence. Marcus Ranum described the situation like this: Imagine that you are the developer of a new piece of software. You can bring your product to market before your potential competitors, but knowing that it is insecure.

If you pick that option, you'll be driving a Ferrari in six months. Or, you can spend the time to fix the bugs. Which option will you pick?

We feel that the investments that software vendors are making in the security of their products will result in more secure products. Even so, it will continue to remain difficult to test this hypothesis in a scientific way. First, as we noted, there is not a single definition of security. Second, simply counting vulnerabilities isn't enough. (A lack of logging functionality may well be a security issue, but it is not a vulnerability.) Vendors are also under no obligation to report vulnerabilities they find and to fix them in their own products. Even if they did, they might have sufficient incentive to game the system and release numbers that are not objective. For prospective customers, the easiest external measure is the number of reported vulnerabilities. Another potential measure is the ability of software products to achieve "certification." Product certification schemes in security suffer from the problem that defining "what is to be tested and how" might turn out to be a can of worms. Government attempts to help, most lately in the form of the "Common Criteria," have produced excellent cures for insomnia at the cost of many trees. They have had few other benefits.

It will continue to be very difficult to evaluate and compare products on the basis of their security. (Some very interesting properties that we would like to know about, such as the number of vulnerabilities waiting to be discovered, turn out to be very hard to measure.) As a potential source of evidence, data about vulnerabilities is intriguing. However, it is challenging to apply well.

Instrumentation on the Internet

Since the late 1990s, academic and hobbyist security researchers have been deploying security sensors on the internet and sharing their results. Some of these sensors are configured to capture a wide variety of network traffic. Others are narrowly configured to detect only very specific behavior. Sensors that are loosely configured might detect an increase in traffic of a given type, but they likely won't be able to analyze it in detail because of the amount of data they must process. Sensors that are designed to detect specific types of attacks miss all unknown attacks. This type of instrumentation has more value when the results are shared quickly, because it allows organizations to determine whether the activity they see is happening elsewhere. To monitor the internet at scale can be quite expensive, but provides a wealth of interesting data.

An important research effort in this space is the Honeynet project. This group connects computers to the internet with the expectation (and hope!) that they will be attacked. The Honeynet project team members then monitor, analyze, and share information about the attacks observed. Their data provides a fascinating look into the mind-set and methods of attackers. Because the computer networks that the Honeynet project establishes are not "real," all the activity they see is hostile. This methodology is powerful because it allows attacks to be easily seen. Unfortunately, it also means that the results are less useful for answering broader questions about why information security fails. Users making mistakes seems to be a major cause of security failures, and that dimension is missing from "honey" experiments.

As a potential source of evidence, instrumentation on the internet provides a useful and focused source of technical data.

Organizations and Companies with Data

A number of organizations sponsor information-sharing efforts. Some organizations also collect, collate, and report on data. In the aftermath of the first internet worm, a Pentagon agency established a Computer Emergency Response Team (CERT) that has been widely imitated around the world. CERT acts as a clearinghouse for information about security vulnerabilities and incidents. Its data set is composed of information that has been voluntarily reported to CERT, and that data is kept secret. (CERT staff have occasionally published their analysis of that data.)

More recently, the United States has introduced Information Sharing and Analysis Centers (ISACs). According to their members, ISAC meetings are a great place to collect business cards but are not particularly useful for anything else. Similar private groups exist, such as the Forum of Internet Response Security Teams. We could go on, but all such organizations try to address their members' concerns about sharing data by making new members jump through hoops. Sometimes these hoops are financial, with substantial dues required. In the end, these organizations tend to focus more on secrecy than on useful information sharing. This essential problem has plagued every information security sharing effort of which we're aware. A sad irony is that some of the most effective information-sharing programs have been set up by the underground to share information about new vulnerabilities. Over the years, members of the underground have set up and operated important information-sharing initiatives, including mailing lists such as Bugtraq and web sites such as PacketStorm and Milw0rm.

Some companies publish reports as a way to market their expertise on a variety of subjects, from the details of attacks that occur to high-level summaries of spending patterns and analysis of new technology trends. It's only natural that companies that sell security products gravitate toward researching problems that their products are designed to fix. Unfortunately, it's rare for such reports to contain their underlying data. This may be because the company believes that the data is proprietary and provides it with some type of competitive advantage. Whatever the reason, this makes it hard for the reader of the report to judge the analysis: whether the data was gathered well and analyzed in a reasonable way, or whether the report might suffer from bias. Authors of such reports fight a battle in the reader's mind to quell the suspicion that the findings just happen to support the need for the product or service that the vendor is selling. If the goal of gathering data is marketing, that objective is likely better served by giving away not only the report, but also the data.

So far we have discussed possible external sources of evidence. Both organizations and individuals have one source of evidence that is readily available: their own experiences. Many organizations remember what went wrong in their past. Sometimes this is stories, and sometimes it is real incident data and analysis. This is a great source to study, but it's tremendously hard to compare. As people move from organization to organization, they may bring analysis methods with them. The data that fed that analysis probably stays where it was, and it may be hard to understand what differences exist between the old organization and the new.

The preceding chapter discussed how our personal and group orientations create a lens through which we see the world. We need to work to overcome those lenses and preferences. We need to accept that cognitive dissonance can be caused by our orientations and the facts not lining up the way we'd like. However, it is only natural that many of the security decisions we make are based on our knowledge and understanding of past situations. This process of making and correcting mistakes and of making and testing decisions can be viewed as a *feedback loop*. Feedback loops are an essential part of how we learn. To tap into those feedback loops of other individuals and groups, and to mitigate the possibly misleading effects of navel-gazing, we need mechanisms for effective information sharing. We have already noted the problems with how today's "information-sharing" organizations operate. Unfortunately, they have failed.

As a potential source of evidence, organizations and companies with data have the potential to be tremendously useful. The content that flows through these channels may not be objective. It can suffer from many of the problems we have outlined in this chapter. But the idea that more information, more evidence, ultimately leads to better decision-making is persistent.

In Conclusion

The sources of evidence that we have reviewed suffer from a number of problems. Analysis is often presented without the underlying data being made available, preventing effective critiques or further analysis. Some of the examples we noted were badly constructed surveys, perverse incentives in the trade press, and the difficulty of tracking vulnerabilities. The result is that the data that emerges from these sources rarely clears that bar where it could be considered *objective*.

The search for objective data on information security is at the heart of the philosophy of the New School. Without objective data, we are unable to test our hypotheses. Since there is a drought of objective data today, how can we know that the conventional wisdom is the right thing to do? That is not to say that the conventional wisdom is *necessarily* incorrect, but as professionals, we find it profoundly unsatisfying to not know the answer either way. Being unable to test hypotheses fundamentally inhibits our ability to improve.

Our feeling is that overall we *have* made substantial progress in many areas and that we have better and more security than if we did not have security practitioners or a security industry. But having to start such a sentence with "our feeling" hurts. It puts us in the same boat as those who decry progress in security—a flimsy boat on the high seas—because we have little to no objective data to justify our position. The lack of objective data means that there can be little or no substantive argument either pro or con, only one based on circumstantial evidence or subjective judgment.

This state of affairs is unsustainable for the commercial security industry and for security practitioners. When individual companies or the economy as a whole suffer a downturn, the information security group and its initiatives are often terminated. "Risk reduction" is too amorphous a concept to fund when expenses are being reduced. For security professionals, self-preservation and rational self-interest should lead us to focus on obtaining objective data about successes and failures and the factors that led to them. The next chapter discusses a new wellspring of objective data—one that comes from an unusual and possibly frightening source. Beliefs and feelings cannot carry us any further. The Catholic Church finally pardoned Galileo because, in the end, it is reality that counts.

Chapter 4

The Rise of the Security Breach

In 1854, London was in the grip of a cholera epidemic. Disease spreads faster and affects more people in the hothouse of a city, and an understanding of the causes of cholera was hard to come by. Physician John Snow had published a theory that cholera was waterborne, but that was only one theory among many about the causes of the disease. In the epidemic of 1854, Snow plotted cholera deaths on a map and determined that one public water pump was the source of the outbreak. That work is considered a pioneering event in the science of epidemiology, and it led to the creation of public health as a discipline.

We have argued that objective data that would enable good security decisions is in short supply. John Snow had the simple remedy of removing a handle from the pump of an infected well. We may not have such a straightforward solution, but better and more data will help. Ideally, we will get it through less traumatic events than an epidemic, but in information security, there may be an invisible epidemic of mistakes being made. As we said in the preceding chapter, failures of information security are not usually widely discussed.

People dislike talking about security mistakes. They fear the consequences. Mistakes are seen as embarrassing failures and a source of potential liability. Although much can be learned from information sharing, it is hard to break out of the pack and be the first to discuss what is happening to you. Opportunities for errors abound, as ChoicePoint, a company based in the Atlanta suburbs, learned in February 2005.

Nigerian con man Olatunji Oluwatosin opened several accounts with ChoicePoint in October 2004. He claimed to be a variety of financial companies that required access to the data that ChoicePoint has on its customers. Over the following months, Oluwatosin accessed the records of more than 163,000 individuals, choosing 800 to fraudulently impersonate and subject to identity theft.

ChoicePoint was one of the first companies to fall under the aegis of a new California law that requires organizations that lose control of people's personal data to notify the persons affected. That law, California Senate Bill 1386, is usually referred to simply as SB1386. Just two years later, it is now one of more than thirty-five state laws of its type. As required by SB1386, ChoicePoint notified 30,000 or so Californians of the security breach. MSNBC reporter Bob Sullivan broke the story. Shortly afterward, thirty-eight state attorneys general wrote to ChoicePoint, asking that their citizens be notified if they were also affected by the incident. Information about the breach from ChoicePoint was fragmented, contradicted by statements from law enforcement, and played itself out over a long background of conflict between ChoicePoint and privacy advocates.

It's ironic that ChoicePoint, a company that provides background checks and so-called "identity verification services," fell victim to such a fraud. That irony contributed to how the issue unfolded, capturing the attention of reporters, analysts, and bloggers. Data breaches became a major subject of stories and analysis. The Privacy Rights Clearinghouse began to maintain a running list of data breaches. One researcher and blogger realized that reports to New York State were subject to Freedom of Information Act requests, so he requested those reports and placed them in the public domain. Those people and groups acted because the data seemed interesting and worth capturing. For them it was a natural response. Those efforts made possible the creation of academic papers in law, economics, and security.

Back to ChoicePoint. It did not want to talk about what happened. Like everyone who has ever suffered from a security breach, ChoicePoint was concerned about the many costs, from the possibility of lost customers to bad public relations. But California's new law compelled ChoicePoint to disclose its breach, so it did. The new laws have shown that all sorts of groups have experienced breaches. As we write, over 700 organizations ranging from schools to governments, from commercial pygmies to giant multinationals, have reported errors. Reports have come not only from the U.S., but also from Canada, the U.K., Bermuda, and Japan. These breach notices offer the first public equivalent of the mortality notices studied by John Snow. Over the next few years, we hope to get more data, both by getting more data per breach and by getting data about more breaches. We hope that breach data will be reported to central resources that will share it, and that this will put the focus on data analysis and alleviate the effort involved in collecting and collating it.

People don't like to talk about any sort of mistake, but in a wide swath of industries they must. From small pills to large airliners, failures are discussed. In aviation, every error is announced and dissected. It is no coincidence that flying is among the safest ways to travel. Errors result in injuries or fatalities that are exceptionally low by mile traveled, by passenger experience, and by total deaths per year. This tight feedback loop within the airline industry is understood to benefit not just passengers, but also the airline industry, which can promote flying as a safe way to travel.

The shame of having made mistakes will recede as more and more organizations admit to them. We predict that the cost of notifying people will drop, and that the effectiveness of remedies offered will improve. New types of solutions more effective than credit monitoring will emerge. The disincentives for companies to disclose will decline, and by the time this book is published, the thunderous headlines will likely have gone away, replaced by a steady rumbling of reports inside the business or local interest sections of the newspaper. The public face of data breaches will diminish (except in extraordinary circumstances), but the data will increasingly become available.

Despite the desire to avoid scrutiny, liability, and other feared effects of breaches, they offer the best opportunity to gather and share objective data about failures in information security today. They also provide the best chance to transform cultural attitudes about discussing security issues. Breach data has less bias than many other possible sources of information about computer security. This is because the mandatory nature of reporting in many circumstances means that we hear about issues that would otherwise be suppressed. Breach data stands in stark contrast with the one-off nature of journalistic reports about security incidents. The public nature of breach data also means that anyone can pick it up and analyze it. More people will take note of the availability of breach data and study it. What follows is a relatively short analysis. As more data becomes available, more detailed analyses will be performed.

How Do Companies Lose Data?

Companies have lost data to fraudsters and crackers, they have lost it by throwing it away accidentally, and they have lost (or had stolen) backup tapes and laptops. We can broadly categorize such failures into two buckets: deliberate and accidental. Examples of deliberate failures are a con man signing up for an account—as with the ChoicePoint incident—and an intruder breaking into a company's wireless network. Accidental failures are events such as lost laptops or backup tapes.

When the breach data that is available today is categorized according to the number of records exposed, the majority of incidents can be seen to relate to lost or stolen equipment or media. This is perhaps not so surprising. An adage in the networking realm says to never underestimate the bandwidth of a truck full of tapes. A list of the names and social security numbers of every American takes up less than 10 gigabytes. This is larger than most of today's thumb drives, but easily within the capacity of a laptop, an iPod, or a couple of DVDs. Most breaches don't involve data that is quite so optimized, so the data may occupy more space, but the largest breaches have been because of lost backup tapes, DVDs, or laptops. There is some irony that auditors carried many of the DVDs and laptops lost in these incidents.

Only between 1% and 2% of total records were lost or stolen as a result of being exposed online. Only 0.5% of records were compromised due to so-called "insider" incidents. This would seem to contradict the conventional wisdom about the perceived enormity of "the insider threat." Either insiders are responsible for relatively few incidents, or they're detected at a far lower rate than other events.

It is possible to also examine trends that relate to organizations that have suffered a security breach. (Here we can only talk about the experiences of U.S.-based organizations, because the U.S. is the only country in which this sort of research has been done.) According to a Harris Research poll released in November 2006, just over one American in five has received at least one notification that his or her private information has been compromised. According to another survey, 62% of Americans had been notified as of mid-2007. Of these, just under half reported that the notification was from a government agency, and just under a third reported that the notification came from a financial company. Less than one in eight reported some other commercial concern, and roughly one in twenty received a notification from an educational institution or health-care facility. These numbers make a fair amount of sense, even though we are highly skeptical of poll data. By its own mandate, the government keeps vast collections of personal details about every citizen. Citizens can scarcely choose not to interact with the government, so the motivation to minimize the collection of data might be smaller. The motivation to protect government data may be slightly higher in the United States, because an inspector general rates each American government agency on its security activities in accordance with the Federal Information Security Management Act (FISMA). Other countries may have similar laws or different civil service traditions. Financial companies collect a great deal of data, with much of that data collection mandated by government. The finance sector has also become highly interconnected, so a breach at a single financial organization might affect more people than a breach at an average hospital, school, or college.

The breaches with the highest potential for headlines and perhaps harm will continue to come from organizations with the most data. It seems likely, however, that the amount of media attention will be proportional to the size of the company, not the size of the breach. Joe's Bait and Tackle Shop losing twenty credit card numbers makes for a poor story, but ChoicePoint losing twenty credit card numbers would be newsworthy because of the slew of earlier stories to refer to. Coca-Cola losing twenty credit card numbers would be noteworthy, because no words need to be wasted explaining who Coke is. Besides, the headlines ("I'd like to buy the world a Coke—with your credit card number") would write themselves. A final factor in what will be reported on heavily are instances in which an organization broke the rules in its collection of data. This was a factor in the stories about the board of Hewlett-Packard spying on reporters, as well as the publicity around the CardSystems Solutions breach (discussed in Chapter 2). At the time of the story, CardSystems was among the largest breaches reported, with up to 40 million credit cards exposed. The press also fed on the fact that CardSystems broke the rules set by Visa and MasterCard in storing data it should never have stored.

Companies have begun to understand that storing personal data is risky. A rational response is to try to reduce the amount of data they collect and to understand where data is stored. A new category of products branded as "data loss prevention" and "extrusion prevention" monitor corporate communications such as email and file transfers. These products block transmissions when it appears that restricted company data is involved. Encryption software is selling briskly to protect data on laptops from being revealed should a laptop be lost or stolen. There is a blending of motivation in some cases, between wanting to protect data and wanting to avoid mandatory breach disclosure. Some ambiguities in existing breach law make it unclear whether the loss of encrypted records must be disclosed.

As science-fiction writer William Gibson said, "The future is already here; it's just unevenly distributed." Breach reporting is also here, just unevenly distributed. Organizations around the world are reporting on failures, but they are doing so unevenly because of legal loopholes and scattered breach laws of varying strengths. But breaches will, for the near term, continue to impact organizations of all sizes and kinds, offering us windows into various worlds. When compared to the potential sources of evidence described in the preceding chapter, breach data is broader and less biased. Breach data that is freely available can be "sliced" by industry, by loss type, by data type, or whatever other measure seems interesting in support of making better security decisions. Naming names enables follow-up research, unlike research based on anonymous data. Examples include studies by Carnegie Mellon researchers on the impact of breach notices on stock prices, and the research we've done on mentions of breaches in Securities and Exchange Commission filings.

Disclose Breaches

Having said all this, an organization that experiences a breach will naturally have questions: Should we disclose? Can't we just cover this up and hope it goes away? The short answer is no. Covering up is a bad short-term strategy and a risky long-term one. As we've discussed, there are also broader implications for society.

The simplest argument for disclosing a breach is that in many cases, it is legally required. We're not lawyers, but if you have customers in any of thirty-eight states or in Japan, disclosure is probably required. It may be possible to spend a good deal of money on legal advice and notify customers in only certain states. Given the increased interest in disclosed breaches, it's possible that the media will start to notice partial notifications, much like what happened to ChoicePoint. Not an experience anyone wants to emulate.

Even in some places where disclosure is not explicitly required by law, authorities have publicly stated that they interpret their data-protection law to include breach notification. (Canada, Australia, and New Zealand fall into this category.) In some places, there might be no duty to notify, but there is an emerging duty of care. Laws, rulings from privacy commissioners, and the argument around duty of care are rapidly moving most of the English-speaking world toward greater disclosure.

There is a recurring theme in news stories about data breaches in which the organizations involved did not quickly disclose the incident. Customers and the general public affected by breaches are shocked that they were not informed sooner. A strong tone of outrage surrounds the idea that consumers and citizens who could be hurt should be notified in a timely fashion. Not only should organizations disclose, but they also should disclose sooner rather than later as a deliberate strategy. When faced with a breach, an organization should aim to get ahead of the news by notifying customers at once with the fullest details available. While lawyers may be able to argue for partial notice or no notice, such analysis would be more expensive and riskier than disclosure. The risk comes from notification coming out later, causing outrage.

There are other possible reasons to embrace breach disclosure. Organizations might promise to disclose as a signal that they are confident in the quality of their security. Companies that commit to disclose all breaches to their customers are making a statement about the investments they have made in security. An organization that lacks confidence in its security would not make such a commitment. This creates a new opportunity for companies to compete on security or privacy.

Many businesses will need to change their external reporting activity as a response to the legal requirements for breach reporting. These changes might initially be uncomfortable, and it might be tempting to respond by trying to roll back breach notification mandates. Not notifying customers or trying to lobby against mandatory breach disclosure would show those companies to be scornful of their customers. That sort of hostility seems a far better way to lose customers than telling them there was a mistake. (This is a hypothesis, and one that could be tested.)

Most companies have made a commitment to treat the data they collect with care. Organizations in sectors such as finance, government, and health may even be under strict legal obligation to do so. A company that promises to protect the information provided to it, fails to do so, and then fails to report that fact, may open itself to a charge of deceptive business practices. What constitutes a deceptive business practice is for lawyers to argue. Working to cover up a mistake runs counter to transparent and honest business practice. It was not the crime, but rather the cover-up, that forced Nixon to resign. Attempts to cover up mistakes are likely to result in harsh penalties in the future. In the event of a lawsuit, data is likely to come out as a result of the legal discovery process in any case. So, yes, mistakes happen, and mature organizations own up to them.

It may be possible to temporarily roll back mandatory disclosure, but this is an inefficient, short-term risk trade-off. If the way we approach security today is inefficient because we lack the data to help us improve, obtaining data is worth a great deal. It is true that the costs of breach disclosure are currently distributed inefficiently. Disclosure offers no immediate payback. In an ideal world, the benefits would be better aligned with the costs, but after years of security failures we've learned nothing. Breach data offers our best chance to overcome this. The future consists not only of mandatory disclosure, but of companies, governments, universities, and trade organizations all studying the reports, learning from them, and refining their processes.

Possible Criticisms of Breach Data

As a result of SB1386 and the ChoicePoint incident, we arrived at breach data as a happy accident. However, the breach data that is available today is not ideal for our full set of needs. We will discuss this topic; then we'll debunk the common criticisms.

The type of breach data that is available today represents only a subset of what we'd like to know. Some security experts note that the number of incidents reported seems low. U.S. government reports, driven by Congressional investigation, have revealed incidents that were not publicly known. Freedom of Information Act requests routinely reveal new breaches that have been missed by researchers scouring the news wires. These newly revealed incidents are both mistakes by government agencies and mistakes reported to them. Other researchers have compared laptop loss figures to reports of lost data and commented that the amount of sensitive personal data on laptops should have led to a lot more reports. Ultimately, we'd like to know about all computer crime, much like the (American) National Crime Victimization survey or the FBI crime statistics provide insight into all conventional crimes that are reported. Breach notices only provide us with data about privacy breaches, and we don't yet know what proportion of security breaches involve personal data. What we do know is that in each of these cases someone tried to protect the data and failed. We also know that other incidents are interesting but are not breaches. For example, denial of service attacks that lead to failures of availability seem to fall outside the meaning of "breach."

Mandatory breach notification laws are an expensive route to the data we'd like. Sending notices to customers affected by a breach costs money, as do other aspects of response, such as staffing a phone bank and perhaps providing credit monitoring or locking services. Much of the published analysis focuses on financial costs such as expected revenue loss from lost customers. It appears, however, that these costs are one-time events and that the stock market has already learned to discount them. Data breaches do not seem to have much of an effect on stock market valuations.

Some people believe that admitting to a security breach will drive away customers. There is research that shows that in most breaches, no more than a small percentage of customers will leave. This research has been published by companies that sell services for responding to breach events, so it might be exaggerating the effect. As people come to expect that mistakes happen, they will be less likely to withdraw their business because of them. This leads us to believe that the churn rate for customers who leave in the event of a breach is probably far smaller today than early surveys of consumers suggested. In the aftermath of one of the largest breaches to date (at the TJX companies, discussed in Chapter 1), sales actually went *up* in the two quarters following the announcements. Over time, we expect that only repeated mistakes and those that are attributed to carelessness might have an impact on share price and customer churn.

The claim is sometimes made that data that is lost by companies won't hurt anyone, so breach notification serves no purpose. However, over half of identity fraud victims have no idea how a criminal got hold of their personal data. (For the half who believe they know, we have no data about how accurate their beliefs are.) That gap in our knowledge can be closed only by analyzing breach data and its correlation to cases of identity fraud. The argument that data that is lost won't hurt consumers is not a valid reason for not disclosing breaches. Logically, if there is no chance of harm, we should be able to discuss each incident openly.

A similar (but contradictory) argument is that because customers have no effective means to protect themselves from identity theft and the other ill effects of the disclosure of personal information, mandatory breach disclosure does not serve the best interests of the general public. This may be somewhat true today, but new businesses are emerging that may help address the problem. If today's technologies cannot or do not help, new businesses with new approaches will emerge. Businesses that help customers "lock" their credit files against account fraud have already appeared. We expect to see a raft of new businesses arise to help companies report breaches, analyze breach data, and protect consumers against the broad set of threats associated with the disclosure of personal information. To the extent that they're effective, we welcome them.

Because of differences in breach disclosure law, the structure and content of breach reports are not standardized. Different data points, levels of detail, and terminology are used to describe the same things. This is somewhat of a challenge, but by no means an insurmountable one. John Snow faced similar challenges. Cholera is a viscious disease, and absent intravenous hydration, it kills young and old alike. The fear of cholera drove people away, and anyone who had a place to flee to during the epidemic did. This meant that sometimes deaths caused by cholera happened somewhere else, so a complete data set was not available. Deaths were a tragic and expensive route to the data. Just about any other data point would have been preferable, but those might not have led to enough information to test Snow's theory. The breach data that is available today is sufficiently detailed to allow us to draw many conclusions. As it becomes more standardized, detailed, and comprehensive, we will be able to draw even more conclusions and do so more efficiently.

Some might say that we don't need detailed or comprehensive breach data because many stories in the popular press discuss high-profile breaches, and we can draw conclusions from those accounts. Again, answering this question has parallels to Snow's work. He wallowed in his subject at great personal risk. He did not simply read newspaper reports and graph data. He went into the infected areas and talked to people about what was happening. He got up close and personal with a deadly disease that no one understood. What caused him to be able to effectively select the information that mattered? Some of it was his orientation as a physician, which led to his theory about the disease. Some of it was the depth of his immersion in the question. The key lesson is that analyzing breach data is far different from reviewing copy written by reporters. Breach data is both richer and broader. Today we get our data from web sites such as attrition.org/dataloss and pogowasright.org.

An analysis of the stories in the press shows that they don't line up with those in the state repositories of breach notices. So, what is in the press is not an accurate summary of the underlying facts. The lessons present within breach data exceed what we can learn from headlines alone. The public availability of breach data also means that our analysis is not limited by the people before us who have sifted, selected, and interpreted the information. There is a strong similarity to historians' preference for original source material. While an early historian may have done a great job of sifting through the documents to put together a narrative, another will do better by returning to the source, seeing the documents themselves, and deciding if other interpretations exist.

The final potential criticism we will note is that breach notices are believed to be career-limiting for the executives at fault, and that, therefore, there is a strong incentive not to report. Again, this is an established myth, but by and large it is false. (If management is at fault, however, it may be both true and appropriate.) More often, what happens is a mistake, and it is seen as a mistake rather than a failure of judgment. As we learn more, what can be described as a mistake versus what can be considered a failure of judgment will become clearer. In the absence of objective data such as breach data, a scattershot security strategy has been the default. So breach data *does* pose a risk to decision-makers. As breach data begins to illuminate the nature of mistakes that are being made, executives will open themselves up to criticism if they do not use breach data to guide their spending on security in the most appropriate manner. There will be security leaders who oppose these new rules—not just because they fear the effects of mistakes, but because they haven't yet joined the New School. They have not yet learned to focus on observation and objective measurement. Those who have know that nothing built by human hands is perfect. They have the maturity that comes from having faced failure and learned from it.

Moving from Art to Science

Breach reports tell us who lost control of data, how it was lost, and how much data was lost per incident. These data points allow us to consider with broad strokes the issues that lead to public reporting. Ideally, we want to be able to evaluate security strategies in detail and understand how various approaches might help prevent incidents. This would also help us identify what methods unequivocally do not help so that we can abandon them. Do people who attend one security training class do better than those who attend another? Is one particular type of security product superior to another? There are many other questions that we cannot answer without evidence.

We don't want to minimize the difficulties involved in answering such questions. We can't arrange a set of companies in test tubes, add heat, and see what comes out. In that respect, our data sources are more like those of astrophysicists or sociologists than those that a chemist or physicist might create by careful design. But this doesn't mean we can't learn from observation. Careful observation and analysis have led to our understanding quite a bit about how the universe is shaped, where it comes from, and what is happening far away. Some of the most interesting observations are even accidental. (When Penzias and Wilson found the cosmic background radiation left by the Big Bang, they weren't looking for it; they had built a radio that picked up a persistent noise that they couldn't initially explain.) It is true that computer security consists of a fog of moving parts, and that lurking near any simplistic analysis is the truism that correlation does not prove causation. At the same time, complex problems do get solved. Investigators bring a broad set of analytic techniques, ranging from explanatory psychological stories that can be seen to jibe with the data, to complex economic models. Some of these may enable hypotheses to be put forth and tested in a scientific manner. Underlying them all is the possibility of collecting objective data against which predictions can be made.

This core aspect of scientific research—the ability to gather objective data against which to test hypotheses—has been largely missing from information security. It is likely that many security strategies that are prevalent today and that were developed as a "best guess" in the absence of objective data will not stand up to scrutiny. Absent measurement, we are reminiscent of medieval scholars arguing about how many teeth a horse has, by reference to Aristotle, rather than by actually looking at a horse. So we need to study horses. "Fortunately," they can now be seen all around us. For a wide variety of interesting questions, it is possible to gather data about the causes of security breaches. It becomes possible to compare insider attacks to outsider attacks, to compare password failures to patch failures. We can apply that data to the questions that matter to us, and chart a new path with a greater degree of confidence than ever before.

Get Involved

We will speak here about how organizations and individuals can embrace the use of breach data. We will build on these thoughts in Chapter 8, when we discuss the application of the New School overall.

Jane Goodall made a career of studying chimpanzees. She spent years in the wilderness observing chimp behavior and group dynamics. Those deep observations made her an expert worth hearing. In a similar fashion, information security professionals should take time to gather and analyze security breach data, and be familiar with the analysis that others are doing. (Fortunately, you can do this from the comfort of your desk.) A security professional making planning decisions on topics related to data loss can better make those decisions by referring to the lessons of breach data. An organization that wants the focus of its security program to be on preventing data breaches can align its spending to protect against the types of incidents that are reported elsewhere. We will discuss in Chapter 6 how security budgets today tend to be set using rules of thumb. But because breach data is now available, spending strategies can be made much more efficient. Managers who approach a problem by investigating and gathering data and then propose solutions based on that data will succeed more often than those who look to generic, entrenched thinking. The most value that any individual or company can receive from breach data is for them to bring their questions and orientations to the data and study it themselves. Studying data doesn't require any theories. It simply requires data. Much like John Snow, getting involved is a great place to start.

As lessons are learned from breach data, those lessons must be communicated to the larger world. Every organization and individual who spends time analyzing breach data should communicate what they are studying and why. People with a variety of backgrounds will be able to bring fresh perspectives to breach data for quite some time, leading to interesting talks, journal papers, and other career-enhancing activity. This variety of backgrounds has been referred to as *hybrid vigor*, a term Dan Geer imported to the security field from biology.

To continue the momentum behind mandatory disclosure, the conversation about data-gathering must also continue. The requirement to report breaches is new, and some people and organizations are deeply uncomfortable with the new. They want things to be as they were, and they are working to roll back the new rules around breach disclosure. The more vibrant the conversation around breach data, the more individuals and organizations will become aware of the positive effects of the availability of that data. The more people who are aware of those benefits, the less likely that forward progress will be slowed. We're confident that the more we learn about breaches, the more value we will see, and the more questions we'll want to ask. It's the natural progression of data collection and analysis.

In Conclusion

When there are things that are not well understood, great scientists know that there is no alternative to getting into the details and *being there*. That is why scientists are willing to travel to a long list of uncomfortable and dangerous places to get near the things they want to observe. It's why natural historians and anthropologists observe not for a day or a week but for years. Seeing what's normal and what's abnormal often requires an immersion in the subject and a willingness to follow trails, not knowing where they might lead or if they'll be a waste. This is what allowed John Snow to succeed: immersing himself in the environment that gave rise to cholera. Fundamentally, medicine and public health involve observation and measurement before theories and diagnoses can be made.

We have identified a source of objective data for information security that is both new and important. We've discussed how that data can transform the way in which we discuss and approach security issues, and we have taken an initial stab at analyzing that data.

Breach data is bringing us more and better objective data than any past information-sharing initiative in the field of information security. Breach data allows us to see more about the state of computer security than we've been able to see with the traditional sources of information. It has also allowed us to demonstrate that some of the reasons why we don't share data are more fears than realities. Crucially, breach data allows us to understand what sorts of issues lead to real problems, and this can help us all make better security decisions.

The concept of gathering data, analyzing data, and being willing to adjust behavior based on the message of the data is at the heart of the New School.

Chapter 5

Amateurs Study Cryptography; Professionals Study Economics

Long before anyone had built a computer, mathematicians were constructing the underlying tools of logic on which all computers are built. The research of mathematicians such as Shannon, Turing, and von Neumann enabled us to understand the limits and possibilities of what computers and the programs running on them might do. Decades of brilliant engineering have allowed us to build increasingly complex systems and make them faster and usually smaller. The underlying mathematics remains unchanged—a testament to the power of good mathematical thinking.

Their origins and very nature make computers mathematical artifacts. Indeed, the deep abstractions of computer science are often indistinguishable from pure mathematics. Mathematicians have defined a subset of their field, applied mathematics, to distinguish it from other areas that have no expected practical application. Applied mathematics would be the black sheep of that scientific family, if not for computer science.

If we consider the challenges that we face within information security to be problems of logic, the answers to those challenges should be found through the application of mathematics. This hypothesis does not ring true with the experiences of most security practitioners. They typically feel that users and other "soft" factors are the reasons why security often fails. It is true that many problems within information security are usefully illuminated by math and logic. Once we have solved those problems, issues emerge from the ways in which computers, societal norms, and people's behavior intersect. This would not have surprised von Neumann, who helped invent game theory and who offered a framework for how to approach games like the prisoner's dilemma.

Looking back at our Turkish hacker from Chapter 1, his plans make no sense expressed in mathematical terms. However, they are entirely sensible when you consider that his victims were human beings and thus prone to making mistakes. Those mistakes allowed the gang to manipulate numbers within computers that eventually became little bits of colored paper that they wanted because other members of society would exchange those pieces of paper for goods and services. So, looking at the failings of computer security absent the context of people and society in which those computers operate is a narrow view that is unlikely to bring us effective solutions.

This is problematic, because people who learn about information security in college are taught a narrow set of lessons about what security is. Many academics think it should be treated as a mathematical problem. Historically, computer security or network security classes at universities and colleges have focused on the study of cryptography. They applied cryptography to rather abstract problems in which various parties communicate in the presence of an adversary. Cryptography is certainly a very useful building block, but most problems in computer security do not exist because of a lack of cryptography. A late 1990s analysis of security issues described in Computer Emergency Response Team (CERT) advisories found that 85% could not be fixed through the application of more or better cryptography. Thus, the time that students spend in security classes tends to be spent on indirect, theoretical aspects of problems that just happen to be mathematically interesting. (Some universities are addressing these issues, but absent good data about what goes wrong, it has been challenging to craft new curricula.)

We are by no means arguing against the use of mathematics, but rather against the application of mathematics to security problems to the exclusion of all else. The New School suggests that because computers are inevitably employed within a larger world, information security as a discipline must embrace lessons from a far wider field. Some of those lessons will come from the fields of economics, psychology, and sociology. Accomplishing this will require individuals such as researchers and practitioners in disparate fields to collaborate and cross-ferment ideas. Some of this intermingling has been gathering steam for a few years in the area of "the economics of information security." Other instances of collaboration between disciplines are just getting started, or have not yet begun.

Cross-disciplinary endeavors can be hard for academics, who benefit from having their work published in prestigious journals that, by their very nature, tend to focus on existing lines of research. Those journals might not be amenable to publishing work that suggests that, in fact, we've all been looking at problems from a wrong or at least skewed perspective. The editorial boards of academic journals might hold such work to a higher standard, so it may be practically discouraged, if not consciously. We're happy to give the benefit of the doubt. We believe that most academics or journal editors will not flinch at the opportunity to advance the field by presenting new perspectives.

This notion that improvement can come from the introduction of new perspectives flows from the approach of observing the world and asking why. We ask why to understand people's motivations—their conscious and unconscious incentives—and in doing so, learn to craft better approaches to security challenges.

The Economics of Information Security

Ross Anderson is a professor of security engineering at the University of Cambridge Computer Laboratory in England. His areas of research include banking, analysis of cryptographic protocols, security of medical information systems, and public-policy matters, among others. In 2001, he published a paper titled "Why Information Security Is Hard: An Economic Perspective." That paper is generally considered the first piece of work to explicitly analyze the broad field of information security from the perspective of economics. It describes how many of today's challenges in information security can be understood using the models and language of microeconomics, such as the theory of incentives, network effects, and liability. Anderson's central observation was that the motivations of the various parties who interact with a system are often the most significant factor that influences its security. In other words, how people are motivated to behave can be as important as, or often more important than, how the system is designed to behave.

What's unique about this idea is that it contrasts with the mind-set that information security is primarily a technology problem, and that ultimately the "solution" can be reached by piling on more and more technology. In fact, there is no data to show that businesses that spend more on security products will *necessarily* experience a corresponding reduction in security incidents. (Ways this might happen include when a company buys products and leaves them on the shelf, or turns them off after too many false alarms.) Multiple factors influence the possibility of a security incident, and the number of security technologies in use within an organization is just one. It may not be a leading indicator.

Security experts often point to user behavior as a factor that leads to security incidents. For example, experts accuse users of selecting poor passwords. The prevailing approach within the security industry is to impose technological solutions that attempt to mandate or constrict users' behavior. Many organizations spend tremendous amounts of energy trying to get users to pick good passwords. Good passwords are a cornerstone of many authentication schemes, and much security fails if impersonation is easy. Unauthorized people can log in and do things they shouldn't. Investigators might then focus on the wrong person. If an organization views this as a technical problem, it imposes its policy through tools that implement arcane password rules regarding capitalization, special characters, and the like. The result is that some of the company's users write down their passwords, and others use the same password everywhere. Still others invest time in inventing password-changing schemes so that they can use roughly the same password with enough changes to satisfy the mechanics of the policy. Of course, writing down passwords violates yet another of the company's security policies.

This cycle, long frustrating to technologists, makes perfect sense when viewed through two economic lenses. The first is that the two sets of incentives are not aligned. Users have no particular incentive to use a complex password. Indeed, they would most likely prefer no passwords at all, or to use very simple passwords across all the systems to which they have access. The second is that the small demands of each system with its own complex password policy accrue in the individuals asked to remember those many different passwords. Therefore, we see people ignore, sidestep, or subvert the policies. There is a saying: "If users are given a choice between security and dancing pigs, they'll pick dancing pigs every time." This quip points out that users' incentives usually are not aligned with the goals of security technologists. At the same time, it exposes the mind-set that users are the enemy, or that they are worthy of condescension. Railing against human nature hasn't been a winning strategy. We'll turn to this subject later in this chapter.

When years of earnest exhortation haven't changed anyone's behavior, perhaps we need a new approach. The systemic failures we see in computer security require more than simply technical analyses—and these broader analyses are starting to happen. Let us now look at some examples of how economics can provide insight into significant or interesting problems within information security.

Why Do Some Security Technologies Fail?

Consider a street with several stores. The stores have suffered a rash of burglaries, so the merchants decide to hire a security guard. A guard would be too expensive for any single store to hire, but it may make sense if they can share the cost. Once the guard is in place, all the stores benefit. They hope the number of burglaries will be reduced. But even if some merchants decide not to pay, they would still receive value from the guard. If too many merchants decide to employ that strategy, there won't be enough funds to hire the security guard in the first place. The only stable state is where there is no guard and none of the merchants are happy. This illustrates two things. The first is what economists call "free-riding." A merchant who does not pay is free-riding on the investment of others. The second is a Nash Equilibrium, in which there is no move that any one player can make that would make anyone better off.

Here is another example of such an equilibrium. In Philadelphia, car insurance is expensive, so some people drive without insurance. If you get into a car accident in Philadelphia, it is more likely, compared to other cities, that the other person involved in the accident will be uninsured. This in turn drives up the cost of car insurance in Philadelphia, causing even more people to drive without insurance. No one individual can do anything helpful to improve the situation.

A final example of an equilibrium is that everyone wants to learn from the security mistakes of other organizations. Everyone would agree that the ideal situation is for everyone else to fully disclose their breaches. Fortunately, breach notification laws have forced organizations to act differently. There are good reasons to disclose breaches, and regulation helped break the equilibrium.

The outcome for any participant in these situations depends on the decisions made by the other participants. In other words, the benefits of your investments can depend on the investments that others make, or choose *not* to make. This same situation exists in the security world and can be applied as a concept for understanding the adoption of security technologies. It can also help us understand how we might influence their adoption.

Many of the network protocols that enable the internet to function are known to have security problems. One example is the Domain Name System (DNS), which is used to convert between numeric addresses and domain names such as news.bbc.co.uk. DNS has well-known, documented security weaknesses, and a newer, more secure alternative exists. But the use of DNS remains systemic, and a mass upgrade to the new protocol that has better security seems unlikely to occur, even in the long term.

If the internet used high-security protocols, we would *all* benefit. This would require ISPs, governments, and companies with an internet presence to adopt the new protocols. Stuart Schechter has pointed out that for these new protocols, a minimal level of adoption would have to be reached before *any* organization would see *any* benefit. As such, there is little to no incentive for any individual organization to upgrade, since the cost to upgrade is greater than the benefit the organization would initially receive. Historical evidence shows that hoping that organizations will act altruistically for the benefit of internet security appears to be a losing strategy. So, what strategies could be used to change this situation?

An authoritarian approach would be to mandate the new security technology. Tell everyone that only the new protocol will be supported at the end of the year, and then flip the switch when the time comes. This approach tends to appeal to certain kinds of security practitioners. But without a "king of the internet" who could perform such an act, it is most likely a pipe dream. A second approach would be to bundle the new security functionality within a product that will be widely consumed, such as a new operating system or piece of network infrastructure, and turn on the functionality by default. This bundling approach is a highly workable strategy, but it depends on vendors understanding and valuing the instrumental role they could play and then acting on that knowledge. Some people think this is fertile ground for industry lobbying of government, to get subsidies for the adoption of the new security technologies through tax breaks. It seems likely that this would inhibit innovation, as the cost of technology becomes distorted through the tax code.

A third approach would be to hope large organizations adopt the new technology for their own internal use. This might make the value high enough for other organizations to also adopt the technology, and then mass adoption would (hopefully) occur. There are working examples of this phenomenon, such as fax machines. Large companies initially purchased fax machines to allow staff at physically distant sites to send documents to each other. This got the ball rolling toward widespread adoption where companies and individuals could communicate not only internally, but also externally. If the internet had only a single computer attached to it, it would be useless. The value of each internet connection goes up as the number of people connected to the internet increases. This is an example of the network effect. The more people who own a technology, the more value there is for everyone else who owns that technology. A weak version of this operates offline. For example, some people buy Hondas because there are lots of Honda repair shops.

Another example of the network effect is in industries such as online gambling. Fraud affects one fifth to one half of all transactions, so digital cash systems that have many of the important properties of cash would be hugely valuable. If you are not knowledgeable about the intricacies of digital cash systems, suspend disbelief for a moment and accept that mathematics makes it possible to create numbers that work as money while preserving privacy, ensuring security, and being transferable between people. Why is such a system not widely available? It is not the mathematical complexity that is the barrier. The mathematics underlying the frequency-hopping, encrypted radio transmissions that make cell phones work is perhaps more complex. The issue is that deploying such a platform requires software on home computers, software at lots of merchants' web sites, and software at the banks. It is hard to get so many different parties to simultaneously commit to the system and embrace it at once. In the case of electronic cash, questions also surround patents, law, and regulation, and raise the cost for everyone involved.

Our analysis above is built on Schechter's paper "Bootstrapping the Adoption of Security Protocols." Related work by Geoffrey Moore argues that markets for products function in stages. Many companies (not just in security) stumble and fall as they attempt to transition their customer base from early adopters of the technology to the mass market. A new product serves some group of early adopters well, and the producer focuses on that group to the exclusion of a broader market that might be reached. The broader-market product is usually simpler and less expensive. For example, the Palm Pilot was not the first handheld computer. It followed the Casio Boss and Apple's Newton. Technologists who remember either can explain (at length) why each of these "should" have been adopted in the mass market. Unfortunately for them, not all worthy technology gets widely adopted. This applies just as much to security as it does to other fields. The adoption cycle that Moore describes is driven by careful attention to the needs of one group, and ensuring that that group's needs are fully met. As that market becomes saturated, it can act as an evangelist to other groups. An example of this type of success in security is a technology called Secure Shell (SSH). The first group that SSH helped was system administrators. Other computer users became aware of the capabilities of SSH because it was being actively used. Those other features, such as "tunneling," were then found to be useful enough that other groups picked up SSH. SSH is now in widespread use, and many other systems rely on SSH for communications security.

We can see that a security technology tends to be adopted in the mainstream when the user directly and immediately perceives the benefit of the technology. Where the adoption of a security technology benefits another party, or where some minimal level of adoption must be reached, we must look at other strategies to propel adoption forward.

Why Does Insecure Software Dominate the Market?

Most software is insecure. Almost all major software packages and platforms have a history of security vulnerabilities. Why do organizations continue to purchase insecure products? Part of the answer is that product features create more easily understood value than security. Even if two pieces of software have roughly the same features, it can be hard to understand which one has better security. There is even legitimate disagreement about what it means to have "good" security, as discussed in Chapter 2. Attempting to measure security requires time and money spent on experts in software security, so the transaction costs involved in evaluating software security are high.

Transaction costs are an important concept in economics. The most obvious transaction costs that people encounter are the "closing costs" incurred when buying a house. These are costs you pay to get the deal done. Sometimes transaction costs are explicit financial costs, but they can also be seen as including time and effort. For example, some credit card companies make their legal terms and conditions complex partly to drive up the transaction costs of comparison and make switching to another credit card more difficult.

In addition to high transaction costs, there are other reasons why assessing software security is hard. The results of security evaluations are rarely consistent. Two different experts with different areas of expertise will likely identify different issues. Getting organizations to invest in evaluating the security of software they are considering purchasing is also challenging. Free-riding on the analysis of others would be a perfectly reasonable strategy for organizations, except that currently no worthy evaluations are being done upon which to free-ride. Most software security evaluation programs are paid for by the vendor that creates the software being evaluated. To our knowledge, none have flunked an applicant.

Because "security" is so difficult for prospective customers to evaluate, it is rarely prioritized above other factors in their purchasing process. As a result, vendors that develop software rationally choose to invest in other factors that are more visible to prospective customers. Hiring programmers and managers who have experience in building secure software is also expensive. Software vendors can reasonably assume that it will probably be years before their decision not to focus on security will have any impact on sales. Lots can go wrong with a fledgling company before then. In the future, new management might be in place to deal with the effects of the prior lack of investment in security.

These factors combine to result in a "market for lemons." This means that it is difficult to distinguish between products that have more or less security, and that no vendor has an incentive to sell a product that has high security. No vendor *wants* its product to be perceived as a lemon. Therefore, the vendor makes a concerted effort to transmit "signals" to prospective customers that its products do in fact have good security. The market today employs two general strategies for trying to do this. The first is to make claims about the processes that go into ensuring security qualities, and producing measurable evidence of improvement. That evidence can be hard to obtain or interpret, as described in Chapter 2. The second strategy is to simply make claims about your software. This often backfires, because the claims made can betray a lack of understanding to people who are experienced in evaluating software security. Examples of this second tactic backfiring include advertising security as "unbreakable" or "virus-proof."

One idea for how to address insecure software is to extend liability to security issues in software. The idea is that liability for a problem should fall where it is cheapest to fix. The thinking goes that imposing liability on software producers will encourage them to invest in software security, and the software that they create will then become better.

This idea has a number of problems. They range from the practical to the theoretical. On the practical end, how far should the liability extend? If a company ships an open-source package (one that is given away), should the company be liable for the product? Apple ships commercial versions of open-source software packages. This allows Apple to provide its customers with high-quality software at a low cost. If Apple were held liable for the open-source software it ships, it would have to either recreate the software in-house or analyze and perfect it. Building perfect software is impossible. As the defects are repaired, there is a risk of new problems being introduced. More worrisome, people don't agree what "secure" means or what a company should reasonably do to make a piece of software "secure." There are many experts with passionately held opinions—a nice scenario for lawyers. Uncertainty around security would cause some projects to be canceled, making for a worse selection of software for consumers and businesses.

Even assuming that "perfectly secure software" could be built, what about user error when the software is used? Perhaps software would include a warning such as "Caution: the software you're about to enjoy is extremely fragile." Alternatively, software might come with thousand-page-long manuals that the user must read in order to get the warranty. Giving software creators an incentive to claim that "all problems exist between the chair and keyboard (PEBCAK)" seems like it would create a new set of problems, perhaps worse than the software security problems we face today. Finally, new liability around security could impede breach disclosure (depending on the precise wording of the law). Companies would find reasons to sweep issues under the rug as a way to avoid liability. This would put the brakes on a very important new source of evidence.

Insecure software persists within the marketplace not because companies that purchase software don't care about security. Companies would consider security part of their purchasing process if it were easier to measure security and if those measurements could be trusted. A market for lemons can be understood as the natural outcome of the transaction costs associated with evaluating software security and a lack of objective data about software security.

Why Can't We Stop Spam?

We'll use spam as a final example where economics can help us analyze an intractable security problem. Spam has blossomed into a resilient ecosystem of people with a variety of products to sell (real, forged, or imagined), middlemen who market these products, and infrastructure providers who send the email messages through the defenses that have been built.

Spammers invest in ways to get their email past your defenses. They have a two-pronged strategy. First, they misspell words, use images, and do everything they can to get past the text filters that most people use. If they went to all that effort, but sent their email messages from only a few computers, it would be easy to knock those computers off the internet or blacklist them. Therefore, spammers employ a second technique—sending their spam from many different "zombie" computers. Because spammers control a shifting pool of hundreds, thousands, or even hundreds of thousands of zombie machines, their operations are very hard to shut down. Spammers may live in places where their money goes further than it would in New York City. It may make sense for them to invest months of effort for a few thousand dollars. This "cost advantage" enables attacks that many people would dismiss as not worth the effort.

Why is it apparently so easy for spammers and other criminals to compromise so many computers, turn them into zombies, and then use them to send spam? And why does this problem persist?

Some countries have made sending spam illegal. The problem is that in lots of other places, spamming is not illegal. Even where it is illegal, there is competition for police resources. Spam is not as important to the police as a mugging or an assault. Catching one spammer takes much time and effort, and the payoff may seem small, especially if the spammer is in another country. Thus, the risks to a spammer are low, because the deterrent effect of the law is so small.

Economists speak of externalities, in which the costs of a transaction are not carried entirely by the people involved. People who drive sport utility vehicles (SUVs) that emit more fumes than smaller cars don't experience any more smog than anyone else. SUV owners don't personally experience the consequences of their actions in a proportional manner. The same problem exists with the security of home PCs. When a PC is turned into a zombie and is used to send spam, the owner of the PC doesn't directly suffer the consequences.

There is no software marketed as preventing a home PC from being turned into a zombie, because consumers would be unlikely to purchase it. Luckily, most antivirus products provide a reasonable level of defense against a home computer being turned into a zombie. Consumers *do* pay for antivirus software, because they don't want to lose their files to a virus. This is bundling, which we discussed in Chapter 2 as a strategy for increasing the adoption of security technologies.

Unfortunately, not every home computer connected to the internet has up to date antivirus software installed. The remainder represent many millions of computers—more than enough for spammers to take advantage of. Even a small fraction of all computers connected to the internet represents a massive number.

Unscrupulous people are making lots of money sending spam. Spammers face hardly any risk of being caught. The combination of these incentives and the externalities, magnified by the size of the internet, means that it is perhaps impossible to stop spam.

We have discussed how ideas from the field of economics can be used to shed light on some specific problems in information security. The same approach can be brought to other challenges, such as the analysis of principal-agent relationships.

Alice wants to sell her car but has very little free time to look for prospective buyers, so she hires Bob to help. But how does she know he won't sell the car to one of his friends at a discount, and tell her that was the best price he could get? Economists call this the principal-agent problem. Alice is the principal, and Bob is her agent. In this simple example, the obvious solution is to pay Bob half the money he gets above the car's book value, thereby rewarding him for working hard.

The principal-agent problem has been studied extensively for lessons about paying CEOs. The board of directors at a company wants their CEO to be sufficiently motivated to increase the firm's value. If they give the CEO lots of stock options, he might take too many risks, aiming for a huge rise in share price. On the other hand, if the CEO has all his money invested in the firm's shares, he may act too cautiously. (If the CEO has options, he may purchase some shares at a given price. If the stock is trading for more than the option's strike price, the CEO can exercise his options at a profit.) Finding the right blend of incentives that motivates the CEO in the ideal manner turns out to be a tricky problem. In a similar fashion, in conversations about hiring security experts, we often hear questions such as "is he a rock star?" Rock stars are people who are so good at what they do, they can choose which projects they want to work on, because they can always find another job elsewhere. Because they are so hirable, and because security experts are scarce, managing the agency problems associated with these individuals can become a challenge.

Addressing principal-agent problems is a key issue in security when considering the work of various groups such as outsourcing partners and auditors. Auditors have an incentive to point out a tremendously long list of problems. (This is commonly called CYA: the auditor points out every possible problem to avoid liability. One of the authors once did a security audit for a civil rights organization. He felt the need to point out that background checks are a very common practice, knowing full well that the organization opposed them.) The auditee would prefer a list of audit findings that allows it to balance risks and the costs to mitigate those risks. Companies that perform outsourced security monitoring might be tempted to save money by performing only superficial levels of monitoring. After all, if they're performing the monitoring for a customer, how likely will the customer be to notice what has been missed?

Psychology

Psychology is another science we can use to better understand information security challenges. One such challenge is the topic of *security patching*. Over time, security vulnerabilities are found in pieces of software, and the vendor issues a security patch. As soon as the user of the software has applied the security patch, she should be protected against the security vulnerability. Patches contain changes to a program. They can be read to understand what those changes are. Using the changes as a map, security researchers can analyze the original program to learn about the vulnerability or vulnerabilities that the patch fixes. With this information, they can create exploit code, which takes advantage of the vulnerabilities.

How long exploit code is widely available before a patch is applied is of crucial importance, because it defines how long systems are vulnerable. (We are simplifying here in assuming that no other work-around to the vulnerability exists, which is not always the case.) From a pure security perspective, there is no reason *not* to apply a security patch, and yet millions of system administrators and individuals regularly choose not to do so. Why is this the case?

An important reason is that applying a security patch could destabilize the system to which it is applied. Because of this, it is common for system administrators to test patches by installing them in an incremental fashion throughout their computing environment. We've seen organizations that have used this incremental deployment strategy. Some took a cautious approach, sometimes with up to seven test groups of computers. This meant that security patches could take a hundred days to be deployed to all the computers that needed them throughout the environment. Research has shown that most bad patches are fixed within ten days. Therefore, there's probably little improvement in patch reliability between eleven days and a hundred days. Also, we've rarely seen anything like a rational basis for how many tiers of tests should exist, how many machines should be in each tier, or expected failure rates for testing.

By understanding that tension exists between the security risk of not installing a patch and the operational risk of installing a patch, we can design a strategy that allows us to balance these incentives in an optimal fashion and time the application of security patches. The key difference is between making decisions based on fear and making decisions based on risk.

Another lesson we can learn from psychology is that psychological effects such as *risk compensation*, also known as *risk homeostasis*, can have surprising effects on how human beings interact with security measures. Understanding these effects can help us design systems that provide better security in a more effective manner. Risk compensation can best be explained by walking through some examples.

An antilock braking system (ABS) improves a driver's ability to maintain control of the car while braking. In Munich, a study was performed on the behavior of taxicab drivers. Two groups of cars were tracked. They were identical, except that one group had standard brakes, and the other had ABS. The taxicab drivers were randomly assigned a car from one of the groups. All accidents involving the two groups were tracked; 747 car accidents were recorded during the three years of the study. The surprising result was that there were *more* accidents involving the cars that had ABS.

If you go skydiving but don't deploy a parachute, you're guaranteed to have a bad day. The major cause of death in the sport of skydiving has been exactly that: failure to deploy a parachute. Observing this, a European company named AirTec designed and built a device called a Cyprus that automatically deploys a parachute at a minimum safe altitude. That technology has been widely adopted by skydivers and has saved many lives. But the number of fatalities per participant in the sport has remained relatively constant, even after the introduction of this important new safety technology. What has happened is that there has been an increase in fatalities from jumpers attempting to perform higher-speed landings—flying their fully deployed canopies into the ground.

One ten-year study of smokers found that those who stopped smoking had fewer instances of lung disease, but their average life span was actually *shorter* than the group who decided to keep smoking. Another study showed that smokers who were given low-nicotine cigarettes inhaled those cigarettes more deeply and more frequently, thereby sustaining their level of nicotine intake.

As one last example, people who wear a seat belt while driving are more likely to survive an accident. However, in the United Kingdom, the number of deaths in car crashes actually went *up* after the law was passed that mandated seat belt use.

All these studies reflect the same underlying tendency. After a particular safety measure is introduced, the participants appear to reset the amount of risk to the level at which they were previously content. The participants do not get "safer"; they simply reapportion the risk elsewhere. Why does this happen? Returning to one of the preceding examples, why doesn't introducing ABS make taxicab drivers safer? The answer, according to risk compensation theory, is that drivers with ABS think they're safer and therefore perform more aggressive maneuvers. A separate study carried out in Oslo found that people who drove ABS-equipped cars drove much closer to the car in front of them, compared to cars with standard brakes. Why doesn't an automatic parachute-opening device reduce the number of fatalities in skydiving? Skydivers take into account the new safety device and perform riskier jumps.

Attempts to reduce risk are continually frustrated when the subjects deem their level of risk to be satisfactory. The insurance field calls this concept "moral hazard." When people know that their assets are insured, they often compensate by behaving in a more reckless manner. The insurance companies build their models to anticipate this effect. Banks provide other examples of moral hazard. The "Savings and Loan" debacle of the 1980s involved U.S. banks insured by the government. With that insurance, they invested in riskier and riskier gambits to earn returns to attract savers. The crisis cost U.S. taxpayers roughly $125 billion. Similar risky loans have led to a crisis in "subprime" lending in the U.S. and the U.K., including a bank run against Northern Rock in the U.K.

Can better approaches to security be designed with the knowledge that moral hazard exists? A 1992 law in Australia made bicycle helmets compulsory. As someone using risk compensation theory could have accurately predicted, the number of cycling deaths remained the same after the law went into effect. Compare the approach of the Australian government with the approach taken in the Netherlands. In the Netherlands, relatively few cyclists wear helmets, but their injury and fatality metrics are comparatively very low. This was accomplished in part by creating dedicated cycle lanes that separated road traffic from cyclists. *A safe environment was created*, with no safety decision put in the hands of the "user." Nobody likes getting food poisoning, but no one in first-world countries chooses to learn about biology to protect themselves from that risk. People rely on the process of inspections that the health and safety board uses to shut down unhygienic restaurants. In fact, no one should have to know that the health and safety board exists, and that is exactly as it should be. They have succeeded when the public is protected from risks without knowing about either the risks or the protection mechanisms.

A twist on this approach, being used successfully in some European cities, is to remove visible safety measures such as crosswalks, speed bumps, and stop signs. The result seems to be that people drive more safely. It may be hard to adapt this thinking to computer environments, where the dangers are less visible and visceral. These aspects of human psychology may hold substantial lessons for the way in which security measures are designed. Visible security measures appear to have the effect of making people take more risks. There are implications for the ways in which we attempt to deliver better security, from interface design to the creation of security policies and the practices of security education and security awareness training.

Sociology

Security practitioners love to exhort. One of the things they exhort people to do is to lock their screens. Almost no one does it. They think that locking their screens sends a message of distrust to their coworkers. That's an uncomfortable message to send. In one of Microsoft's security teams, a prank has evolved where it's acceptable to bend company policies by "borrowing" a computer left unlocked and sending prank email to the team. (There are strong limits on what pranks are acceptable. No one should do this to anyone involved in producing a security update. The mail sent should also clearly say "Fire me!") The effect is that everyone on the team locks their screens.

This is a clever way to influence people's behavior. Experts have been trying to get people to lock their screens for a long time. Designing this solution would require an understanding that the issues with locking screens are not simply laziness or externalities. Rather, it's an issue of how people interact with one another. Sometimes those interactions are economic, but other times, sociology may be a better guide to how people act around each other. How people behave on the security team we used in our example could easily be described in terms familiar to anyone who has studied sociology. There is team formation, the setting and communication of norms, and activities that signal membership in a group. It's a practical application of sociology to a question of security.

Another area where sociology can help is in understanding risks of monoculture. Diversity is a wellspring of new perspectives. We've discussed the idea that people from different fields bring different perspectives to their work. It's not just different fields that can bring different perspectives. Research regularly finds that the more diverse a group, the better the solutions that emerge. A chapter that proclaims the benefits of incorporating diverse new perspectives and ideas would not be complete without noting that the professional information security community is not very diverse. The conferences we attend on information security topics are a sea of middle-aged white men. By observation, such conferences seem less diverse than the broader computer and IT professions. The same applies to the apparent ethnic origins of computer security practitioners. Since we don't have numbers, we'll just say that sitting in front of a screen all day doesn't turn everyone that pale.

Assuming that our observations are representative, why is computer security such a monoculture? Is it worth trying to change, and, if so, what might we do about it? One of the main "feeder routes" into computer security is IT. In the U.S., IT tends to be full of white men, and this might not appear especially attractive to other groups. This may be an example of a self-perpetuating state, without malice by anyone involved. Like many of the examples in this book, it might be a situation where the majority want things to be different but don't understand the reasons that perpetuate the status quo.

Another observation is that the subculture within computer security, most notably at hacker conventions, has evolved to a point of remarkable hostility and exclusion. There is often an assumption that women in the technology field must work in sales, marketing, or some other nontechnical role. Not only is this exclusion profoundly wrong, but the homogeneity of orientation and experience robs us of new insights. By embracing the New School principle of opening security problems to examination through the lens of other sciences, it is our hope that the field of information security can become more diverse not just in its perspectives, but also in its makeup.

Externally visible characteristics such as gender and race are the most obvious aspects of how we appear to others. All of us attempt to influence, or try to influence, how others see us. Some things are hard to change (gender or race), but others, such as style of dress, are easier.

Some people are quiet sports fans, and others adorn their offices or cars with displays of devotion. Other people display their religious or secular devotion by placing symbols on their cars, such as the symbol of a fish—or a fish with feet. Other signals include clothing or the use of jargon. Men's clothing ranges from T-shirt to suit and tie. Each is chosen to present a particular image, and some people choose carefully for the crowd they expect to see. As people go from place to place and role to role, the ways in which they present themselves changes.

We might present a different face at home, at work, at sports events, or at church. The hard-driving executive may be a loving and supportive parent. The sports fanatic may spend all day at a football game with his buddies, but might not talk to them the rest of the week. People even use different names, from James at the office to Jim at home. These names may help people separate the ways in which they present themselves. We can't be "on" all the time, but the distinction is often lost on people designing systems.

Work in computer security surrounding "identity" tends to default to the idea that each person has one identity. (This narrow thinking helps perpetuate the idea of identity theft.) Most of us have multiple overlapping identities. Systems that fail to respect the context of each of these identities are more likely to make their users feel uncomfortable. This in turn makes users more willing to bypass security policies. We've been told of people refusing to give their cell phone number for a disaster-recovery plan, convinced that their employer would use the information in situations well short of a disaster. This perceived lack of respect for separation of identity adds real risk to the plan.

Helen Nissenbaum, a professor at New York University, has presented the idea of "contextual integrity" as an explanation for how people respond to privacy issues. The idea is that when the context of a situation is broken, people get upset. Students post pictures and comments on social networking web sites, intending that only their community of friends will see them. They never think about prospective employers viewing their pictures and writings. This is the "context" of the sharing: their friends, not their employers. Maintaining that contextual integrity is an important aspect of privacy.

People tend to respond strongly and emotionally to behavior that is wrong for the situation. For example, members of the Westboro Baptist Church hold demonstrations at the funerals of fallen soldiers. Many people who respect their right to protest feel strongly that funerals are the wrong place for such protests. The idea of contextual integrity has been used to great effect to explain why some privacy issues blow up, others "feel wrong," and still others are accepted with barely a whimper.

Economics and psychology provide new insight into people's behavior. Understanding social pressures and context might also help. Opportunities to better understand security by learning from sociology have barely been explored.

In Conclusion

The title of this chapter is not meant to be facetious. If the security world can better understand the nature of its challenges, this will lead to better, more focused solutions. Even if we discover that the causes of the problems actually lie outside our control, we can at least react in other ways that might help us compensate.

Today, we can begin to find answers to many of the challenges we face in an emerging field of study: the economics of information security. For security professionals, reading the output of this new area of research is like switching on a light in a dark room. The findings provide long-needed justification for many widely held beliefs and demolish others. They provide answers to problematic questions, reveal nuances, and create new areas of research. Other sciences will hold similarly valuable insights into the challenges we face. The application of ideas from other fields is a key discipline within the New School. The goal is to transform information security into a multidisciplinary field in which technologists work closely with experts in "soft issues" such as public policy, economics, and sociology.

Lessons from other sciences allow us to observe the world, ask why, and *receive an answer*.

Chapter 6

Spending

All organizations face three universal questions about their security spending: *why* spend, *how much* to spend, and *on what* to spend. The efficiency of spending is clearly important to companies. The effectiveness of security spending matters to business partners, and ultimately to customers. Spending is clearly also an economic activity with psychological aspects and ties to many of the New School ideas that we have described in the previous chapters. As such, spending provides us with the opportunity to evaluate current thinking through the lens of the New School.

Spending is where decisions become concrete. The allocation of scarce resources shows what people think is worthwhile. A frequently quoted statistic is that organizations spend more on coffee than on information security. The implication is that this is a broken state of affairs, and something must be done to improve things. If companies were spending too little on security, they'd be going out of business left and right. Perhaps it's OK to spend more on coffee. With better data and better analysis, we could actually tell.

This chapter addresses the questions of why to spend, how much to spend, and on what to spend. We will focus predominantly on the perspective of businesses, but these questions are universal. Governments, nonprofit organizations, and consumers all have incentives to spend on security. Where their spending strategies might diverge from businesses, we'll discuss their perspectives.

Reasons to Spend on Security Today

The justification for spending on security used to be straightforward. It was to protect us from viruses and then from the internet. It's gotten a little more complex since then. There are a few common answers to the question of "why to spend." In examining these answers, it is important to remember that different types of companies have different needs, so different answers may make sense. The question of how to allocate resources scales from poor to rich, and from small to large. Either in time or money, the issue of allocation is common, even as the answers vary widely.

One frequent answer to the question of why to spend on security is to try to avoid loss. In theory, loss avoidance is a great reason to spend money on security, but this raises important questions. First, how much money could be lost, and how? Second, will security spending realistically prevent the loss? Will it do so consistently, or only sometimes? Later in this chapter we will describe why these are very difficult questions to answer in the absence of good data about what goes wrong. Specifically in this case, we don't have actuarial data like insurance companies do.

Another reason to spend that relates closely to monetary loss is damage to reputation or brand. Chapter 4 discussed the many myths surrounding breach disclosure. We have good evidence that the share price of a company that discloses a breach recovers within a few days. Contrary to expectations, few customers leave. Nevertheless, the immediate cost and distraction of dealing with a breach can justify spending on security.

A common reason for organizations to spend money on security is to enable a new business process. Some new processes carry such obvious risks that, without security, they could never be launched. An example is selling stock over the internet. The new process is no doubt expected to make lots of money. But the process might also expose the business to risk, so spending money on security might be considered appropriate. Spending money on security analysis early, to find and address risks, is usually a better choice than spending money later on "mitigating technologies" or "compensating controls." If you don't know and can't easily discover what your risks are, it's likely that other people will find them and start exploiting them.

Some business processes require compliance with externally imposed standards. For example, if a company wants to accept credit card payments, it must comply with Payment Card Industry (PCI) standards. A fast-growing thicket of laws concerning security, privacy, and operations regulates corporate behavior. Complying with the law has been one of the fastest-growing reasons to spend on security in recent years. Some of those laws impose fines and even jail time for noncompliance, so compliance spending has been viewed in some cases as "spending to keep the CEO out of jail."

In the United States, information security law is mostly sectoral, covering finance and health. The Sarbanes-Oxley Act, often simply called SOX, is the broadest of these laws. It imposes new levels of due care in record keeping by public companies. If the computers that records are stored on are insecure, how secure can the records be? SOX has been a boon to compliance departments in U.S. companies and those that list on U.S. stock markets, because SOX is often seen as a blanket reason for spending. Unfortunately, compliance spending has often been accomplished through diverting security funds. SOX controls that are constructed only to allow an auditor to "check a box" are unlikely to be very effective.

Some privacy laws in the U.S. are sectoral (covering finance and health, but also more mundane areas such as video rentals). Others are broader in scope but more local. For example, California has laws that impact any company that stores certain data about a California resident. California Senate Bill

1386, which we discussed in Chapter 4, provides a good example of how justifications can overlap. Spending here can protect a brand while avoiding the costs of notifying customers about a breach. Other places have stronger data-protection laws, such as the European Union's Data Protection Directive and Canada's PIPEDA. Companies affected by these laws must spend money to comply.

Governments have different motivations for why they might spend on security. Sometimes the data is involved in national security, such as the identities of spies or nuclear launch codes. Other times, the obligation has to do with the mandatory nature of the data collection and the social contract that surrounds it. It is worth noting that in government, there are no *competitive* reasons to spend on anything per se (including security), because there are no competitors. Governments rarely "go out of business" because of mismanagement. For a business or individual to switch to a new government is much more challenging than it is to switch to a new ISP. Two other notable motivations affect a government body: avoiding investigation and maintaining a sufficient level of trust such that most citizens won't lie to them. One of the worst things that can happen to bureaucrats is being brought before the legislature for an investigation. Such investigations can paralyze an agency (think of Iran-Contra, the Clinton scandals, or the corruption investigations into associates of Brazilian President Lula da Silva). Incidents of government employees being jailed for incompetence or malice seem to be quite rare, even when incompetence, sloth, or malice have an impact on people's lives. When government agencies are seen as untrustworthy, people avoid them, lie to them, and otherwise prevent them from doing their job. This can be seen in the black markets that exist in corrupt economies around the world. The same sorts of issues that make it hard for consumers to evaluate the security posture of a company or a piece of software can apply to a citizen trying to evaluate a government. The added interference is that the government can classify a problem, making it illegal to disclose or discuss. If people believe that their data will be unprotected, they may choose to lie to protect themselves. Data security concerns can then play into data quality, and governments may choose to spend on security for this reason. As we write this, Congress gives the average American federal agency a D grade for information security management. When some agencies start to improve, this may also motivate others to do the same.

Many of the reasons that a nonprofit organization would spend money on security mirror those of a business. There may be an additional ethical dimension, however. Planned Parenthood has case files that it has not only a legal obligation to protect, but ethical reasons as well. If an organization has unusual ethical commitments to security, it is worth structuring investments to reinforce those commitments. This motivation is powerful, and if it exists, it is worth spending to maintain and enhance it.

Individuals invest in security and privacy for a wide variety of reasons. The most compelling reason is to prevent theft. People do not want their private or confidential documents to be stolen. These documents might include nominally secret information that would allow fraud by impersonation or identity theft. They may be searching for a job without their current employer's knowledge, or they may be researching an embarrassing personal problem. But it is hard to know who is watching, or how. It is hard to estimate the future costs of information leakage. Even if these problems can be solved, people will continue to engage in what economists call "hyperbolic discounting," trading immediate pleasure for long-term risk. Social web sites, such as Facebook, exhibit similar economics. People provide tremendous amounts of personal information without considering possible negative effects. Facebook rose to prominence on college campuses, where it became an essential part of dating. Cigarette smoking is perhaps the canonical example of this behavior. Many smokers enjoy having a cigarette, or the socializing that goes with it. There's more than a one-in-three chance that smoking will kill you in twenty years, but smokers continue to tell themselves that "one more cigarette won't matter..."

Non-Reasons to Spend on Security

Sometimes a business chooses to spend money on a security measure as a visible deterrent, such as a guard at the door. This idea doesn't carry over to the online world very well. The cost of tracking down and prosecuting an attacker is high. It is relatively simple to detain and search someone as he leaves a retail store. The same thing can't be done with an online transaction—at least not cheaply. The high cost stems from the extensive investigative effort that would be required, support for law-enforcement activity, and the difficulty in tracking down an individual who may have laundered his connection through many jurisdictions and countries. Extraditing and prosecuting electronic criminals can be very hard. That's not to say it's never worth it, but the costs should be considered early on. A deterrent effect depends on the likelihood and severity of punishment. In the case of online crime, the likelihood of prosecution is very low.

Chasing attackers is hard, but it can also be a lot of fun. The book *The Cuckoo's Egg* made its author, Clifford Stoll, into something of a hero for catching crackers who worked for East German intelligence. The two-year pursuit came after he noticed a 79-cent error in accounting and soon after uncovered strong evidence of serious wrongdoing. But unless the costs of investigation and forensics fall dramatically, it will be hard for any individual company to justify making them.

For several years, it seemed that spending on technologies to protect against fast-spreading internet worms would be an excellent reason to spend on security. Staying up to date with security patches will slow or stop most worms, but patching can be a time-consuming activity. It also seemed likely that worm authors would focus on using vulnerabilities for which no patch existed. A number of products that were brought to market tried to identify worm behavior so that it could be automatically blocked. However, it appears that attackers have lately become more oriented toward attacks that have a financial payoff. Spreading a worm has little payoff, other than notoriety, and today worms are rare.

Chapter 2 discussed some of the sales tactics that security vendors employ. The security industry often portrays security issues as black and white. An example is the "insecurity of wireless networks." Groups of people publicize how many insecure access points they've found this month. These folks have no way of knowing if those wireless access points are secured in accordance with policy. All they know is that the access point is accessible. This chapter was written on a laptop that is wirelessly connected to the internet. That internet connection is deliberately left open, in accordance with policy, but it would certainly be counted as an insecure access point in such a survey. Fears based on selectively interpreted data are not a good reason to spend money on information security.

Newly minted security managers or Chief Information Security Officers (CISOs) often point to a history of noninvestment in security within a company as a reason to invest. A historical lack of investment is not, in itself, a reason to invest. This is simply selling security through fear, and adding guilt. This strategy can be quite effective, because it aligns with whatever reasons caused the organization to create the new security leadership position. This thinking also involves a degree of self-protection. No executive wants to have spent nothing on a potential problem and then have that problem occur.

The vast majority of businesses should not expect that spending on security products will lead to sustainable competitive advantage over their competitors. Most businesses do not develop security technologies in-house, nor do they typically customize the open-source security tools they might use or the commercial security products they purchase. The result of this pervasive "buy rather than build" philosophy is that most businesses employ nearly identical sets of security technologies in almost identical ways. Consequently, nothing stops competitors from acquiring the same functionality, either from the same vendor or from another vendor whose product has similar features. Almost all security technologies are available for purchase on the open market. Without some unique way of using a particular technology, organizations should not think that spending on security products will enable them to sustain any advantage over their competitors. Even with a unique technology, or way of using a technology, it may be challenging to explain the benefits effectively to prospective customers. In comparison, a sustainable price advantage needs no explanation.

Spending on security products is unlikely to lead to competitive advantage, but spending to improve processes that benefit security might. More efficient processes can help an organization spend less overall and achieve improved capabilities in key areas, as discussed in the next section.

Emerging Reasons to Spend

We see a number of emerging reasons to spend on information security. None of these are yet mainstream, but they are being explored, so we'd like to highlight some that we find interesting. Some of these justifications for security spending may become omnipresent and overtake the current justifications.

Others might fill niche roles within certain sectors and be used by businesses with particular needs.

Emerging security technologies provide opportunities to do business in new ways. A class of technology called Digital Rights Management (DRM) offers a new approach for placing security around documents and other types of files. DRM technologies use cryptography to control who can see files and provides a certain level of assurance that files can be used only by authorized individuals. For example, accounting and other financial documents could be "locked" so that only the accounting department and management could see them. In a development studio, source code could be locked so that only software developers could have access to it. The key difference between DRM and previous access-control technologies is that the protection that DRM technology provides travels *with* the data. This means that if a confidential document were to travel outside the company network, DRM technology could stop it from being read. This functionality is appealing, and companies might find it irresistible not to spend money on DRM security products. The downside of DRM technology is that the administrative overhead of creating the various permission lists could be overly complex and perhaps burdensome. Also, DRM in the consumer world has a bad reputation, because it is used to restrict the use of goods such as music files. No user would choose to pay for DRM, but they are forced to because it is tied into products they want. Further, some DRM technologies have introduced security vulnerabilities into the computers DRM has been installed on or even removed from.

A lot of buzz surrounds spending on security to try to create *trust*. This differs from spending to avoid brand damage because it focuses on a message, rather than on a technology or its effect. Trust may help a company sell its goods or services. Consider the advertising of biotech firms involved in the bioengineering of crops and the "green" advertising of oil companies. Dangers to the public are often accompanied by concerted efforts to influence the perception of those risks. Companies that are involved in activities that have information security risks increasingly seem to see brand management as a good reason to spend funds on security. At a minimum, they want to avoid looking inferior to the competition. Note that we are not arguing here for spending on superficial security measures that create the mere *appearance* of security, but rather for security measures whose worth can be measured objectively and then communicated. However, if an organization's customers are concerned about ghosts or phantoms, it may make sense to spend money to reassure them. Otherwise, they might spend their money elsewhere. Even though what they are concerned about isn't real, it may be easier to behave as if it is real, and invest in "security theater."

Another emerging reason for security spending is to satisfy demands from partners. Some large organizations require their business partners to provide evidence that their processes include certain security activities, or that certain security technologies are deployed before allowing them to connect into their environment. The thinking behind such approaches is driven by the realization that modern IT infrastructures have very significant inter-dependencies. Business processes extend upstream and downstream, into clients, into outsourcing partners, into service providers, and so on. When your security is dependent on the actions of someone else, how do you control that? Standard mechanisms and protocols for businesses to communicate and coordinate their security capabilities are emerging. Within forward-thinking companies, the desire to achieve those capabilities certainly exists and will likely continue to grow.

A business that sells software needs to consider how much security to put into its products. For a very long time, the rational answer was "very little." Prospective customers saw cost or speed or functionality as more important than security. As a result, software manufacturers did not consider security properties to be an important part of their products. Even when vendors invested in security features, they tended to be built to overcome objections that "this isn't secure." This orientation still exists, but many large software vendors now claim security as one of their top priorities. The driver is often the desire to try to avoid competitive *disadvantage*. This shift in mind-set has largely been driven by consumer disgust at virus infections on home computers, weariness at having to patch constantly, the inconvenience of malware, and rising operational costs driven by the insecurity of software products. Nobody wants to give their competitors an advantage in the sales process, so spending on security for this reason is likely to rise. This increase will, at the start, be driven by efforts to be "good enough" and will focus on easy-to-deploy, easy-to-use systems for increasing security. Tools such as automated code analysis, compiler enhancements, and so on are likely to figure prominently, as will a focus on the security aspects of the software development lifecycle.

It is possible to view spending on security as an investment in control efficiency. This is perhaps the most subtle emergent reason for spending on security. When security processes are implemented, they often provide a level of visibility into and control over the technology environment that was previously unattainable. If organizations think about this when spending on areas such as SOX, they will be able to reap more benefits from that spending. This is because security goals and the goals of other aspects of IT are increasingly convergent. Security technology that protects against distributed denial-of-service attacks has valid applications in other areas, such as bandwidth monitoring and shaping, traffic monitoring, retrospective link utilization reporting, and service-level monitoring. Along these lines, there is a growing realization that security capabilities can be used to enhance IT operations. As we said in Chapter 2, inventory management, change management, and configuration management are all activities that underlie IT security. Inventory management is essential for understanding what needs to be defended and for prioritizing security efforts. Without change management, it is impossible to determine if a change to a system was authorized or malicious. Configuration management can be used to ensure that systems are configured according to their functional and security needs. Operational and security concerns are an integral part of each of these activities. When a company spends money in these areas, it reaps both operational and security benefits.

When a business builds and standardizes mechanisms and processes that address security concerns, it increases its ability to react to change. Each time a major change occurs, the business doesn't have to go back and ask fundamental questions. The joining of two IT infrastructures as the result of a merger or acquisition is easier and quicker if established security mechanisms are available that are well understood and easy to deploy. In this way, security controls promote flexibility. This is likely to be seen as a good reason to spend on security as evidence of its effectiveness emerges.

How Much Should a Business Spend on Security?

Now that we have touched on conventional and emerging justifications for spending on security, we will delve into the question of *how much* to spend. This question is especially difficult when the goal of the spending is defined in overly broad terms, such as "to avoid security incidents." If an organization invests in security and then subsequently doesn't suffer a security incident, was the investment in security worthwhile, or did the organization just get lucky? This is a pivotal economic question. If failure never occurs, how can an organization know if spending was justified, or how much spending was justified? When possible, focus security spending on measurable goals, such as standardizing on security technologies across an organization to reduce cost. Doing so makes it easier to determine whether the investment has paid off.

Today, businesses use a number of general strategies to determine their level of security spending. These include waiting to see what breaks and then fixing it, striving for a complete set of security technologies, setting spending levels according to external direction, and using traditional project valuation techniques.

The first, tacit approach is to simply wait until a security incident occurs and then spend whatever amount is necessary to recover. For many businesses, this strategy of "wait and see" is not adopted consciously, but rather by default. Most security practitioners recoil at the very notion, because it suggests an implicit disregard of due care. But from an economic standpoint, it may be a rational strategy if the benefits of security technologies and processes are too difficult to measure. Some very advanced companies have consciously adopted what appears to be a similar approach, although they reach it through a very different route. These businesses have spent extensively on their security programs over several years. They have reached the point where they realize that spending funds on additional defensive measures will lead to only very small additional gains in security. These companies now focus their spending on their ability to recover from incidents, rather than trying to prevent them upfront. The number of businesses in this situation is probably a small fraction of all organizations. But there is an interesting similarity to how both ends of the spending spectrum focus on a reactive strategy, albeit for very different reasons.

The opposite of the "wait and see" strategy is "buy one of everything." This is the strategy of the completist, and it is more likely to be championed by a politician within the organization rather than a technologist. It creates lots of noise and visibility, which is often the intended result. In other words, the manager has lots of positive progress to report. Concrete systems installed, people trained, and lots of activity that management should know about, and, thus, positive exposure for the security manager and his budget. Unfortunately, this strategy is predicated on the assumption that buying and deploying a "complete" suite of security tools will actually deliver operational security. Given our observations about the commercial security industry in Chapter 2, this is likely to be one of the most inefficient spending strategies an organization could employ.

A third approach to setting spending levels, which is probably the most widespread today, is to set the level of security spending according to external measures or according to the advice of third parties such as analysts or consultants. If a research firm like Gartner says that the average security budget is between 6% and 7% of the overall IT budget, many companies simply follow suit and commit to that number in their budget. For the same reason that "no one gets fired for buying IBM," spending decisions made on the basis of external "experts" are politically defensible. That strategy has its place. For example, ensuring that your spending covers an externally provided list such as COBIT or ISO 17799 may be a helpful part of a defense in a lawsuit. Thoughtful organizations recognize that they can be more efficient by determining their optimal level of security spending. The goal is to ensure that a balance is maintained between underspending and going too far past the point of diseconomy, where each additional dollar spent on security provides a progressively smaller benefit. Accomplishing this balance requires objective data about what security measures are effective based on real incidents. If such data was to become available, businesses would be able to use it to set spending levels much more efficiently than setting their level of spending on security at a certain percentage of IT budget simply because that's what everyone else does.

We now turn to traditional project valuation techniques as possible ways to determine how much to spend. One well-known technique is return on investment (ROI). It's easy to calculate ROI. It's the size of the investment divided by the gain. Unfortunately, the methodology has many failings when used to consider possible projects. For example, it doesn't incorporate the chance that a project might fail or the possible benefits of spending the money on something else. Net present value (NPV) and economic value added (EVA) are two techniques that are far more sophisticated and useful than ROI. Many security practitioners are happy to use ROI because it's easy to understand, but that doesn't mean it's right or even useful.

Generally a "return on investment" means how much money someone would make. Security practitioners typically turn this on its head and talk about the "return" from avoiding potential losses. They define the ROI of a security measure as the extent to which it can reduce losses. Those losses are typically calculated using annual loss expected (ALE), which is the probability of a loss event multiplied by the expected cost of the event. So, if a security incident would cost a business $1 million, and it has a probability of 0.4, the ALE would be $400,000. If the cost of the new security product that could stop that security incident is less than $400,000, the business "should" purchase it. This looks good on paper, but the approach doesn't stand much scrutiny. The problem today is that the *probability* of the loss event is very hard to predict, as is (to a lesser extent) the event's expected impact. This makes it hard to use ROI, NPV, or EVA for security.

To calculate the risks to a house, a home insurance company studies the actuarial data related to that type of house and its location. This includes whether its exterior is brick or wood, whether it sits in a floodplain or tornado alley, and so on. Analyzing historical data and extrapolating those trends is a scientific approach to the task of calculating the probability that a house might be destroyed. But as noted in Chapter 4, only recently has data on security incidents begun to flow into the public domain. This is primarily because businesses have had no reason to publicize the fact that their security has been compromised. In the absence of mandatory breach reporting or the belief that reporting is the right thing to do, it was predictable that businesses would cover up security breaches because of worries about reputation. Thus, relatively little data is available to predict the probability of an incident.

Trying to determine the full impact of a breach used to be a similar quagmire. There was a joke about a business wanting insurance against losses stemming from an information security incident. Not knowing how to calculate the level of risk involved, the insurance company's reply to the business was "How much is your company worth? That's your premium—send it in!" This joke reflected the difficulty in determining the costs of a security incident. For a long time, people wondered how significant a security breach would have to be to provide sufficient incentive for customers to switch to a competitor. The value of a brand could be calculated by asking what it would take to build an entirely new brand. They also believed that this would represent the upper limit on the possible cost of a breach (to have to build a whole new business from scratch). This is one area, however, where we now have some objective data that we can use to shed light on these questions. As noted in Chapter 4, the data on security breaches that is now in the public domain shows that the impact on companies that disclose a breach is, on average, quite small. It's certainly much less than the cost to rebuild a brand. Large numbers of customers have not yet pulled their business from companies that have suffered a breach, although the capital spent to recover from a breach has been significant in some cases. Although we have better data on breaches than ever before, until we have many years of actuarial data on loss events that have occurred and their impact, it will remain difficult to apply economic models to security spending decisions.

Some proponents of using traditional economic techniques are honest and upfront in characterizing the uncertain nature of their numbers: "We don't know what the probability of an attack is, but let's just say that it's X." A good deal of modern financial analysis involves working with lots of uncertainty. That's OK if everyone understands the assumptions. It is important that everyone involved understands and communicates the weaknesses when working with these models.

One reaction to this state of affairs might be to focus purely on the lowest common denominator for spending decisions: their total cost of ownership (TCO). Most organizations can estimate the costs of a purchase. This calculation includes the purchase cost, costs of training, integration costs, the cost of licensing, and so on. It is always possible to assign a lower boundary to TCO, at least in terms of cash outlay. Determining the upper boundary for security technologies can be tricky, because the operational costs over time tend to be more significant than the capital expenditure. Intrusion detection systems are a good example, because many businesses do not anticipate the operational cost of having to respond to the false alarms that those systems can generate. The TCO for firewalls in any rapidly changing environment is dominated by the operational aspect of updating firewall rules. The TCO for a patch management solution within an enterprise is dominated by the need for appropriate testing of patches before they are deployed. The cost of the technological deployment system is relatively small in comparison.

Looking forward, new research is beginning to shed light on the question of how much to spend. Lawrence Gordon and Martin Loeb are professors of accounting and information assurance at the University of Maryland's Smith School of Business. They have worked on problems within the economics of information security, including the question of how much a business should spend to protect a given information set.

In their paper "The Economics of Information Security Investment," they present a mathematical model that incorporates vulnerability and potential loss. Their model shows that it is not appropriate to invest in security measures up to the level of the expected loss, because there are diminishing marginal returns. That is, additional money spent brings less value than the earlier money spent. Gordon and Loeb calculate that the maximum amount that a firm should spend on protecting an asset should be only a fraction of the expected loss. Specifically, a firm should not spend more on security measures than 37% of the expected loss.

On its surface, and because we have glossed over many of the details, saying that the amount spent on protection should be no more than 37% of the expected loss may seem a little like saying that the answer to life, the universe, and everything is 42. However, this number comes from clearheaded analysis, and we suggest those who question it refer to the paper. It is exactly the type of research that the security field needs and should pursue, until we have sufficient actuarial data. It is a simple but powerful model that produces a workable rule of thumb and is based on economics, not fashion or fear.

The Psychology of Spending

One of the ideas within the New School is examining security challenges through the lenses of other sciences, such as psychology. When we spend, we have to consider that psychological factors might be influencing our spending. Does anyone really need to buy a Porsche or a Range Rover, or does the desire to project a certain image influence the decision? In the same manner, it would be useful to know what factors can typically affect your decision-making when you're considering spending on security.

As we have described throughout the book, fear is a strong emotion that is actively manipulated to influence spending decisions. But even without such attempts, studies have shown that when people are presented with a number of descriptions of a scenario, the majority will remember the most alarming one. In other words, human beings tend to react to risk in an emotional way, and we are typically most influenced by the high-water mark for the severity of the possible outcome. In its most extreme form, this can create the desire to want to drive out *all* risk from our lives. Some parents do not allow their child to play alone outside because of fears of child abduction. In reality, figures from the FBI and other law enforcement agencies show the number of child abductions by strangers is small—about 200 to 300 per year. Most children who go missing do so in custody disputes and are taken by someone they know and trust. The advice to "never talk to strangers" doesn't address the main cause of children going missing, and it puts them at risk when they become lost. In 2005, 11-year-old Brennan Hawkins got lost in the Utah mountains. For four days, he avoided searchers because he was afraid to talk to strangers.

An aversion to risk can result in security measures that greatly inhibit the underlying processes they are trying to protect. The security restrictions imposed by the U.S. government have damaged the airline industry. Many people now prefer to drive rather than fly, or they choose to fly less often. The crux is that the government would be held accountable if an airline security incident occurred, so this creates a very risk-averse mind-set that results in laborious and often nonsensical security procedures. (And for the observant reader, this is yet another example of incentive failure, since the government isn't measured on how happy or frustrated airline travelers feel.)

Risk aversion can have the same negative effects in the IT sphere. The bad press around security vulnerabilities in wireless networking has caused many companies to be so worried about the risk that they have told employees not to use their laptops' wireless capabilities. In this situation, it is likely that some employees will activate wireless anyway because they want to be able to connect to their home network, or to work while sitting in a coffee shop. Attempting to ban a technology comes with the trade-off that the benefits of that technology will not be realized while the risks may persist.

A "big event" within an organization such as a worm infection can create a risk-averse mind-set. Depending on the enormity of the situation, the company might swing from having little or no desire to spend on security to an overwhelming desire to spend to avoid a future occurrence of a similar incident. The concern here is that money might be thrown at the problem in a reactionary and consequently unfocused way. There may be a parallel in boom and bust cycles in banking. After a problem, the board of directors hires a risk-averse CEO. The CEO takes a while to clean things up, and memories of the problem recede. The board brings in someone more aggressive and willing to take risks. Risks accumulate, and eventually one of them goes very sour. It was about twenty years from the savings and loan crisis to the subprime lending crisis.

One of the authors of this book once advised a law firm that had just suffered a worm infection. The infection had kept the partners in the firm from getting work done (and when partners charge $750 an hour, this is a big deal for the firm). They had cleaned up the infection manually but were extremely worried about a similar infection happening again. The IT manager thought his job was at risk. He was grasping at straws and was dead set on purchasing a suite of security technologies from a particular vendor, simply because that vendor had made its pitch the previous week. Work-arounds could have been put in place, at least for the short amount of time it would take to step back and objectively assess the situation, but the IT manager went ahead with the expensive purchase of the new product suite. Normally, evaluating the type of product they had in mind would take only a few weeks, but the risk to his job loomed too large in his mind. This made him act to "do something" but left him with a suite of products that security practitioners generally considered to be inferior at preventing a recurrence of the problem he so feared. (This is another example of a principal-agent problem. Management was relying on the IT manager to make good decisions in his area of expertise.)

A major security incident can have such an emotional impact that it creates the desire to "fight the last war." If a computer server is compromised because of a missing operating system patch, the limited resources of the security team might be swung around to focus on operating system patching. But on balance, there might be more risk in the applications running on the servers, so the focus is misdirected.

Presenting security numbers without context can create an emotional effect and lead to misdirected or inefficient spending. The number of vulnerabilities within an environment would seem at first blush to be a good number to know. It's appealing because the presence of vulnerabilities implies risk. It is also a number in which taking action to patch systems would "move the dial" and create a positive trend. The tool most often used to gather data on vulnerabilities on a network is a vulnerability scanner. For any medium to large environment, the number of vulnerabilities the scanner will find will be astronomical. It will be on the order of tens of thousands or even hundreds of thousands of vulnerabilities. A vulnerability assessment report often resembles a telephone directory when printed. The reason for this is that in the formative years of the market for vulnerability-assessment products, it was easy to convince prospective customers that the more vulnerability "checks" that could be performed, the better the tool would be. The result was that vendors of vulnerability assessment tools were spurred onward to incorporate ever-increasing numbers of vulnerability checks into their products, even for things that could only tenuously be considered a "vulnerability." A vulnerability scanner will report a large number of "vulnerabilities" for just about any environment. This is as much a product of competition between vendors as it is an indication of the state of the systems scanned. On the other hand, an environment might really be riddled with vulnerabilities. It is useful to be aware of the flawed methodology and its possible psychological effect.

On What to Spend

We would like to be able to provide detailed direction on what security technologies and services organizations should purchase, but alas, we cannot. The organizations at which the readers of this book are employed differ from each other. Technology's role in their products or services differs. The competitive pressures each faces are different. The makeup of their technology environments are different (centralized or decentralized, geographic span, underlying complexity, and so on). Lastly, their appetites for risk are almost certainly different.

We *can* provide two things. First, when considering "on what to spend," there are some framing questions to ask. Second, businesses often spend money on things that don't jibe with the New School. We think they're probably good things to avoid to save money, and we'll highlight two examples.

When considering spending on a security product, a useful first question to ask is whether the core capabilities that the product would provide are already available within the organization's IT infrastructure. The functionality provided by standalone security technologies increasingly overlaps with the functionality of other products that many businesses already own. Most network security monitoring technologies operate in a very similar way to network management software and can record similar data in many cases. If a business is not using the extensive log-generation capabilities of its existing assets, such as network routers and servers, buying new security-monitoring products is questionable. It is also important to consider how much better the security product works, how manageable it is, and whether the difference is worth the cost. Those costs might be better spent developing skills and processes to use the existing technologies.

Another framing question to consider is whether the security functionality you want will be delivered at some point in the future within the infrastructure that the organization already owns or expects to own. Software vendors such as Microsoft, Oracle, and Cisco are increasingly implementing security functionality in their products. Platform and infrastructure vendors are well placed to deliver security that is integrated enough to scale, yet transparent enough to the user to be effective. Before buying new technology, organizations should see if their major vendors have similar capabilities either in place or available soon. At the same time, no company is expert in everything, so getting some functions from other specialized vendors might make sense. As auto manufacturers integrate in-dash GPS systems, the "aftermarket" starts to look for new features to add. This competition is healthy. Even with healthy competition, no product is perfect, and no product will perfectly meet your needs. The question is how to find products that most effectively meet your needs. It may be that a smaller vendor will be more responsive, so it may be worth the additional cost to work with that vendor. The key point is to employ a realistic strategy for meeting your security needs.

As described in Chapters 2 and 3, a common orientation surrounds the expected elements of a security program. The examples that we have chosen to note next as being incongruent with the New School do not relate to specific technologies, but rather to widespread practices. These are popular because they are "so obviously good ideas" that it is hard to argue against them. But given the lack of evidence for them, it is difficult to believe that they provide value in proportion to the amount of resources that are typically invested in them.

The first is the notion of "employee security awareness training." It follows this logic: "If the employees are trained about security, they will be more likely to make the right security decisions, which will lead to better security within the organization as a whole." This idea is popular, and some companies cater to the idea of delivering the "message" of security. However, people are surprisingly resistant to indoctrination against those cases where there is a payoff for breaking the rules. Several studies have shown that people will reveal their passwords in exchange for a candy bar or for some other frivolous reason. In April 2004, the BBC reported the results of a study that showed that more than 70% of the respondents would reveal their computer password in exchange for chocolate. Certainly, the passwords revealed might have been false, but to even jokingly violate the first lesson of security awareness training ("never reveal your password") illustrates our point. Few people would jokingly violate the first rule of firearm safety by pointing a gun at someone, even for a candy bar.

In general, breaking a safety or security rule usually makes life temporarily *easier*. It is possible to act faster or more directly. When people evaluate a decision in terms of its costs and benefits, and they perceive that relatively little risk is associated with a lot of benefit, they have a strong incentive to act. Breaking a safety rule is reinforced by the positive consequences of doing so, and human beings find it very difficult to ignore a payoff. Most people have broken the speed limit when driving, simply because they were in a hurry to get somewhere.

Lower-paid staff and temporary workers often fill positions that entail a great deal of trust. Since receptionists and assistants to managers and executives can access the accounts of those important people, it is logical to think that they would be targets of social engineering attacks. These are confidence tricks in which an attacker tries to convince the target to reveal his password, or something similar. We no longer live in a world of lifetime employment. People expect to change jobs, so they feel less loyalty toward their employers. As a consequence, user "training" is less likely to influence behavior.

The second idea we will critique is security policies. Having a comprehensive suite of security policies is a cornerstone of conventional wisdom within the security field. Security policies are documents, blessed by management, that describe how the employees of an organization must act when confronted with situations where the employees' actions might affect security. An organization typically has a variety of policy documents, targeted at different roles within the organization.

A number of problems exist with both the expectation of the value that security policies will deliver and how they are traditionally employed. First, we have spoken in this chapter and the preceding one about how mandating behavior is unlikely to work. The reason is the many psychological and motivational aspects that influence people. If an organization employed a zero-tolerance policy for violations of security policy, making it a firing offense, employees might study the policy closely. But without that mandate, security policies in their traditional form (typically a large, dry document) are unlikely to be read. We have seen security policies literally gathering dust on a shelf.

A second problem is that security policies are typically written in very clean, simple language that speaks about high-level, theoretical ideas such as "threats" and "risks." This conceptual way of thinking about security can be seductive to security practitioners, who are often disillusioned by the complexity and difficulty of implementing security at a technical level. Sometimes a security team begins focusing on policy setting and retreats into this abstract world. When that happens, the security team spends its time writing security policies instead of actually making practical changes within the organization.

These problems with security policies suggest that the value they provide is low in comparison to their cost.

In Conclusion

The effects of spending decisions within an organization ripple outward, affecting partners, customers, and the bottom line. As with many other aspects of the security field, emotion is ever-present, rising up to cloud judgment and misdirect.

The New School approach to security spending incorporates an understanding of forces both internal and external to the organization. Proponents of the New School consider and evaluate psychological factors and employ sensible economic valuation techniques. They are also on the lookout for how they can create changes in the larger world by changing how they spend. Acting in this way allows them to question existing approaches and evaluate the effectiveness of their actions.

Where this new approach obviates old-school ideals, we should put aside those old tenets and go forward. Good money should not be thrown after bad.

Chapter 7

Life in the New School

There are not always easy answers. Solutions that might apply in the general case are not necessarily applicable in every case. We have spoken in the previous chapters about how applying ideas from the New School will create positive effects. It is possible to achieve a future in which information security is not riven by opinion and demagoguery. Using objective data and embracing other sciences can trump both fear and fashion. We have also spoken throughout this book about how there is no *single* solution to the majority of the challenges that exist within information security. We have railed against the notion that any one product is a "silver bullet," or that there is some special framework or methodology that an organization can simply employ. The New School is neither a product nor a service. It is an approach to the world that embraces the scientific method, new sources of objective data, and new perspectives from diverse fields from which new theories and approaches flow.

The turn toward the New School will influence how we speak about problems. It will alter our immediate and considered reaction to news, shifting the emphasis from overdramatization to a more calm assessment of the facts. The New School will influence how individuals and organizations purchase security technologies by providing better answers to questions such as "how big is this problem?" The model of employing scare tactics to drive sales will decline, because anyone will be able to search for information about problems and determine how prevalent they really are. It will also be easier to find out what approaches to problems actually work. These changes will influence which information security products and service offerings are brought to market and which become successful.

Even though life in the New School will be a much more productive and enjoyable experience than in the old, it will not be a utopia. In acknowledging this, we hope to differentiate ourselves from those ideologues and snake oil salesmen in the information security industry who refuse to see the weaknesses in their own argument, product, or service. This chapter describes some areas and challenges in the field of information security for which the New School either does not provide an immediate solution or does not suggest a solution at all. We'll talk about human nature, the limitations of breach data, externalities, risk compensation, language, and organizational issues such as skills shortages.

Lastly, we hope and expect that the ideas within this book will be challenged. We look forward to that debate. By engaging in a conversation about how to make better security decisions, the New School can only be strengthened.

People Are People

The New School won't be a utopia, because people are people, and so why should it be? People still smoke despite the long-term risks because of the immediate pleasure it provides them. People don't exercise, even when they know they are overweight and at risk of heart disease and diabetes. People often make such choices knowing the risks. In many places, cigarette packs are decorated with horrifying pictures of people with diseases caused by smoking, or they carry harsh warnings such as "Cigarettes cause strokes" or "Tobacco use can make you impotent." People still choose to smoke, but doctors no longer endorse cigarettes. The availability of objective data allows better choices to be made by those who seek out that data and act on it. We expect that most will do so, and that better choices will be made in aggregate. It seems inevitable that some individuals and organizations will continue to make choices that are bad, confusing, or morally distasteful to some.

Poor decision-making, stubbornness, and apathy can be expected. They are part of the human condition. Some of the reasons people might not embrace the use of objective data to make better security decisions are more subtle. A number of psychological effects come into play in security decisions. In Chapter 6, we discussed how an unnecessarily risk-averse mind-set can be created by the fear of loss, even when the probability of loss is low. This aversion to risk can lead to inefficient and misdirected spending as a response, even when data suggests a better, more optimal course of action. In America, car accidents kill a far greater number of people than acts of terrorism, yet spending on antiterrorism measures dwarfs spending on road safety. The spectacular, horrific nature of terrorism creates a strong emotional response. Studies have shown that people find it difficult to think rationally about risks that carry heavy costs. As we noted in Chapter 2 when we discussed security surveys, the way in which questions are framed and situations are posed also has a strong effect on people's expressed opinions and their subsequent actions. Even as we move from fear to data, data can still be manipulated to create an emotional response, and people still tend to put their own interests first. Participants in the New School seek to overcome these psychological effects by using objective data and its analysis as the key factor in effective decision-making. They also recognize that people do not always behave rationally.

Chapters 5 and 6 highlighted the use of economic models. Those economic models are typically predicated upon certain assumptions. A common assumption is the notion of a "rational actor," which is a model of human behavior in which individuals are expected to behave in ways that maximize the utility of their efforts. These types of simplifications allow economic models to be built at the cost of glossing over underlying complexities. Security models often break down when the user violates assumptions. A classic example that is known to all security practitioners is the class of attack known as the "buffer overflow." In this attack, the programmer writing a program assumes that the user will not enter input that exceeds a certain length. The attacker deliberately enters more than the expected amount of input, possibly changing how the program runs. We can perhaps expect that economic models are no different from security models, in that the assumptions they make can be their undoing. Research has shown that human beings deviate from conventionally defined economic rationality. In other words, people sometimes *choose* to behave in a risky manner.

When we discussed economics, we spoke of "agency problems." Although the economics of information security might enable us to propose strategies for making better security decisions, agency problems won't go away. Individuals and organizations will continue to be swayed by subjective or emotional factors. Some security executives promote themselves by pointing to their embrace of the latest security technologies. They might continue to pursue certain security projects that are seen as attractive and use them for self-promotion. Many security practitioners also want to obtain practical experience using the latest technologies because of their desire to increase their marketability. It would be naive to believe that the availability of economic models that can guide security decisions will have the universal effect of purging personality and organizational politics from decision-making. They will help, though.

Similarly, if a market continues to exist for security products that make the buyer feel better, but only superficially solve problems, companies will continue to provide products and services to satisfy that market. A case in point is antibacterial soap, which seems to make people no healthier than standard soap and leads to more-resistant bacteria. Chapter 2 noted that many of the commercial information security products that exist today seek to correct only the symptoms of problems rather than the problems themselves. Companies build and sell these products because the effort involved in "solving" the more superficial aspects is less than would be required to address the problems at their root. Those who are responsible for making purchasing decisions within an organization might not realize the fundamental nature of their challenges, so they might unwittingly support that market. As more objective data becomes available, this behavior will be reduced, but some people might have the misfortune of remaining unaware of the benefits of using the data.

Some people choose to hoard data or form cliques to restrict its distribution, and this might be a difficult habit to break. Within the security field there is a great deal of secrecy around topics such as new vulnerabilities and attack techniques. Groups and cliques form to create or maintain power structures, often based on the secrecy of the knowledge they hold. As Lord Acton said, "Power tends to corrupt; absolute power corrupts absolutely."

Some cliques are commercial endeavors. A number of "information-sharing" organizations charge a membership fee. These fees are often structured such that only the wealthiest organizations can afford to be members. Perhaps this makes sense, to ensure that the organization will send appropriately senior representatives. Or the reason for the high fees might be elitism. In either case, the exclusivity of such organizations stands in opposition to the notion of free and open data sharing that is championed by adherents of the New School. A countervailing force to such cliques are truly open information-sharing initiatives. All else being equal, groups focusing on open information sharing and analysis will create more value than those who invest in secrecy and exclusion. The open group will also reap the benefits of more diverse membership.

Breach Data Is Not Actuarial Data

Chapter 6 looked at traditional methods for attempting to calculate the value of security-spending decisions. We noted that these methods fail without actuarial data. Some of them require knowing the *likelihood* of a loss event such as a security incident. Without actuarial data, reliably determining that likelihood is very difficult. The breach data that is in the public domain today goes a significant way toward meeting that need. But to achieve an actuarial-like quality, it would need to be more detailed than it is today, and we would need more data to derive trends. This is not to say that breach data can never reach that required threshold, only that it does not do so today.

A complicating factor in creating actuarial data for information security that needs to be overcome is that the technology landscape is changing much more rapidly than, say, the techniques of home building. A house can be expected to have a wood, stone, or steel structure, and there are a relatively small number of choices for how the ceilings and interiors can be constructed. The *risks* to houses are also well known: floodplains are well mapped out, as are tornado-prone areas. Insurance companies only need to track a relatively small number of variables to generate actuarial data. The risks for other insurance markets, such as asbestos-related problems, can also be calculated. (Callous as it may seem, the upper boundary for asbestos insurance is the medical costs for everyone who has worked or will work in the asbestos industry.) In contrast to these topics, the technological landscape that affects the ease or difficulty of attacking or defending computer systems fluctuates as new technologies are introduced, as technologies are configured and reconfigured, and as the security of systems decays over time.

If an insurance company offers homeowners' insurance only in Florida, it has a different exposure to hurricane-related risks than a company that offers homeowners' insurance only in California. There is a thriving business in which insurance companies sell part of the liability for their portfolios to re-insurers. Re-insurers then work hard to ensure that their portfolios are balanced across the existing pools of risk. The number of factors they must balance is rather small relative to those that might come into play in the electronic world. For example, criminals can execute electronic attacks at scale, with no consideration for issues such as geography. These factors make it difficult to create a model that would allow information security risks to be priced appropriately. (Whoever figures it out will make a mint.)

Breach data is a profoundly useful source of information, and the availability of objective data about successes and failures in information security will greatly improve our ability to make better security decisions. However, challenges still exist to obtaining actuarial data that would support insurance markets.

Powerful Externalities

Chapter 5 discussed externalities—costs that are not felt by the organization or individual who performs the action that creates them. One of the examples we used was of drivers of larger vehicles such as SUVs not experiencing more smog than drivers of smaller cars. Although SUV drivers create more smog, they do not feel the effects of poor air quality in proportion to the amount of air pollution they create. There are analogues to this type of situation in the security world. Failing to keep up to date with security patches might cause a computer to become compromised. The compromised computer might be used to attack other computers. The impact of those attacks is an externality to the owner of the computer used to launch them. Assuming that the computer owner suffers no consequences for the attacker's actions, all the cost is borne by the party being attacked.

There are negative externalities, but also positive ones. Using the same example, an organization that invests in security measures creates *positive* externalities for the companies with which it interacts electronically. This is true because the organization's computers are less likely to become compromised or infected and therefore are less likely to spread a compromise or infection to the business partners. All sorts of social parallels exist, such as using immunization to reduce the spread of disease.

Within the study of the economics of information security, some strategies have begun to be identified to overcome these challenges. We've discussed some of them, such as product bundling and the use of incentives and penalties. Even so, the market today exhibits powerful externalities that work against security. An example is the level of security quality that software vendors, particularly start-ups, choose to implement in their products. The marketplace tends to reward companies that are the first to market in any new product space. This causes many companies to not worry about security properties for the first versions of their products. They might include some security features, such as encryption, but not worry about vulnerabilities in their code or design. The orientation of their programmers doesn't include worrying about security. The costs are borne by the customers of those products, due to their insecurity and the effort involved in improving their security later. Applying economic thinking to identify these challenges and propose solutions is extremely useful. However, the ingrained nature of many of the current problems suggests that the point at which positive effects will begin to be widely seen might be some time away.

The Human Computer Interface and Risk Compensation

Great user interface design is hard. There are more examples of bad interfaces than good ones. It's also much easier to point out that an interface is bad than to point out that it's good. (This has much in common with security.) For a long time, usability wasn't part of what sold software, never mind security software. Security was even supposed to be *hard* to use—to stop the user and force him or her to *think!* Interfaces are often designed to support particular tasks. If the designer's understanding of those tasks is wrong, the interface won't help the users get to their desired results. Thinking about usability requires thinking about the user, and that's a different orientation from thinking about the code. When a programmer thinks about the user, he often makes what he thinks are small, useful changes to the system, such as improving the Open and Save dialog boxes to "be more intuitive." In the programmer's view, these little visual tweaks are helpful. The customers may see lots of little tweaks from lots of places, and this can all add up to a cacophony. Icons aren't seen as the designer intended. The word the user searches for isn't the one the programmer thought the user would use. And all that is before security is considered.

People often think of security and usability as being at odds. Security certainly can prevent things from "just working." Unfortunately, if you can get to your files from anywhere without a password, so can anyone else. Security decisions often involve situations in which the computer can't make the decision by itself, so the user must get involved. Is the web site really the bank's, or is it a clever imitation? It might be easier if there was only one bank on the internet, but we bet they'd have lousy customer service.

Usability might seem to be a subjective set of questions, with fuzzy definitions and no way to resolve them. But usability professionals have rallied around testing their ideas as a way out of the mess. Great usability experts believe in testing, refining, and testing again as a way to improve designs. (Security can learn a lot from usability.) Some of the challenges involved are that people are complex. They're very observant, and sometimes they pick up on subtle clues, which is great when it works but is hard to rely on. Returning to our accused Turkish hacker, only 0.3% of the potential victims fell prey to the false email. To put it another way, 99.7% of the people didn't fall for it. What happened to the others? Maybe they were on the phone as they were looking at their email. Maybe something distracted them, and they clicked the wrong link. Maybe we can use people's risk thermometers to keep them cautious, or maybe such attempts would blow up in our face. It's hard to test such things. Telling experimental subjects that a study is about security changes their behavior. Not telling them may violate ethics rules. Studying behavior that only three people in a thousand exhibit may require a very large sample. Making software usable is an empirical and iterative process, based on designing and running good tests.

Innovative work on these challenges is being shared at the Symposium on Usable Privacy and Security. Some of these papers have been assembled into an excellent introductory book, *Security and Usability*. This field is still in its infancy, and a great deal remains to be done. Even when we have done a generally good job of making security understandable and usable, attackers will still be motivated to find places where they can induce confusion and then guide users into making the wrong choices. This seems likely to be the case for as long as software is as complex as, say, a VCR. We know things can get better, but perfection isn't coming anytime soon.

Even when things have improved substantially at a technical level, the effects of risk compensation will keep things interesting. We've discussed how psychological factors can influence security decisions. The phenomenon of risk compensation (also known as risk homeostasis) can have a negative effect on security measures. Because risk homeostasis can weaken security measures or render them ineffective, it would be useful to know how to construct systems so as to ward off, or at least mitigate, its effects. One approach we have described is designing security measures so that their operation is invisible to those who receive the protection. Good security design involves putting the "right" security on the default path. However, a great deal of today's software depends on end users making the correct security decisions. During the installation of a popular web-based collaboration product, the installation program presents a message that states "Always click 'Yes' or 'Always' when receiving messages from your web browser when using this program." This desensitizes the users to the decisions they are making.

As described in Chapter 6, we are skeptical of the traditional responses to this problem, such as the "security awareness training" of end users. First, there does not seem to be any good evidence that training users causes them to behave differently weeks or months after the training. Second, risk compensation allows us to suggest that users will believe the risk in any given situation will somehow be mitigated by other protective controls. Third, even if security awareness training were shown to be effective, the "weakest link" principle applies. In other words, an attacker needs to convince only *one* employee to make the wrong choice. People are people, and if end-user security awareness training would make a difference, everyone would exercise regularly, practice safe sex, and never smoke cigarettes.

We are stuck, then, between ideals of how to construct security systems to be secure and usable, and the reality that there are pervasive, deeply entrenched systems that are not implemented with those design goals in mind. Those platforms can improve, and they *will* improve as these concepts within economics and psychology are more widely understood, but much work remains to be done. If computer security improves dramatically, people are likely to believe that computers are more secure. Believing that computers are more secure, people are likely to be more willing to accept instructions to perform risky actions. Risk compensation may well interact poorly with user interface improvements. We'd like to be clear: we are not arguing that people are stupid or careless. We are arguing that people are hard to change, and that we need to strive to help them in full recognition of these difficulties.

The Use and Abuse of Language

A great many of the words we use when discussing security, including trust, threat, risk, safety, privacy, and security, can have multiple meanings. Each is evocative and carries with it cultural baggage. We often find ourselves talking past each other because of the inexact nature of these terms. This is not an argument for prescriptivism in language. Languages are successful when and because they are vibrant means of communication. If we can think and speak clearly, we can do so in spite of imprecise terms. If we can't think clearly, having precisely defined terms won't help us.

Language can be abused, and it *is* abused. Chapter 2 discussed some of the sales tactics used within the commercial information security industry. Describing a product as "secure" reinforces the fallacy that security is somehow a binary value—that something can be either "secure" or not. That kind of black-and-white distinction works with, say, pregnancy, but not for security. Without active intervention, the security of a computer system degrades over time. This happens because new vulnerabilities emerge that can affect it, and because of a process akin to natural decay in which operational changes become security issues. Something that is "secure" can at the most only be said to be "secure right now." What is "secure" today is unlikely to be "secure" tomorrow. Another example is referring to certain security architectures as having an "assured" security model. In fact, no security can unequivocally be "assured." In cryptography, a debate is raging over the use of the term "proven," for much the same reasons.

Some security practitioners understand that when they refer to something as "secure," they are implicitly including an unstated corollary of "...depending on this, that, and the other thing." Trying to define this, that, and the other thing—the external factors on which the security depends—is a game of infinite regression. The term "secure" might be seen as a simplification to cope with the situation's inherent complexity. This abstraction makes it easier for people to function practically in their jobs, but not everyone understands that subtlety. The preceding section discussed the challenge of making a system "secure and usable." We spent quite some time discussing a way to say this without using the word "secure." In the end, we decided to hope that you would see it as an example of a place where "secure" is easier to say, while glossing over underlying complexity.

Security companies often invent new terms for things. "Pharming" is a name for attacks against the Domain Name System. The meaning of "pharming" is not obvious. That makes it a poor name. The same criticism can be leveled against other terms within security, such as "pretexting." This was the technique used to illegally collect information about the Hewlett-Packard board of directors in 2006. Pretexting is actually "social engineering," which is just another word for lying.

Arguments about terminology have been unresolved for many years, and we will not solve them here. Attempts to create strictly defined vocabulary within information security are likely doomed to failure as long as English remains a living language.

Skills Shortages, Organizational Structure, and Collaboration

There's never enough time in the day. Much like our allocation of resources and dollars reflects our priorities, the allocation of time and training shows what skills an organization values.

There is much talk in the security industry about the need for more security practitioners. Given the state of information security in the world, the value of having more people to perpetuate the status quo might be questionable. Chapters 2 and 6 discussed how security needs merge into, and in many cases form a subset of, traditional activities within information technology. It seems that, rather than needing more people to think about security all the time, we need people with responsibilities in areas such as enterprise architecture, planning, and operations to think more effectively about security.

This change has two primary aspects. First, as long as secrecy and tribal knowledge are at the core of the information security field, practitioners in other fields will be unlikely to consider security. Tribal knowledge doesn't help us answer questions and justify our answers. Using objective data, security decisions can be more easily understood, and their benefits more easily expressed. Second, companies should consider how best to structure themselves to allow security thinking to spread throughout the organization.

Chapter 1 described how "phishing" attacks exploit the difficulty of distinguishing between real and fake email, and between real and fake web sites. We spoke about how some organizations send email that is difficult for their customers to authenticate. These organizations have no conscious desire to confuse their users and put them at risk, but within those organizations, the left hand is unaware of what the right hand is doing. The team responsible for communicating with customers does not collaborate with the information security team. This is in fact another example of an externality. When an organization sends mixed messages about security, the cost is borne by the customers of that organization. Customers might rightly be confused by an organization that deploys new security technologies to increase the security of its web site but then sends email that can lead to phishing attacks. Such costs also reflect on the organizations at fault. They take the form of increased customer support costs, customers using channels such as the phone that are more expensive but more easily understood, and perhaps a few customers leaving. (Understanding and measuring the externalities imposed by companies on their customers and others might be a valuable research project for a consumer advocacy group.)

Put frankly, the availability of objective data and the embrace of other sciences does not solve problems of organizational structure or a lack of collaboration. In its favor, the New School is a set of ideas that can be understood and applied at all levels of the organization, regardless of technical aptitude.

In Conclusion

We have spoken throughout this book about challenges within the field of information security such as viruses, spam, and identity theft. We have also discussed structural issues within the security industry in which the traditional ways of approaching problems can actually cause them to be sustained. The New School reveals new approaches to many of these problems. As in other fields, however, some seem surmountable, whereas others appear more difficult or even intractable given the environment that created them.

We feel it is important to describe the challenges still ahead. To do otherwise would be to peddle the next panacea. Where economic models break down, or where decisions are made ignoring data, those failures must be identified and used to craft better approaches. That approach *is* the New School: to identify causes of success or failure and use that information to improve.

A collective effort is still needed. We must continue to work. We can make things better.

Chapter 8

A Call to Action

Beginning in the 1960s, foreign competition took a heavy toll on the manufacturing industry in the United States. The ability of developing countries to manufacture goods at a very low cost in comparison to American factories created significant incentives for companies to manufacture their products outside the U.S. As a result, American jobs in the manufacturing sector began to decline in the early 1970s. What had been the "manufacturing belt" of the U.S. became the "rust belt."

Some might say that the challenges faced by the information security industry aren't so bad, so there is no need to change. Those people risk creating their own rust belt. As with the effects of globalization on the manufacturing industry in the U.S., forces and trends that are pushing on the field of information security will have a major impact. After decades of information security being driven by fads and trends, organizations are tired of being told that they must invest in what seems like a black hole. At the same time, security practitioners and those working in IT want to be able to understand and measure the effects of their security initiatives. They want to be able to make *good* security decisions that balance identifiable benefits and costs.

Some time ago, these trends germinated the seeds of a New School of Information Security. That New School has grown and taken shape as two core ideas. First is the pursuit of objective data about real-world outcomes to enable better security decision-making. Gathering, analyzing, and acting on the lessons of objective data is the only way for information security to become a science not only in its academic aspects, but also in how it is used on a day-to-day basis. Second, the New School looks outward to the sciences to identify new strategies and objectively assess current approaches. In contrast, the inward-looking nature of today's security industry has created a bubble.

Confronting the new involves questions of how to fit in, whether existing skills and habits will adapt well or poorly, and how to maximize profit from changes while minimizing loss. These are the sorts of questions that confront both companies and individuals. Companies must adapt when the market shifts, such as when new competitors or technologies appear. Individuals must also learn new skills or risk unemployment. Opposing these needs is the all-too-human trait of becoming set in a comfortable, routine way of thinking and operating. Often, it is easier to ignore the need for change and keep doing things the same old way. The rust belt beckons.

The risks and unknowns of embracing a new approach can be scary, but here the opportunity costs are slight. The New School does not mandate the purchase of any particular product or service. All the New School requires is an investment in a way of thinking about problems—to observe the world and ask: why? If time is money, time spent thinking deeply about security challenges can pay large dividends. The sorts of questions to be examined are those such as, how can security practitioners be empowered with sufficient knowledge to enable them to make good decisions? Within organizations, how should approaches be examined for objective evidence of their success or failure? What areas should universities, national laboratories, and others focus on and invest in? This book has touched on many of these questions, but this chapter addresses them succinctly and head-on.

Much of the advice that the New School offers is universal. It can be employed by a small nonprofit organization or a multinational corporation. We will speak to these universal ideas first and show how to apply them. Then we will drill down into advice for some specific industries and groups.

Join the New School

Joining the New School first requires an understanding of some of the structural issues that affect the information security industry. These issues have contributed to the long life of many security problems. The people and organizations that make up the security industry are a mélange. They have different backgrounds, and they often have divergent and sometimes competing interests. Chapter 2 showed that any one group, seeing only the piece of the puzzle that is most visible to them, might act in a way that does not serve collective best interests. We have also made the observation that commercial concerns imposed by the market can contribute to a narrow, short-term view of what problems can or should be tackled. These structural issues can be understood in terms of the orientation that each group holds, and those orientations tend to be reinforced by regular interactions within those groups. To avoid the tunnel vision of a narrow orientation, we need objective data about where security measures are successful, and where they fail. That data must feed experiments or analysis and convince people to change their current approaches. Shared data can be the catalyst for unifying disparate views (and for debunking some, too). For this to happen, the information must be both widely disseminated and freely available.

Gather Good Data

Where will this good data come from? As we discussed in Chapter 3, many of the traditional sources of information about the state of information security are flawed. Today's security surveys have many problems, creating wide variations in the results. These problems include selection bias and the likelihood that security people who are "in the trenches" dealing with operational issues might perceive the world to be a more dangerous place than it really is. The trade press as a source of evidence has its own set of problems. Some of these are self-imposed, such as when time-critical information about security vulnerabilities and threats is published in a monthly print magazine. Trade periodicals and magazines also have a natural incentive to provide good product reviews for products that are sold by the vendors that pay to advertise in those same magazines. A focus on products can also make the reader believe that spending more on security products will necessarily lead to better security. (It might, but again, only good data allows us to test that hypothesis.) Other apparent sources of information have their own subtle problems, and problems can blend together.

Faced with these weaknesses, it is opportune that a new source of objective data on information security has emerged. That source of information is the legally imposed breach notifications that have become widespread since the ChoicePoint incident in 2005. Breach data reveals *who* lost data, *how much* was lost, what *type* of data was lost, and often *how* it was lost (although not to a very detailed level today). By correlating breach data to stories in the media about those breaches, we can also examine aspects of data breach incidents such as the behavior of the reporting company, how the market responds, and what subsequent events transpire over time. This breach data and its analysis provide tremendous benefits. The data can be used to guide security spending decisions in a more optimal way. It also reveals whether existing approaches are effective. (On the whole, given the current data, it appears not.)

We have pointed out that success in security is often silent or invisible. Failure can also be silent. Prior to breach notification laws, it might have been thought that because there was no raft of publicized breaches in the press, nothing was going wrong. This in turn created a sense that current approaches were satisfactory, which contributed to the malaise. Gathering data is the first step in joining the New School.

Analyze Good Data

Organizations and individual practitioners should examine the analyses of breach data and put them to use. Where avoiding data loss is a priority, these analyses can be used for strategic planning. They can also be used to guide tactical decisions about protective measures. Companies and individuals can bring their unique perspectives, backgrounds, and questions to the data. Findings should be published and shared. Open, noncommercial, information-sharing organizations are the ideal venue for doing so, as are new media such as blogs, most of which are open to all comers. Analyzing and sharing data are key to joining the New School.

The availability of breach data has in many respects been a happy accident. Collectively, we must build on the opportunity by identifying new sources and types of objective data and bringing them into the public domain. There is no qualifier for what data might be useful. It seems best to focus initially on data that could be used to make better spending decisions. The financial lever is an important one, because it provides a way to create real changes in behavior within companies and within the security industry as a whole. As data proliferates and more discoveries are made, many of the security strategies that are employed today might be found to be inefficient, or perhaps even ineffective. (Chapter 6 noted some that we suspect of being in this category, such as end-user security awareness training.) As we move forward with this new mind-set that places data at the heart of decision-making, we should never be afraid to put ingrained ideas to the test of evidence, and in doing so, challenge the conventional wisdom. The people and organizations that embrace the New School will receive returns on that investment. By bringing forward new analysis, they will be seen as forward-thinking, and they will save their organizations money while advancing their goals.

Seek New Perspectives

Joining the New School requires organizations and individuals to seek new perspectives on their security challenges by looking outside their own professional orientation, and even outside the security field itself. Today, the research shared at the Workshop on the Economics of Information Security (WEIS) provides one of the most significant of these diverse views. This new discipline applies ideas from the study of economics to security challenges. It has provided explanations for many of the most notable security problems that exist today. One of the most interesting and useful new ideas to emerge from the economics of information security is the realization that the incentives of the various parties who interact with a system are often the most significant factor in that system's security. When incentives are not aligned, incentive failure can occur, closely followed by a breakdown in security. This finding will lead to better-designed security measures.

All the sciences have the potential to provide new insight into information security. In the same manner, the diversity of contributors and their backgrounds is important for creating the greatest probability that new, useful approaches will be found. Security practitioners on the whole are a monoculture: white and male. This is a deep-rooted, structural problem that organizations can take positive actions to address. Doing so is not just a warm and fuzzy approach to the world. Research consistently shows that more diverse teams tend to make better decisions.

Embrace the New School

Embracing the New School means changing aspects of how each of us behaves. As we gather and analyze information through a variety of new lenses, we need to use that data to change our behavior—specifically, how we teach, how we act, and how we react.

Change How You Teach (and Learn)

Universities are ideally placed to champion the New School. Their syllabi already include teaching the scientific method and analyzing data. The goal of a university is not simply to educate students about fundamental concepts, but to teach them how to think about and solve the practical problems they will encounter in their work life. When the topic is information security, this increasingly means considering not just the technological aspects but also facets that relate to economics, psychology, and other fields. Information security is becoming a multidisciplinary endeavor, from both an academic and practical perspective. Universities need to accommodate this shift, and they are ideally positioned to do so. Some are also well placed to foster interdisciplinary research. In the next several years, research programs in information security might come to resemble those in economics, sociology, and criminology as much as they resemble those in computer science. There is a virtuous circle for institutions of higher learning here, because great faculty are attracted by the opportunity to perform interesting research, which in turn attracts top students.

University faculty and the graduate students who serve under them are adept at gathering data to fuel their research. These skills are easily transferred to the search for objective data about information security. Today, individuals, hobbyists, and one tiny nonprofit organization collect security breach data. These individuals and groups are frustrated by the lack of objective data with which to make security decisions. They are also curious about what failures have occurred. This collection of breach data is a time-consuming activity, but it is not rocket science. *Analyzing* breach data requires only an inquisitive mind and the desire to perform the task. This means that researchers at all levels can contribute to pushing forward the state of the art in computer security, not just Ph.D. candidates working on thorny technical challenges.

Outside of universities, the majority of teaching information security professionals takes place at professional training courses. As knowledge of the benefits of the New School begins to become widely evident, these courses might shift their focus from the overwhelmingly technical to a view that encompasses the wider perspectives of the New School. In the meantime, we suggest that seasoned security professionals broaden their horizons and delve into other fields by reading and attending classes or even conferences. There are lessons all around for how to better approach security problems.

Change How You Act

The lessons of the New School are universal, but here we will be more specific and speak to how organizations act.

The New School provides a number of filters and concepts that are useful when considering spending decisions. One of these is the realization that the same core problems may underlie many apparently disparate symptoms. Seeking to treat the symptoms of these problems by purchasing the latest gee-whiz security product is likely to provide only fleeting, superficial gains, because the underlying problems will remain. These underlying problems for most companies relate to fundamental IT objectives rather than pure security objectives. They include configuration management, inventory management, and change management of systems. If software is developed in-house, the security aspects of the software development life cycle are also fundamental.

This is not to say that spending directly on security cannot provide benefits; it can. Some of the most interesting benefits are also some of the more subtle. Spending on security can be viewed as an investment in *flexibility*, allowing changes within the organization to be handled in a modular and therefore efficient manner. Spending on security can also be the catalyst for activities that simplify and consolidate IT infrastructure within the environment. But it is important to remember that spending on security technology is unlikely to create sustainable competitive advantage for most companies, because the technologies employed are widely available.

When considering how much to spend on security, it is inefficient to focus on negative goals. For example, if the goal is "no security incidents," and an incident never occurs, it becomes very difficult to calculate how much may have been overspent. Arbitrary rules such as "spend 7% to 11% of the IT budget on security" are just that: arbitrary. They may be politically defensible because an industry analyst suggested that the figure was appropriate, but this approach is likely one of the most inefficient spending strategies a company can employ. (Companies don't go bankrupt because they spend at this level, but few companies go bankrupt because of failures in their security.) Traditional techniques for supporting spending decisions such as ALE and ROI are effectively crippled when applied to security-spending decisions today because of the current lack of actuarial-like data that could predict the probability of attack. Rules of thumb based on economic models are useful until that data becomes built up, such as with the Gordon and Loeb model described in Chapter 6.

Security capabilities and properties tend not to be built into early versions of software because of powerful incentives that exist within the market. This is a key topic when considering on what to spend, as discussed in Chapter 5. Software that becomes successful in the market usually builds in security capabilities over time. Large companies often do this by buying small companies. Organizations considering the purchase of a security product should first ask themselves whether the desired security capabilities exist within the core platforms they already own. (This is a valid strategy only if the vendors that are implementing the security functionality are doing it well.) Second, will the desired functionality soon be built into those platforms? "Wait and see" by tailing the technology market becomes a plausible purchasing strategy. If an organization wants to be more proactive, it should focus its security efforts on working with the vendors it can influence. For larger organizations that have more purchasing power, it makes sense to work with the vendors of the organizations' core platforms. Smaller organizations can free-ride on these efforts, but they might not be able to exert much influence over the large software companies. They might then have good reason to partner with smaller vendors that might be more receptive.

Examining breach reports and looking at the ways companies have lost data, certain trends emerge. These trends hold lessons for organizations. A common type of incident is for companies to lose data by misplacing media such as backup tapes. They also lose data through stolen devices such as laptop computers. Data given to consultants and auditors that goes awry is another persistent trend. Beyond the obvious recommendation to "look after your stuff," companies can try to reduce the amount of personally identifying information they store. They can also focus on the security measures placed around or preferably *with* data. This contrasts with the general focus today on the security of the components through which the data travels (the IT infrastructure).

On the other side of this coin is the commercial security industry. A superficial view of problems creates superficial markets. Once the New School becomes more widely understood, vendors will be forced to make changes in the products they bring to market. They will also have to alter how they sell these products, moving from the widespread use of fear as a sales tactic to objective measures of value. The good news for security vendors is that new markets and opportunities will emerge. In anticipation of these changes, their first step should be to arrange and align their offerings to satisfy the growing desire for objective data.

Change How You React

There can be both madness and wisdom in crowds, so it is incumbent upon each of us to contribute to the pool of good information and reject the bad and the obscured. If a company suffers a breach, it should acknowledge what happened. Those who disclose security incidents can be safe in the knowledge that they are not the only ones. They should also know that the best analyses of the data have shown that there is unlikely to be any long-term effect on their company's share price. It has been demonstrated that customers do not flee from companies that suffer a breach. It is in the interest of the company, its shareholders, and its customers to notify early, and to do so publicly. These, unequivocally, are the New rules of breach disclosure.

Make Money from the New School

We have spoken throughout this book about the need to understand people's motivations. While we expect that some will embrace the New School for reasons of intellectual honesty or long-term professional advancement, others are no doubt wondering how they can use the New School to make money. This is to be expected and embraced. The motivation of some has always been the desire for fame, fortune, and power. Let us be clear that the New School is not a get-rich-quick scheme. However, making money is a reasonable and common motivation, and some of those who are on the fence may embrace the ideas we present in order to enrich themselves. To not recognize this fact would be to stick our heads in the sand, so we provide the following advice in the hope that the goals of the New School will be best served.

We spoke earlier about the changes that companies who provide security products can make to better align themselves with the New School. Customers will increasingly demand objective evidence of the results that security products and services provide. The crucial word is *objective*. The sales pitch based on fear will massively diminish in power. In many respects, this shift toward the objective is a change that security companies must respond to—they simply have no choice. That said, *choosing* to be on the cutting edge of change provides opportunities for companies to best position themselves within these new markets and to promote themselves as thought leaders.

Another opportunity for companies might be to gather and sell data, or to analyze data and sell that analysis. Pointing out this possibility might seem to contradict our persistent calls for the open and free sharing of data, but there are real parallels to existing markets for information. Stock quotes delayed by twenty minutes are freely available on the internet, but real-time stock quotes are sold at a price. A market could be created for the timely delivery of security breach data. It is very likely that a market will exist for the in-depth analysis of breach data and the analysis of other objective data related to security.

An obvious set of consulting services will become more profitable as the New School gains traction. These include consulting services for responding most appropriately to an incident or breach, for gathering objective data about security, and for analyzing it in support of decision-making.

We believe that doing well and doing good can overlap in information security and that opportunities in this regard will exist for both companies and entrepreneurs.

Final Words

Those who have worked in IT or information security who have taken the time to read this book have likely alternated between interest, amusement, and perhaps annoyance. We hope that the preeminent emotion has not been the latter, because we have attempted to carefully justify our skewering of sacred cows. To be clear, our intention is to criticize results, not motivations. We have had to present a lot of bad news to reach the good, but the opportunity to make better security decisions motivates our inquiry.

As such, we ask for your honest engagement with the ideas contained herein. We are hopeful that the arguments we have put forth will convince you that positive changes *are* possible. We hope that our broad analysis is helpful in organizing and structuring your thoughts, and that it will cause you to consider the New School when making security decisions. We hope that you will use your position of influence to encourage the collection, analysis, and sharing of objective data. We also hope that you will set the bar higher for products that claim to solve a problem but simply address one narrow aspect of it. We can never entirely eliminate security risks. We *should* ask "how effective are we?" and "are we investing in the right things?"

Finally, we have hung our argument not on our wisdom but on the quality of our analysis. That analysis is doubtless wrong in some particulars, but we are confident that an empiricist approach to information security will act as a tremendous catalyst for change within the field. The journey of gathering and using information better has been the story of many industries in the last quarter century. In public health, in the insurance markets, and in the management of financial portfolios, objective data is sought out and embraced. They have done it. So must we.

Endnotes

Chapter 1, "Observing the World and Asking Why"

In December 2006, Turkish authorities announced the arrest of Ali Y'nin and nine accomplices for bank fraud.

Ufuk Koroglu and Bunyamin Demirkan, "Turkish Hacker Depletes 10,000 Bank Accounts," *Today's Zaman*, Istanbul, December 20, 2006, www.todayszaman.com/tz-web/detaylar.do?load=detay&link=39364.

At the time of writing, there was no additional information about the resolution of the charges.

Some large companies are dedicating resources to helping police forces investigate attacks that matter to them, but it is not clear if this strategy is a good investment.

Companies doing this, including Microsoft, do it because they think it's a good investment. We're taking a broader societal perspective of "is this how a neutral social planner would approach the issue?"

The assistance approach assigns the cost to those who stand to benefit most from the investigation. Is that good public policy? What about those who can't afford to support an investigation? Should we only investigate crimes that hurt the rich and powerful? Shouldn't the police investigate crimes? Wasn't making justice available to all behind the creation of professional police forces? Should the police be reliant on outsiders? Isn't one of the core reasons we pay taxes for the enforcement of laws? We don't yet have answers to these questions of how to investigate transnational crime, especially as it grows in volume.

Mark Klienman, "Microsoft helps FBI bust Chinese gang," *Daily Telegraph* online, July 25, 2007, www.telegraph.co.uk/money/main.jhtml?xml=/money/2007/07/24/bcnmicro124.xml.

Federal Bureau of Investigation press release, "Over 1 million potential victims of botnet cyber crime," June 13, 2007, www.fbi.gov/pressrel/pressrel07/botnet061307.htm.

American brokerage houses have found themselves losing millions of dollars to schemes in which criminals use other people's money to "pump and dump" the stock market.

For example, in 2006, Ameritrade compensated customers for $4 million in losses due to pump-and-dump schemes, and E-Trade compensated customers for $18 million in losses.

Eric Lai, "Identity thieves hit customers at TD Ameritrade, E-Trade," *ComputerWorld* Online, October 24, 2006, www.computerworld.com/action/article.do?command=printArticleBasic&articleId=9004416.

Ideally, security shows up first and allows us to preempt problems, but that seems to be a rare occurrence.

It might seem that way, but if built-in security actually works, we might never notice the successes we've had. They're harder to notice than failures.

Spam, and Other Problems with Email

In 1994, a law firm decided that the internet would be an ideal way to advertise its legal services.

See, for example, Robin Rowland, "Spam, Spam, Spam: The Cyberspace Wars," CBC News Online, November 24, 2003, www.cbc.ca/news/background/spam/. Wikipedia also has a well-maintained article at en.wikipedia.org/wiki/Spam_%28electronic%29.

The first are companies you did business with once, which then send you emails forever. Even if you ask them to stop, the mail keeps coming. Consumers see this as spam.

For a marketer's perspective on this, see John Whiteside, "Expedia should consider the only definition of 'spam' that matters," The Opinionated Marketer blog, April 3, 2007, http://opinionatedmarketers.blogspot.com/2007/04/expedia-should-consider-only-definition.html.

Sometimes this was and even still is true, but often the adware is embedded in other software and installs itself without the meaningful consent of the PC's owner. (By meaningful consent, we mean that the person installing the software understands what he is getting into.)

The basic principle of contract law involves a meeting of minds and the exchange of value. The surprising and surreptitious installation of software seems a far cry from a meeting of minds, and the idea of an irrevocable installation seems like it may carry additional requirements of clear notice.

Today, some experts say it can be more cost-effective to reinstall a computer than to remove a bad adware infection.

Ryan Naraine, "Microsoft says recovery from malware becoming impossible," eWeek.com, April 4, 2006, www.eweek.com/article2/0,1895,1945808,00.asp.

In January 2006, more than six billion emails were recorded as part of 15,000 different phishing scams.

SonicWall, quoting the Anti-Phishing Working Group, "SonicWall Phishing IQ Test, Phishing Facts," http://sonicwall.com/phishing/. Undated page, visited December 22, 2007.

In a test of people's ability to distinguish real email from fake, only 6% got all the answers right, and only half of real emails were recognized as being real. Even so, many companies that do business online have not yet adopted some simple measures that would help protect their customers.

One of us (Adam) offered a number of suggestions in August 2005 in "Preserving the Internet Channel Against Phishers," www.homeport.org/~adam/phishing.html. Most entail making it easier for mail recipients to act to avoid phishing, rather than requiring them to investigate and avoid it.

Rather than take these measures, many companies have instead made things more difficult for their customers by registering new web addresses, using confusing web addresses, and using certain technologies in their web pages that make it easier for fraudsters to camouflage their actions.

There seems to be no general survey of all the bad practices out there. Some works that list problems are Peter Seebach, "What you can do about phishing," IBM Developer Works, January 4, 2006, www.ibm.com/developerworks/web/library/wa-cranky60.html, and S.A. Mathieson, "Gone phishing in Halifax," Elsevier Infosecurity, October 7, 2005, http://infosecurity-magazine.com/news/051007_halifax_email.htm, which describes how a bank sent email that the bank's own staff identified as a fake.

In "certain technologies," we include the use of Flash or JavaScript on bank web sites. If someone wants to use HTML without executing programs, he or she can no longer do so. JavaScript, with methods such as on.mouseover and on.click, makes it harder to understand the real content of URLs. Flash conceals them entirely. Some banks (such as Citibank's "Account Online" site, as of December 2007) go so far as to intentionally take the user to a different page if JavaScript is ever off.

To be fair, some companies have sought to address the problem of phishing by implementing a new breed of authentication technologies. ... For example, in a 2007 study, one of the market-leading products in this space was shown to be ineffective 92% of the time.

One reviewer suggested that this is intentional "security theater" designed to convince people to feel better, rather than prevent fraud. It's bad security and worse theater, because research shows that people don't notice its absence.

See Stuart Schecter, Rachna Dhamija, Andy Ozment, and Ian Fischer, "The Emperor's New Security Indicators: An evaluation of website authentication and the effect of role playing on usability studies," IEEE Symposium on Security and Privacy, May 2007, www.usablesecurity.org/emperor/.

Hostile Code

For the last twenty years, the majority of anti-virus (AV) products have relied on explicit knowledge about every virus that exists in the world. That knowledge is codified within a *signature*.

For an excellent reference on antivirus technology and its evolution, see Peter Szor's *The Art of Computer Virus Research and Defense*, 2005, Symantec Press.

But this technology can struggle with distinguishing between hostile and benign actions, and it can have an error rate of 50% or more.

To be specific, by "error rate" we mean a false positive rather than false negative error rate. See Andreas Marx, "The false positive disaster," Virus Bulletin, November 1, 2005. In that study, one particular AV product, when presented with 896 nonmalicious files collected from the internet, flagged 10 as infected and 709 as "suspected infected."

There was no fundamental difference between the methodology or techniques used by those modern incarnations of worms and the original Morris Worm.

The Morris Worm exploited poor passwords, stack-based buffer overflows, host trust features, and the "WIZ" backdoor in Sendmail. Examples of each of these are still with us twenty years later.

See either J. Reynolds, "The Helminthiasis of the Internet," RFC 1135, December 1989, or Mark Eichin and Jon Rochlis, "With Microscope and Tweezers: An analysis of the Internet virus of November 1988," 1989 IEEE Symposium on Research in Security and Privacy, www.mit.edu/people/eichin/virus/main.html.

Security Breaches

The personal data that was compromised included customer information related to purchases and returns, and it contained credit and debit card numbers.

The data also included some driver's license data as part of an antifraud program around returned merchandise. See Office of the Privacy Commissioner of Canada and Office of the Information and Privacy Commissioner of Alberta, "Report of an Investigation into the Security, Collection and Retention of Personal Information, TJX Companies Inc./Winners Merchant International L.P.," September 25, 2007, www.privcom.gc.ca/cf-dc/2007/TJX_rep_070925_e.asp.

Eighteen months was enough time for the attackers to thoroughly ransack the TJX computer network.

Evan Schuman has documented how attackers moved 80 GB of data from the TJX network and installed a traffic-capture/sniffing program that went undetected for seven months.

Evan Schuman, "TJX Intruder Moved 80-GBytes of Data and No One Noticed," StorefrontBacktalk blog, October 25, 2007, http://storefrontbacktalk.com/story/102507tjxrevisedcomplaint.

Over half of all Americans have been sent notices that their personal data may have been compromised in one of the many breaches that have been disclosed. This number seems low given the vast number of databases containing personal information, the rates of reported laptop theft, and how personal information is bought, sold, and traded.

In July 2006, the U.S. Office of Management and Budget started requiring reports of security incidents that expose personal information. By June 2007, agencies were reporting about fourteen incidents per day. By October 2007, that had risen to thirty per day. It seems unlikely that security got dramatically worse during that time. A better explanation is that the requirement became more widely known. Numbers from Jill Aitoro, "Reports of federal security breaches double in four months," Government Executive.com, October 23, 2007, www.govexec.com/story_page.cfm?articleid=38348.

The point about laptop theft rates is from Ed Moyle, "Strange things are afoot with breach disclosure," Security Curve blog, November 3, 2006, www.securitycurve.com/blog/archives/000476.html. He points out that the rate of laptop theft would seem to indicate that much more data is being lost than is being reported.

According to the Ponemon Institute, "2007 Consumer Survey on Data Security," June 25, 2007, 62% of respondents to a web survey had received such a notification.

Identity and the Theft of Identity

We use other identifiers to identify people, such as "Dad." Dad is not a *unique* identifier, but most people are pretty sure whom they mean when they say it.

This lovely little example is from L. Jean Camp, *Economics of Identity Theft*, 2007, Springer-Verlag.

A bank with eight customers named John Wilson needs to be able to differentiate between them.

Carl Ellison first used John Wilson in an example in "Improvements on Conventional PKI Wisdom," First Annual PKI workshop, April 2002.

The problem is that many of these identifying fragments were never designed for the ways in which they are being used.

There are hard questions of how to best identify a customer who has forgotten his or her password. Many organizations are using "secret questions" such as "What was the name of your first pet?" or "What's your mother's maiden name?" to deal with this situation. With online genealogy databases, mothers' maiden names are scarcely secret anymore, but system designers seem not to know that.

The SSN was not designed to be secret, and yet it is widely believed to be secret and often is treated as such.

The Social Security Act of 1935 doesn't even mention the SSN, never mind the word "secret" or "confidential." It simply "authorized the creation of some type of record keeping scheme." The Social Security Administration, "Social Security Number Chronology," www.ssa.gov/history/ssn/ssnchron.html. The first mention of confidentiality in that chronology is in 1971.

Some states have proposed "identity theft passports" to help victims of identity fraud. However, the more we tighten the security of identity systems, the less willing authorities will be to believe they can be compromised and defrauded.

For example, Virginia has such a "passport," as documented in the web site of the State Attorney General, "FAQ Identity Theft," undated web page, visited December 22, 2007, www.oag.state.va.us/FAQs/FAQ_IDTheft.html. The origin of the term "passport" for such documents is unclear and strikes us as more than a little bizarre.

Should We Just Start Over?

Even if we "just" tried to recreate the most popular pieces of computer software in a highly secure manner, how likely is it that no mistakes would creep in?

This strategy of outright replacement is advocated by some security professionals, most notably Marcus Ranum, "How to really secure the Internet," Blackhat Briefings, 1997. To be fair, Ranum does call it "an amusing thought" and says it won't happen.

It seems likely that errors in specification, design, and implementation would occur, all leading to security problems, just as with other software development projects.

Specifying and designing software is hard. There are a tremendous number of decisions that have to be made, and reinvention has its own set of problems.

So, after enormous expense, a new set of problems would probably exist, and there is no reason to expect any fewer than we have today, or that they would be any easier to deal with.

We think there would likely be more, and new and exciting issues would creep in.

Much of the usefulness of the internet comes from its open-platform nature that allows new ideas to be developed and incubated.

The internet is designed as a dumb network that simply passes packets. This is in contrast to telecom networks, which have lots of smarts in phone company computers and none in the phones. AT&T didn't invent the BlackBerry or the iPhone. Text messages are an afterthought in the GSM mobile telephony standard. In other words, the ability to deploy new services doesn't require help or approval from the center.

The internet's success depends to a large degree on an open philosophy, which in turn requires accepting a certain amount of insecurity.

There are several thoughts behind this. The first is that if a network were designed to block new things, it might well be more secure, in accordance with a general philosophy of "allow only what is explicitly permitted." Getting a new service approved by some "authority" would inevitably take time. Such an authority would likely block some useful new services because "security isn't baked in." (After all, that's the authority's job.) The web might never have come about. Who'd want to show web pages to *unauthenticated* users?

The next thought is that in building connections, not needing to configure cryptographic security removes a barrier to successfully connecting. Because security barriers are often large, if new internet connections had required security configuration, they would have taken longer to set up and been more expensive. Some number of users would have given up or stuck with services such as AOL or Prodigy, which had better commercial support.

Finally, as a reviewer commented, there's a relation to people's willingness to sacrifice liberty for a little temporary security. The value of liberty is that it allows new things, some of which are dangerous.

Chapter 2, "The Security Industry"

If the prisoner's dilemma is a good model of the security industry, then yes. (We may be oversimplifying, but it illustrates our point.)

The prisoner's dilemma is by no means a perfect model of the security industry. Many security professionals find their careers crossing repeatedly with each other, which would make an iterated prisoner's dilemma more accurate. In an iterated prisoner's dilemma game, very different strategies can take hold. Within game theory, there are models of emergent cooperation, such as with stag hunt/assurance games. Additionally, people in the real world can communicate with each other. Regardless, the simplification is illustrative, even if it's imperfect. For a fascinating (if academic) analysis of assurance games, see Brian Skyrms, *The Stag Hunt and the Evolution of Social Structure*, 2003, Cambridge University Press.

Where the Security Industry Comes From

The computer security industry couldn't get started until computers existed, and many of the earliest computers and networks were built by the military.

Very important work in computers was done as part of the effort to crack the Enigma cryptosystem that was used by the German military during the second world war.

This led the U.S. military to fund early and influential research in computer security.

We're thinking of Jack Anderson's Computer Security Study, the work of Biba and Bell-LaPadula on formal models of security; and some of the Multics investigations into computer security that were all funded by the U.S. Department of Defense. Work carried out by the Advanced Research Projects Agency led to the internet. No other military has been as influential on information security, with the possible exception of the British military investments to break the Enigma.

In the 1980s, the Department of Defense wrote and published security standards and then required that the IT vendors the government did business with meet those standards in their products.

The archetypal example here is the "Orange Book," otherwise known as the Trusted Computer System Evaluation Criteria (TCSEC). The Orange Book defined various levels of security. Vendors were supposed to demonstrate that their product met the relevant level for use in each government facility. In some cases, vendors were able to compensate for weaknesses in their product by simply removing a particular piece of hardware from the machine being tested, such as a floppy disk drive. The certification process could also take so long that the products being tested were sometimes off the general market by the time the certification was achieved.

The "C2" standard was intended to represent the security offered by products in the market, such as RACF, a security product from IBM.

Contrary to widespread belief, the military does not have access to any special data set that would enable it to make better decisions than, say, a large corporation.

See the U.S. House of Representatives, Committee on Oversight and Government Reform, "Seventh Report Card on Computer Security at Federal Departments and Agencies," April 12, 2007. The Department of Defense was given a failing grade. If the U.S. military could make better security decisions than other organizations, that should have been reflected in their security standards. The military does have a number of differences from companies, such as the ability to issue orders and the relatively easy availability of armed guards. It also has specialized expertise in attacking systems, which does not translate cleanly into better defending its own.

We use the traditional meaning of the word hacker: someone who is adept at pushing a system beyond expected boundaries, and not usually with malicious intent.

Hackers experience intellectual joy in seeking out the assumptions upon which the security of a system is based and then confounding those assumptions. Most people do the same thing in their everyday lives, at least to some extent.

Most audit work is performed by junior employees, who have relatively little technical skill and are less able to influence the selection of security products in use.

Auditors may have some influence on feature sets but are unlikely to convince a company to replace one product with another.

To make lots of money in security, an entrepreneur must find a problem that customers can understand and that can be solved with technology.

Having spent three years trying to sell complex privacy technology to people who understood neither the problem nor the technology offered to solve it, Adam is a strong proponent of working on problems that customers can easily understand. That said, that is not the only type of problem that we are in favor of effort being spent on. As the chapter notes, the most useful problems to solve might be the hardest to describe.

One of our reviewers suggested (somewhat cynically) that entrepreneurs would be better served if they found a problem that can be understood using pretty graphs.

This can channel entrepreneurs and start-ups in security into a narrow market, focused on a small subset of the important problems.

And, perhaps, a great many not-so-important ones that are easily marketed.

This is an important source of innovation, and many important security products have come from the open-source world.

Obvious examples include SSH, snort, nmap, and OpenBSD.

Analysts are often given in-depth briefings by companies, and the quality of their analysis hinges on the rigor they place on gathering and interpreting data. ... A cynical view of the advice that research firms such as Gartner provide to business is that "no one ever gets fired for implementing Gartner recommendations."

The earliest version of this advice we're aware of was "no one ever gets fired for buying IBM."

It would be interesting to review the predictions made by business advisory firms regarding information security topics. How right were they? Or how wrong? We are not aware of anyone carrying out such a research project, but we would love to see it.

In a paper published in 1999, Stefan Axelsson, a researcher in Sweden, explained that the value of these products hinges not on their ability to detect attacks, but on their ability to suppress false alarms that drive up operational costs.

Stefan Axelsson, "The base-rate fallacy and the difficulty of intrusion detection," ACM Transactions on Information and System Security (TISSEC), 3(3), pp. 186–205, ACM Press, ISSN: 1094-9224, 2000.

(The other farsighted paper was Ptacek and Newsham's work describing how an attacker can evade the technology.)

Ptacek and Newsham show that without an understanding of matters external to an intrusion detection sensor, it is extremely difficult for that sensor to return results that can be confidently relied on. Thomas Ptacek and Timothy Newsham, "Insertion, Evasion, and Denial of Service: Eluding Network Intrusion Detection," 1998, Secure Networks, Inc. technical report.

Orientations and Framing

We're using the term *orientation* as defined by John Boyd in his Observe, Orient, Decide, Act (OODA) concept, often simplified and called a loop.

Boyd spent his career in the U.S. Army. He published few essays, but he did publish a number of highly evolved briefs (presentations). This lack of a clear corpus of work makes his work challenging to understand. The easiest introduction to his work is Robert Coram, *Boyd: The Fighter Pilot Who Changed the Art of War*, 2004, Back Bay Books. The most in-depth is Frans Osinga, *Science, Strategy, and War: The Strategic Theory of John Boyd*, 2006, Routledge.

In his brief "Organic Design for Command and Control," Boyd wrote: "Orientation, **seen as a result**, represents images, views, or impressions of the world shaped by **genetic heritage**, **cultural tradition**, **previous experiences**, and **unfolding circumstances**." (Emphasis in original.) John Boyd, "Organic Design for Command and Control," 1987. Available at www.d-n-i.net/boyd/organic_design.ppt.

What we see as conventional wisdom is to a large degree shaped by our personal and social preferences, since what is convenient to believe is often greatly preferred.

The last phrase is from John Kenneth Galbraith, *The Economics of Innocent Fraud: Truth for Our Time*, p. x (front matter), 2004, Houghton Mifflin.

Compliance practitioners within corporate security teams view security problems in terms of their possible effect on audit findings. They might dismiss a gaping security hole because they don't believe it will impact the bottom line.

It is only natural that many of the security decisions we make are based on our knowledge and understanding of past situations. This process of making and correcting mistakes and of making and testing decisions can be viewed as a feedback loop. Finding effective feedback loops, where important issues are noticed and processed in useful ways, is a key part of Boyd's theories.

What Does the Security Industry Sell?

The security industry advertises on buses, billboards, and taxicabs. It publishes trade magazines, runs conferences and award shows, operates security news and information portals on the web, provides training courses and professional certifications, creates security products, and delivers security services.

Awards shows for security executives deserve special mention as an example of incentives gone wrong. One particular company that operates "information security executive awards" presents regional "people's choice" awards. Rather than rewarding leadership or innovation, the vendors that sponsor the awards ceremony nominate people for the awards. This means that the person who has bought the most security products likely becomes the winner—a dubious honor. The attendees of the awards event vote for the main "information security executive of the year" award. Nominees (or their employers) pay a large sum (on the order of $1,000) per table of five attendees. Nominees have an incentive to bring as many of their coworkers to the awards ceremony as they can, to stack the voting in their favor. Award winners get to pad their résumés. As a mechanism to reward leadership and innovation in information security, such awards shows fail miserably. As an exercise in gaming the nominees, they succeed admirably.

See also the paper from Ulrike Malmendier and Geoffrey Tate, "Superstar CEOs." It shows that the firms of CEOs who achieve "superstar" status via prestigious nationwide awards from the business press subsequently underperform relative to the overall market. Available at SSRN: http://ssrn.com/abstract=972725.

The use of network firewalls to restrict the types of traffic that can flow into and out of private networks has led directly to the current situation in which every application developer simply makes all the traffic flow over port 80.

This is not completely true. The situation is actually worse. Some applications, such as Skype, are much more clever in their deliberate evasion of firewalls.

Now businesses have to purchase *application* firewalls in addition to their normal firewalls.

There's irony here, since early "application layer" firewalls such as the DEC SEAL or TIS Firewall Toolkit were beaten in the marketplace by faster "packet filtering" firewalls made by companies such as Checkpoint. The less secure design won. It's not clear whether this happened because "fast" was the most important feature or because the transaction costs involved with evaluating firewall products were too high for most organizations.

Bugs and misconfigurations arise from complexity, and a security bug is simply a bug with security implications.

This idea was put forth by Robert Morris, "If your software is full of bugs, why would you think it's secure?," keynote address, 4th USENIX Security Symposium, October 4–6, 1993, Santa Clara, California. The title of the address is not listed on the USENIX web site, but it is taken from Steve Bellovin, "Re: CERT Reports and system breakins," in *Risks Digest* 15:28 (Peter Neumann, ed.), November 15, 1993, at http://catless.ncl.ac.uk/Risks/15.28.html#subj8.

One response has been the emergence of a market for security certifications, which now are available for many different specialties in the field.

It is in the interests of the companies that offer such certifications to develop new certifications over time to continue generating new revenue. This creates a treadmill for professionals who feel obligated to achieve the highest level of certification.

Because security has become an important business topic, this has led people to pursue security certifications in the hopes that they will become more marketable.

There's an element of signaling here, as Spence pointed out. Michael Spence, "Job Market Signaling," *Quarterly Journal of Economics* 87 (3): 355–374, 1973.

This is perhaps not true of all seal programs, but a 2006 analysis of TRUSTe, a major seal vendor, showed that its seal participants were more likely to show up in a large database of malware distributors....

See "Adverse Selection in Online 'Trust' Certifications," by Benjamin Edelman, a working draft as of October 15, 2006. Available at www.benedelman.org/publications/advsel-trust-draft.pdf.

How Security Is Sold

Even so, many newspapers around the world published headlines such as "Killer bug ate my face" and "Flesh-eating bug consumed my mother in 20 minutes."

The Culture of Fear: Why Americans Are Afraid of the Wrong Things by Barry Glassner (2000).

Sales of duct tape spiked after the Department of Homeland Security announced that all Americans should include duct tape and plastic sheeting in "home disaster kits."

See "U.S. stuck on duct" on cnn.com at http://money.cnn.com/2003/02/12/news/companies/ducttape/index.htm.

One vendor that ran five "hacker challenges" in the 1990s was hacked on the fifth. As of late 2007, the vendor had not paid the $50,000 "reward" it advertised.

The vendor was Argus, and the challenge was won by the hacking group "Last Stage of Delirium." Kevin Poulsen, "Hacking Challenge Winners Allege $43,000 Contest Rip-Off," SecurityFocus, November 26, 2002, www.securityfocus.com/news/1717. Validated by personal communication with Last Stage of Delirium alumnus Tomasz Ostwald in June 2007.

We are referring only to "proof by unclaimed reward" here. Organizations, including many open-source groups and Microsoft, provide early access to products in the hopes of learning from and collaborating with hackers.

In an issue of one such magazine, the average rating for the twenty reviewed security products was four stars out of five.

The magazine in question is the February 2005 issue of *SC* magazine. In that issue, 25% of the products reviewed (five products) were awarded five stars. The magazine also contained a half-page advertisement for product review reprints, which could be purchased by the product vendors. Quote: "A reprint of an article in SC magazine can help you in your company's marketing efforts. If you've had a product reviewed ... please call us for further information about obtaining professional reprints." We're not implying that the magazine is unethical for selling things; we're pointing out that its objectivity might be called into question.

In a number of cases, companies that were certified to the PCI standard have suffered spectacular failures in their security.

Certifications come in three flavors. They may be paid for by the creator of the thing being certified, by the consumer, or by a third party acting in the public interest, such as government or a consumer-advocacy group.

The first form carries a risk that the buyer will shop around for the least expensive option. That least expensive option is conveniently the least likely to do an in-depth job. In the second form, reviews paid for by consumers, there is either much duplication of work or a review agency subject to some form of regulatory capture, a risk also created by government reviews.

One of the most well known occurred in 2005, when CardSystems Solutions suffered a security breach in which attackers stole 40 million credit card numbers.

Eric Dash and Tom Zeller, Jr., "MasterCard Says 40 Million Files Put at Risk," *New York Times*, June 18, 2005, www.nytimes.com/2005/06/18/business/18cards.html.

"We followed the Visa rules to the letter, and the people who did the work are longtime security experts," the leader of the audit team was quoted as saying.

Bill Hancock, as quoted by Eric Dash, "Weakness in the Data Chain," the *New York Times*, June 30, 2005, www.nytimes.com/2005/06/30/technology/30cards.html (page 3).

Much like the U.S. Department of Agriculture (USDA) promulgates nutrition guidelines, there must be some equivalent like a National Institute of Computer Security.

We originally wrote "the National Institutes of Health," and only while fact checking discovered that the guidelines are from the USDA. The security industry is not unique in that our advice is created by biased sources, passed through regulatory bodies subject to capture. For more on regulatory capture, see the work of George Stigler, who defined regulatory capture as happening when a regulated entity works to reorient its regulator to see the world as the regulated do, and to make decisions favorable to the regulated.

Many security practitioners perceive the pursuit of "best practices" as defining a diligent security strategy.

Gene Kim and colleagues did a study in which they selected 25 measures of performance across a variety of organizations. They then examined organizations that followed some of the 63 practices defined by COBIT. They found that 21 of those 63 COBIT practices had a major impact on performance, with 4 being key. Organizations that did not follow those 21 practices performed poorly in comparison to those that did. If the research is accurate, a full two thirds of the studied practices are a waste of time and money.

Information Technology Process Institute, "IT Controls Performance Study," www.itpi.org/home/performance_study.php, as described by Gene Kim, "Prioritizing Processes and Controls for Effective and Measurable Security," CERIAS Security Seminar, September 20, 2006, www.cerias.purdue.edu/video/secsem/secsem_20060920.mp4.

Each of those groups has a vested interest in the security decisions that are made, and anyone can (and does) call their advice a "best practice."

A quick search (in October 2007) shows that the top ten Google results for the phrase "security best practice" include a small consultancy whose web site is "copyright 2003"; the SANS institute; Cisco; three general IT industry magazines; two university web sites with grab bags of ideas organized quite differently; and a similar (corporate) Yahoo! page. The Yahoo! page includes advice from "Ensure you're patched," to detailed advice about writing code free of cross-site request forgeries.

People find it difficult to argue against an authority or a perceived majority.

Most strikingly, Milgram's obedience experiments showed that people had a shocking willingness to risk hurting others when directed to by authorities. The series of experiments and reactions to them are described in Thomas Blass, *The Man Who Shocked the World*, 2004, Basic Books. A fascinating experiment showing people's willingness to go along with the majority is described in Asch, "Effects of group pressure upon the modification and distortion of judgements," pp. 151–162, D. Cartwright and A. Zander (editors), *Group Dynamics, Research and Theory* (Row, Peterson, Evanston, Illinois, 1953), cited in Duncan Watts, *Six Degrees: The Science of a Connected Age*, Norton, 2003, which describes the experiments on pp. 207–214. While we're mentioning these, Watt highlights a fascinating set of questions about Milgram's "six degrees" experiment (see page 132).

In Conclusion

In 2003, Michael Lewis published *Moneyball*, a book about how the Oakland A's baseball team uses statistics to decide which players to buy or sell.

Michael Lewis, *Moneyball: The Art of Winning an Unfair Game*, W.W. Norton & Company, Inc., 2003.

Chapter 3, "On Evidence"

We must do likewise with security, because if security can't be measured, it continues to be impossible to say whether we have more of it today than we did yesterday.

A good book on the subject is Andrew Jaquith, *Security Metrics: Replacing Fear, Uncertainty, and Doubt*, Addison Wesley, 2007.

The Trouble with Surveys

Psychologists talk about the "valence effect," which is people's tendency to overestimate the likelihood of good things happening rather than bad things.

David Rosenhan and Samuel Messick, "Affect and expectation," *Journal of Personality and Social Psychology*, vol. 3, pp. 38–44 (1966), as cited in Wikipedia, "Valence effect," visited January 1, 2005, http://en.wikipedia.org/wiki/Valence_effect.

Security professionals who are "in the trenches" will likely experience a *reverse* valence effect: believing that things are worse than they really are.

We say "likely" because we cannot test this hypothesis without data. Both our personal experience and the results of security surveys in which security practitioners are asked to describe their feelings about the state of security suggest that a dark and gloomy outlook is predominant.

One of the best-known surveys in computer security is the annual survey performed by the Computer Security Institute (CSI).

The CSI Computer Crime and Security Survey has been carried out since 1991. As the chapter notes, the respondents to the survey are both anonymous and self-selecting. The survey organizers mention the anonymous but not self-selecting nature of the respondents in their 2005 edition, although in a rather oblique way, stating: "Because the survey is based on anonymous responses, it's not possible to perform direct longitudinal analysis that might more definitively support these conclusions." This survey is commonly known as the "FBI/CSI survey"; however, in 2006, the FBI withdrew its participation.

Two professors at George Washington University analyzed the fourteen security surveys that were the most widely publicized from 1995 to 2000. They found that those surveys were replete with design errors in the areas of sample selection...

Julie J.C.H. Ryan and Theresa I. Jefferson, "The Use, Misuse and Abuse of Statistics in Information Security Research," Proceedings of the 2003 ASEM National Conference, St. Louis, Missouri.

Today's security surveys have too many flaws to be useful as sources of evidence.

Responding to this critique, in 2006, the U.S. Departments of Justice and Homeland Security asked the RAND corporation to run a National Computer Security Survey at a higher standard of quality. As we write this in the last days of 2007, the results have yet to be published. http://ncss.rand.org/faqs.html.

The U.S. Government Accountability Office (GAO) has presented the flawed data from security surveys to the U.S. Congress, possibly influencing government policy.

The Ryan/Jefferson paper just referenced describes how data from the CSI/FBI survey has made its way into documents such as the "GAO Report to the Committee on Government Affairs, U.S. Senate: Information Security Serious Weaknesses Place Critical Federal Operations and Assets at Risk." That report cites "a 16 percent increase in security breaches within the last 12 months" and names the CSI/FBI survey as the source of that data.

(Refreshingly, the Lords were skeptical of the value of such surveys.)

House of Lords, Science and Technology committee, "Personal Internet Security" report, July 24, 2007. In particular, Chapter 2, paragraph 30; Chapter 6, paragraph 15; and Appendix 5 for presentation of "self-selected" survey data. www.publications.parliament.uk/pa/ld200607/ldselect/ldsctech/165/16502.htm.

A prime example in information security is the claim that 70% of all security incidents are caused by insiders.

One of our reviewers commented: "This cracks me up because when I started in security, the figure was 50%. Then about 3-5 years into my career, as security became more and more productized, the figure grew to 60%. Now I am hearing 70%. This is FUD growth at its best."

Steve Lipner recalls that Bob Courtney of IBM used the 70% figure in 1972. Courtney was manager of data security for IBM's Systems Development Division.

A well-known technology research and advisory firm has written that "70% of security incidents ... involve insiders."

The report, from Gartner Research, is headlined "High-Profile Thefts Show Insiders Do the Most Damage." In the body, the report states "Two recent cases show that insiders—not outside cyberattacks—are responsible for most incidents that case real losses." A sample size of two cannot support that conclusion.

Gartner, Inc., "High-Profile Thefts Show Insiders Do the Most Damage," *Gartner FirstTake*, FT-18-9417, John Pescatore, November 26, 2002.

In our research for this book, we were unable to find *any* credible evidence in support of the claim that 70% of all incidents are caused by insiders.

Several reviewers put forth vigorous arguments, including pointers to work at CERT. We think the authors of the CERT work make the essential point better than we could: "The cases studied here may or may not be representative of cases not mentioned in media, court, or Secret Service databases. As noted, organizations may be reluctant to expose these incidents, even to law enforcement. This report and others from the study will articulate only what we found among these known cases. *This limits the ability to generalize the study findings* and underscores the difficulty other researchers have faced in trying to better understand the insider threat. This limitation does not, however, diminish the value in analyzing these incidents. This study provides insight into actual criminal acts committed by insiders." (Emphasis added.)

Quotation from Dawn Capeli and Michelle Keeney, "Insider Threat: Real Data on a Real Problem," CSI Conference, Washington D.C., November 2004, www.cert.org/archive/pdf/CSI-Presentation.pdf.

We agree strongly with the value of studying incidents. We wish that, for those incidents studied based on court records, the incidents had been identified to allow for follow-on research.

A commonly quoted source was a survey carried out by the Association of Certified Fraud Examiners, but its focus is fraud and white-collar crime; the document does not even contain the word "security."

See Association of Certified Fraud Examiners, "Report to the Nation on Occupational Fraud and Abuse," 2006, www.acfe.com/documents/2006-rttn.pdf.

Unless we know how many security incidents occur, we have no way of figuring out how many are caused by insiders.

In the wake of many breach reports, the U.S. government began collecting this information in July 2006. A *Goverment Executive* magazine story states: "The Office of Management and Budget issued a memo in July 2006 requiring agencies to report security incidents that expose personally identifiable information to the U.S. Computer Emergency Readiness Team within one hour of the incident. By June 2007, 40 agencies reported almost 4,000 incidents, an average of about 14 per day. As of this week, the average had increased to 30 a day, said Karen Evans, administrator of the Office of Electronic Government and Information Technology at OMB." (Precise quote by Evans unclear in source.) It seems likely that as word of the reporting requirement spread, more reports came in, rather than the number of incidents doubling in four months, but we don't know.

Jill Aitoro, "Reports of federal security breaches double in four months," Government Executive.com, October 23, 2007, www.govexec.com/story_page.cfm?articleid=38348.

But let us not have our analysis of the larger problem domain be swayed by catchy memes or "movie plot" stories.

The term "movie plot" threat originated with Bruce Schneier, "Terrorists Don't Do Movie Plots," Wired Online "Security Matters" column, September 8, 2005.

The Trade Press

Early stories in the media introduced and popularized new attacks. An example was the "salami attack," in which a rogue programmer took rounding errors from thousands of accounts and put those fractional amounts into his own account.

Thomas Whiteside, *Computer Capers*, Mentor Executive Library, 1978, pp. 33–35.

More recently, books such as *The Cuckoo's Egg* have told the story of East German spies breaking into U.S. defense department networks over the nascent internet, using a university astronomy department as a jumping-off point.

Clifford Stoll, *The Cuckoo's Egg*, Doubleday, 1989.

Those attackers will look to automate attacks that they only previously carried out manually, increasing the number of attacks observed.

We might also have better observation tools.

Vulnerabilities

A number of databases freely available on the internet provide data about many years of vulnerabilities found in major software packages, including operating systems.

The Common Vulnerabilities and Exposures (CVE) project at MITRE is likely the most robust of these efforts. It provides a structured list of names for vulnerabilities and other security exposures. It can be found at http://cve.mitre.org. For the record, Adam is an emeritus member of the CVE editorial board. Other such databases include the U.S. National Vulnerability database and the open-source vulnerability database (OSVDB). The "underground" has been a valuable source of such data, with lists such as bugtraq and sites such as PacketStorm Security.

Software vendors have started trying to differentiate themselves from their competitors on the basis of the security of their products. Oracle has advertised some of its products as "unbreakable," even going so far as to claim that unauthorized users "can't break it" and "can't break in."

Mary Ann Davidson, "Unbreakable: Oracle's Commitment to Security," an Oracle white paper, February 2002, www.oracle.com/technology/deploy/security/pdf/unbreak3.pdf.

Wikipedia, "Oracle Corporation," visited January 1, 2008, http://en.wikipedia.org/wiki/Oracle_Corporation.

Kevin Poulson, "Breakable," SecurityFocus, visited January 1, 2008, www.securityfocus.com/news/309.

The space shuttle has been held up as a paragon of software-development virtue, but even its code has bugs.

The software that runs the space shuttle is very good, but the system as a whole has had a tragic failure rate.

Charles Fishman, "They Write the Right Stuff," Fast Company, December 1996, http://fastcompany.com/magazine/06/writestuff.html.

There have been cases where a vulnerability has been found in a piece of code that was written ten or twenty years earlier and reviewed many times.

There are many examples of this phenomenon. One notable example is the history of security vulnerabilities in the piece of software known as Sendmail. Sendmail has been in widespread use for many years. Even though "many eyes" have examined the Sendmail package for security vulnerabilities over the years, it has continued to have a history of security problems.

For another example, see Bryn Dole, Steve Lodin, and Eugene Spafford, "Misplaced Trust: Kerberos 4 Session Keys," proceedings of the 1997 ISOC Conference, for the story of how a bug in the Kerberos random-number generator avoided detection for a number of years. Kerberos 4 was released in the late 1980s. See also J.G. Steiner, B. Clifford Neuman, and J.I. Schiller, "Kerberos: An Authentication Service for Open Network Systems," in Proceedings of the Winter 1988 USENIX Conference, February 1988. Adam recalls the discussion as saying that the issue was present from the early releases of Kerberos 4 until the advisory, with Dole and Lodin stating that they had looked at the Kerberos source for a well-implemented PRNG and were shocked by what they found.

In 2004, an internet worm used a single vulnerability in a security product line to compromise approximately 12,000 computers.

This internet worm was named the Witty worm because its source code was found to contain the phrase "insert witty message here." It attacked Internet Security Systems' RealSecure intrusion detection product. Three internet researchers who analyzed the worm's spread determined that the initial point of infection was a European internet service provider and that the worm specifically targeted a U.S. military base.

Abhiskek Kumar, Vern Paxson, and Nicholas Weaver, "Exploiting Underlying Structure for Detailed Reconstruction of an Internet-scale Event," proceedings ACM IMC, 2005.

Instrumentation on the Internet

An important research effort in this space is the Honeynet project.

The project is online at www.honeynet.org and has released an interesting book, *Know Your Enemy: Revealing the Security Tools, Tactics, and Motives of the Blackhat Community*, Honeynet Project, 2001, Addison-Wesley Professional.

Their data provides a fascinating look into the mind-set and methods of attackers.

Attackers have transformed some monitored systems into chat services, allowing the Honeynet project team members to monitor conversations.

Organizations and Companies with Data

In the aftermath of the first internet worm, a Pentagon agency established a Computer Emergency Response Team (CERT) that has been widely imitated around the world.

Carnegie-Mellon University press release, "DARPA established Computer Emergency Response Team," December 13, 1988, www.cert.org/about/1988press-rel.html.

There are now roughly 38 "National Computer Security Incident Response Teams" listed at www.cert.org/csirts/national/contact.html.

More recently, the United States has introduced Information Sharing and Analysis Centers (ISACs). According to their members, ISAC meetings are a great place to collect business cards but are not particularly useful for anything else.

We don't mean to understate the value of establishing personal connections. After all, personal connections provided us with anecdotal evidence as to the limits of ISACs, although the members asked that we not quote them by name. However, it seems rare that ISACs are used for the confidential communication of information or its analysis.

Chapter 4, "The Rise of the Security Breach"

In the epidemic of 1854, Snow plotted cholera deaths on a map and determined that one public water pump was the source of the outbreak.

See Edward Tufte, *Visual Explanations*, 1997, Graphics Press, pp. 27–37, and Steven Johnson, *The Ghost Map*, 2006, Riverhead Books.

Opportunities for errors abound, as ChoicePoint, a company based in the Atlanta suburbs, learned in February 2005.

Bob Sullivan, "Database giant gives access to fake firms," February 14, 2005, MSNBC, www.msnbc.msn.com/id/6969799/.

That law, California Senate Bill 1386, is usually referred to simply as SB1386.

California State Senate, "An act to amend, renumber, and add Section 1798.82 of, and to add Section 1798.29 to, the Civil Code, relating to personal information," was approved by the governor September 25, 2002. http://info.sen.ca.gov/pub/01-02/bill/sen/sb_1351-1400/sb_1386_bill_20020926_chaptered.html.

It's ironic that ChoicePoint, a company that provides background checks and so-called "identity verification services," fell victim to such a fraud.

If ChoicePoint's services were foolproof, Oluwatosin would not have been able to sign up as a customer using the fax number of a Kinko's copying store.

Not only is it ironic that ChoicePoint fell victim to impersonation, it's also ironic that a problem at ChoicePoint led a set of people with a blistering contempt for ChoicePoint's collection and commercialization of data to also collect, catalog, and distribute data.

One researcher and blogger realized that reports to New York State were subject to Freedom of Information Act requests, so he requested those reports and placed them in the public domain.

New York State mandates that reports be sent to several government agencies. Reports covering both public and private sector breaches are made available.

See Chris Walsh, "A request," blog post January 3, 2007 on the Emergent Chaos blog, www.emergentchaos.com/archives/2007/01/a_request.html.

We hope that breach data will be reported to central resources that will share it, and that this will put the focus on data analysis and alleviate the effort involved in collecting and collating it.

Today, the data is gathered and shared by hobbyists at Attrition.org, PogoWasRight.org, and a few other sites. The only one with funding (as far as we know) is the Privacy Rights Clearing House. The effort of simply collecting, archiving, and classifying these reports can take upwards of an hour a day.

This tight feedback loop within the airline industry is understood to benefit not just passengers, but also the airline industry, which can promote flying as a safe way to travel.

Danger was a strong deterrent to flying. The Wright brothers flew within living memory, and air travel used to be far less safe than it is today. The airline industry grew dramatically by improving its safety record. For a personal recollection, see Bill Gurstelle, "When Planes Fell from the Sky," December 22, 2006, Notes from the Technology Underground blog, http://nfttu.blogspot.com/2006/12/when-planes-fell-from-sky.html.

We predict that the cost of notifying people will drop, and that the effectiveness of remedies offered will improve. New types of solutions more effective than credit monitoring will emerge.

After we wrote this, the Ponemon Institute released its "2007 Annual Study, U.S. Cost of a Data Breach." "Other costs associated with a data breach decreased 15 percent from 2006. The costs include investigations, notification of impacted individuals, and services such as offering free credit monitoring. This decrease appears to indicate that organizations are learning from past breach responses..."

Additionally, early alternatives to credit monitoring, such as Debix, have already emerged. We expect more such companies to emerge to assist with the various parts of the breach response process. (Adam is a shareholder in Debix.)

How Do Companies Lose Data?

There is some irony that auditors carried many of the DVDs and laptops lost in these incidents.

Existing security technologies are almost all predicated on the idea that security controls surround data. This model breaks down when the data is moved to a location where those controls don't exist, such as a USB drive or a DVD. Relatively new technologies such as Digital Rights Management (DRM) seek to address this issue. We discuss DRM in Chapter 6.

Only between 1% and 2% of total records were lost or stolen as a result of being exposed online.

Adam Shostack and Chris Walsh, "Data About Data Breaches," slide 27, June 2007, presented at FIRST conference in Seville, Spain.

According to a Harris Research poll released in November 2006, just over one American in five has received at least one notification that his or her private information has been compromised.

HarrisInteractive, "Many U.S. Adults Claim to Have Been Notified That Personal Information Has Been Improperly Disclosed," The Harris Poll #81, November 10, 2006, www.harrisinteractive.com/harris_poll/index.asp?PID=708.

According to another survey, 62% of Americans had been notified as of mid-2007.

Ponemon Institute, "2007 Consumer Survey on Data Security," June 25, 2007.

There is a blending of motivation in some cases, between wanting to protect data and wanting to avoid mandatory breach disclosure. Some ambiguities in existing breach law make it unclear whether the loss of encrypted records must be disclosed.

The term ambiguity covers a swath of issues. Some, like encryption, would seem on their face to be good reasons to believe that the data poses no risk to anyone. Unfortunately, it's hard to encrypt data well. For example, encryption keys may be written to disk by a virtual memory manager, or the key may be weakly derived from a bad password, or otherwise be available to an attacker. Further, the password may be lost along with the data, for example, on paper in a laptop bag.

Examples include studies by Carnegie Mellon researchers on the impact of breach notices on stock prices, and the research we've done on mentions of breaches in Securities and Exchange Commission filings.

Alessandro Acquisti, Allan Friedman, and Rahul Telang, "Is There a Cost to Privacy Breaches? An Event Study," Proceedings of the International Conference of Information Systems (ICIS), 2006. Adam's research initially found nothing. Gregory Fleischer provided some advice on how to search. It's available at Adam Shostack, "Breaches in SEC Reports," blog post on Emergentchaos.com, May 3, 2007, www.emergentchaos.com/archives/2007/05/breaches_in_sec_reports.html. Fleischer's improved search shows a growing awareness of the risks in SEC filings, but not of actual breaches.

Disclose Breaches

We're not lawyers, but if you have customers in any of thirty-eight states or in Japan, disclosure is probably required.

Note that this is the location of your customers, not your place of business. The list will likely be longer by the time you read this. For data on the Japanese law, see Kunihiko Morishita, James Minamoto, and Nobuhito Sawasaki, "Notifications of data security breaches: Japan" at Bird & Bird, www.twobirds.com/english/publications/articles/Notifications_data_security_breaches_Japan.cfm. Charts of the U.S. laws are maintained by many law firms, including Perkins Coie and Scott and Scott.

(Canada, Australia, and New Zealand fall into this category.)

See Rob O'Neill, "It's campaign time on data-breach disclosure," *ComputerWorld*, June 11, 2007, http://computerworld.co.nz/news.nsf/scrt/23D66D5FDB5AC8C0CC2572F40000D29C.

In some places, there might be no duty to notify, but there is an emerging duty of care.

First revelations of a breach by HMRC in the U.K. took this approach. See Ian Cowie, "HMRC loses personal details of thousands," *Daily Telegraph*, November 3, 2007, www.telegraph.co.uk/money/main.jhtml;jsessionid=1FXKWDK0CVD2NQFIQMFCFGGAVCBQYIV0?xml=/money/2007/11/03/cnhmrc103.xml.

When faced with a breach, an organization should aim to get ahead of the news by notifying customers at once with the fullest details available.

Breach notification is a form of apology. All analysis of corporate apologies that we are aware of argues for making apologies and moving on. See, for example, Barbara Kellerman, "When Should a Leader Apologize and When Not?," *Harvard Business Review*, April 2006, pp. 73–81.

Possible Criticisms of Breach Data

Other researchers have compared laptop loss figures to reports of lost data and commented that the amount of sensitive personal data on laptops should have led to a lot more reports.

Ed Moyle, "Strange things are afoot with breach disclosure," Security Curve blog, November 3, 2006, www.securitycurve.com/blog/archives/000476.html. He points out that the rate of laptop theft would seem to indicate that much more data is being lost than is being reported. (Also referenced in Chapter 1.)

Data breaches do not seem to have much of an effect on stock market valuations.

Noted above in the section, "How Do Companies Lose Data?"

There is research that shows that in most breaches, no more than a small percentage of customers will leave. This research has been published by companies that sell services for responding to breach events, so it might be exaggerating the effect.

"Following a data breach, organizations suffered an average increased customer churn rate of 2.67 percent, up from 2.01 percent in 2006. Four out of the 35 organizations suffered abnormal churn rates of more than 6 percent." Ponemon Institute, "2007 Consumer Survey on Data Security," June 25, 2007, p. 13. The survey does not explain what the pre-breach variance is or state whether other possible cofactors exist. Secrecy regarding the participants prevents additional analysis. We don't mean to imply that the Institute is exaggerating the effect (or would), but a potential conflict of interest exists.

However, over half of identity fraud victims have no idea how a criminal got hold of their personal data.

Federal Trade Commission, "2006 Identity Theft Survey Report," November 2007, www.ftc.gov/os/2007/11/SynovateFinalReport-IDTheft2006.pdf.

An analysis of the stories in the press shows that they don't line up with those in the state repositories of breach notices.

Adam Shostack and Chris Walsh, "Data About Data Breaches," June 2007, presented at FIRST conference in Seville, Spain.

Get Involved

This variety of backgrounds has been referred to as *hybrid vigor*, a term Dan Geer imported to the security field from biology.

Dan Geer, "Shoes for Industry," keynote address, Shmoocon, 2006.

In Conclusion

We have identified a source of objective data for information security that is both new and important.

Adam wrote about ChoicePoint on February 15, the day after Bob Sullivan broke the story. He spoke publicly about ChoicePoint on February 16, 2005, at a panel at the RSA Conference. Over the next several months, the Emergent Chaos blog became a widely read source of news and analysis on breaches. Over several years, Emergent Chaos has been a central source of ongoing analysis and attention for breaches as a problem and then as an opportunity. See www.emergentchaos.com/archives/2005/03/why_choicepoint.html and www.emergentchaos.com/archives/2005/02/choicepoint_won.html. ("We need more routine disclosure of security incidents. We need to know what caused them, what mechanisms were used to get in, and how they were detected, so we can learn from them." February 26, 2005.)

This conversation included many people. Bob Sullivan, Ian Grigg, and others contributed. Nevertheless, Emergent Chaos was one of the first players, and it was a platform that continued to carry a clear message about the importance of breaches as a data source, not simply as a privacy issue.

In a 2003 paper, Stuart Schecter and Michael Smith discuss using breach disclosure as a deterrent, but not as a source of data to mine. ("How Much Security Is Enough to Stop a Thief?" *Financial Cryptography*, 2003.)

Chapter 5, "Amateurs Study Cryptography; Professionals Study Economics"

The title of this chapter comes from Alan Schiffman, who describes the phrase as "an aphorism that captures my feelings about where the effort in building secure systems needs to go." Alan Schiffman, "Instant Immortality,": (blog post, Recondite), July 2, 2004, http://webpages.charter.net/allanms/2004/07/instant-immortality.html.

This would not have surprised von Neumann, who helped invent game theory and who offered a framework for how to approach games like the prisoner's dilemma.

Like many examples of hybrid vigor, only part of his insight has thrived. When new fields come together, there's an explosion of new perspectives and approaches. Then, as the collaboration becomes ongoing, new norms emerge, and a more rigorous filter is applied to new ideas. This isn't necessarily a bad thing, but it does reduce the vigor that comes from looking to other fields. The process of reaching out and taking new ideas must be an ongoing one, in looking for new data, new data sources, and new approaches.

This also ties into Boyd's approach to keeping orientations fresh, or Kuhn's approach to scientific revolutions. Without new observations and a willingness to adjust, approaches become stale.

A late 1990s analysis of security issues described in Computer Emergency Response Team (CERT) advisories found that 85% could not be fixed through the application of more or better cryptography.

National Research Council, "Trust in Cyberspace," 1999, as quoted in Steve Bellovin, "The State of Software Security," Information Security Law: Software Security and Vulnerability Reporting, Seton Hall University School of Law, November 2002, www.cs.columbia.edu/~smb/talks/vuln-legal.pdf.

The Economics of Information Security

In 2001 he published a paper titled "Why Information Security Is Hard: An Economic Perspective."

Ross Anderson, "Why information security is hard: an economic perspective," Applications Security conference, 2001, www.ftp.cl.cam.ac.uk/ftp/users/rja14/econ.pdf.

That paper is generally considered the first piece of work to explicitly analyze the broad field of information security from the perspective of economics.

There are narrower statements, such as Eric Hughes saying "All crypto is economics." The earliest instance we can find is a 1994 message to the Cypherpunks list, in which Tim May quotes those words. The context (and Adam's personal recollection) suggests that the statement was made earlier. See http://cypherpunks.venona.com/date/1994/08/msg01330.html.

What's unique about this idea is that it contrasts with the mindset that information security is primarily a technology problem, and that ultimately the "solution" can be reached by piling on more and more technology.

In addition to the comments in the chapter, it is important to note that spending on security technologies has an "opportunity cost" (as does all spending). When funds are spent, those funds are not being spent on something else. In other words, there might be a lot of benefit from spending $3 million on a suite of new security tools, but that money could also have been spent creating a new line of business. Before deciding to buy a new security technology, businesses should honestly examine other areas that might provide more value.

Why Do Some Security Technologies Fail?

The only stable state is where there is no guard and none of the merchants are happy.

Of course, this is not *really* a stable state. If markets for thievery are efficient, robbers will appear to take advantage of the lack of guards. All models involve some simplifications, and even useful models, such as Nash Equilibria, can obscure important details.

The second is a Nash Equilibrium, in which there is no move that any one player can make that would make anyone better off.

We're grateful to Steven Landsburg for the examples. For a more detailed introduction, see Wikipedia, "Nash equilibrium," visited January 8, 2008, http://en.wikipedia.org/wiki/Nash_equilibrium.

DNS has well-known, documented security weaknesses, and a newer, more secure alternative exists.

There's a conflating factor, which is that the definition of what security DNS should offer is open to disagreement. Particularly around DNS, there are smart people on all sides of the debate. See, for example, the NSEC3 versus DNSSEC-bis debate, which revolves around a fundamental question of confidentiality versus denial of service. Such requirements tension can also be seen in the challenges we discussed in Chapter 1, in the section "Should We Just Start Over?"

Related work by Geoffrey Moore argues that markets for products function in stages.

Moore defined the stages of the market as visionary, early adopter, early and late mass markets, and laggards. Geoffrey Moore, *Crossing the Chasm*, 1991, HarperCollins.

The adoption cycle that Moore describes is driven by careful attention to the needs of one group, and ensuring that that group's needs are fully met.

Geoffrey Moore, *Inside the Tornado*, 1995, HarperCollins.

Why Does Insecure Software Dominate the Market?

The results of security evaluations are rarely consistent. Two different experts with different areas of expertise will likely identify different issues.

This is another effect of the secrecy surrounding the field. Each textbook (and many a practitioner) brings a different worldview and taxonomy, and the "right" answer is hard to discern. See also the earlier note about DNS Security and the tension in requirements.

These factors combine to result in a "market for lemons." This means that it is difficult to distinguish between products that have more or less security, and that no vendor has an incentive to sell a product that has high security.

We are referring here to George Akerlof, "The Market for 'Lemons': Quality, Uncertainty and the Market Mechanism," *Quarterly Journal of Economics* 84 (3): 488–500, 1970. This Nobel-prize-winning paper in economics describes how, in the absence of information about the quality of goods, a market can be created in which the incentive for sellers is to portray their low-quality goods as having higher quality than they really do. The market for used cars is a classic example. It is difficult to evaluate a used car that is for sale and determine whether it is of good quality. The best guess on the part of the prospective buyer can only be that the car is of average quality. This means that owners of good-quality cars have no incentive to sell them, which in turn drives the market toward one in which only low-quality used cars are for sale.

If a company ships an open-source package (one that is given away), should the company be liable for the product?

Open-source means that the source code is available and includes a set of rights given to users, such as the right to alter and redistribute that source code. The Open Source Initiative defines ten principles in its Open Source Definition.

Open Source Initiative, "The Open Source Definition," last edited July 7, 2006, www.opensource.org/docs/osd. See also the Wikipedia entry "Open source," visited January 5, 2008, http://en.wikipedia.org/wiki/Open_source.

Alternatively, software might come with thousand-page-long manuals that the user must read in order to get the warranty.

Manuals this long already exist but aren't mandatory. For example, Mark G. Sobell, *A Practical Guide to Red Hat Linux*, Second Edition is 1,136 pages, and Ed Bott, Carl Siechert, and Craig Stinson, *Windows Vista Inside Out* is 1,132 pages. David Pogue's *Mac OS X Leopard: The Missing Manual* is 912 pages. These were the first hits we got searching for comprehensive-looking books on Amazon. In our experience, these are not unusually long for technical books.

Giving software creators an incentive to claim that "all problems exist between the chair and keyboard (PEBCAK)" seems like it would create a new set of problems, perhaps worse than the software security problems we face today.

Technical support organizations have long used PEBCAK as a polite way to write "idiot user."

Finally, new liability around security could impede breach disclosure....

Thanks to Nicko van Sommeren for pointing this out.

Why Can't We Stop Spam?

When a PC is turned into a zombie and is used to send spam, the owner of the PC doesn't directly suffer the consequences.

If the malware has quality issues, the PC might suffer instability, annoying the owner. This should tend to drive up the quality of malware, to make it less intrusive to the PC's owner.

Even a small fraction of all computers connected to the internet represents a massive number.

This is an example of the "law of large numbers." Even a very small fraction of a large number is a large number. For example, millions of people switch jobs each year. If, to control immigration, we validate papers and 1% of people are falsely rejected, that's still 10,000 people per million. Actual rates for the pilot program seem to be closer to 3% to 5% of applicants falsely rejected.

Psychology

Therefore, there's probably little improvement in patch reliability between eleven days and a hundred days.

Steve Beattie, Seth Arnold, Crispin Cowan, Perry Wagle, Chris Wright, and Adam Shostack, "Timing the Application of Security Patches for Optimal Uptime," USENIX 16th Systems Administration Conference (LISA 2002), Philadelphia, Pennsylvania, December 2002.

By understanding that tension exists between the security risk of not installing a patch and the operational risk of installing a patch, we can design a strategy that allows us to balance these incentives in an optimal fashion and time the application of security patches. The key difference is between making decisions based on fear and making decisions based on risk.

See the preceding note.

In Munich, a study was performed on the behavior of taxicab drivers.

M. Aschenbrenner and B. Biehl, "Improved safety through improved technical measures? Empirical studies regarding risk compensation processes in relation to anti-lock braking systems," "Challenges to accident prevention: the issue of risk compensation behavior," Styx Publications, 1994.

What has happened is that there has been an increase in fatalities from jumpers attempting to perform higher-speed landings—flying their fully deployed canopies into the ground.

Vic Napier, "Risk Homeostasis: A Case Study of the Adoption of a Safety Innovation on the Level of Perceived Risk," 14th Annual Meeting of the American Society of Business and Behavioral Sciences, Las Vegas, Nevada, February 22, 2007, www.vicnapier.com/riskhomeostasis.htm.

One ten-year study of smokers found that those who stopped smoking had fewer instances of lung disease, but their average life span was actually *shorter* than the group who decided to keep smoking.

G. Rose, P. Hamilton, L. Cowell, M. Shipley, "A randomised control trial of anti-smoking advice; 10-year results," *Journal of Epidemiology and Community Health*, vol. 36, pp. 102–108, 1982. The study results describe how both groups tend to die of the same diseases.

Another study showed that smokers who were given low-nicotine cigarettes inhaled those cigarettes more deeply and more frequently, thereby sustaining their level of nicotine intake.

Kenneth Warner and John Slade, "Low tar, high toll," *American Journal of Public Health*, January 1992, vol. 82, no. 1.

However, in the United Kingdom, the number of deaths in car crashes actually went *up* after the law was passed that mandated seat belt use.

John Adams, "Cars, cholera, and cows: the management of risk and uncertainty," Cato Policy Analysis No. 335, 1999.

A separate study carried out in Oslo found that people who drove ABS-equipped cars drove much closer to the car in front of them, compared to cars with standard brakes.

S. Fosser, I. Saetermo, and F. Sagberg, "An investigation of behavioral adaptation to airbags and antilock brakes among taxi drivers," *Accident Analysis and Prevention*, vol. 29, no. 3, May 1997.

A 1992 law in Australia made bicycle helmets compulsory. As someone using risk compensation theory could have accurately predicted, the number of cycling deaths remained the same after the law went into effect.

Mayer Hillman, "Cycle helmets: the case for and against," Policy Studies Institute, 1993.

A twist on this approach, being used successfully in some European cities, is to remove visible safety measures such as crosswalks, speed bumps, and stop signs. The result seems to be that people drive more safely.

Andrew Curry, "Giving Drivers the Benefit of the Doubt," *U.S. News & World Report*, March 18, 2007, www.usnews.com/usnews/news/articles/070318/26traffic.htm.

Sociology

They think that locking their screens sends a message of distrust to their coworkers.

Dirk Weirich and Martina Angela Sasse, "Pretty Good Persuasion: A first step towards effective password security in the real world," 7th New Security Paradigms Workshop, pp. 137–143, 2001, and Dirk Weirich, Sacha Brostoff, and Martina Angela Sasse, "Transforming the 'Weakest Link': a Human/Computer Interaction Approach to Usable and Effective Security," *BT Technology Journal*, vol. 19, no. 3, pp. 122–131, 2001.

Research regularly finds that the more diverse a group, the better the solutions that emerge.

For a good book grounded in hard science, see Scott Page, *The Difference: How the Power of Diversity Creates Better Groups, Firms, Schools, and Societies*, Princeton University Press, 2007.

Our statement is a slight misstatement of the research, which shows that diversity of opinion, approaches, and backgrounds (what we'd call orientation) leads to good results, and diversity of desires or goals leads to difficulty in making good decisions.

We might present a different face at home, at work, at sports events, or at church.

This section draws fairly heavily from Irving Goffman, *The Presentation of Self in Everyday Life*, Anchor, 1959.

We've been told of people refusing to give their cell phone number for a disaster-recovery plan, convinced that their employer would use the information in situations well short of a disaster.

Adam, respecting the privacy of the storyteller.

Helen Nissenbaum, a professor at New York University, has presented the idea of "contextual integrity" as an explanation for how people respond to privacy issues.

Helen Nissenbaum, "Privacy as Contextual Integrity," *Washington Law Review*, vol. 79, no. 1, February 4, 2004, pp. 119–158, http://crypto.stanford.edu/portia/papers/RevnissenbaumDTP31.pdf.

Chapter 6, "Spending"

Reasons to Spend on Security Today

Spending money on security analysis early, to find and address risks, is usually a better choice than spending money later on "mitigating technologies" or "compensating controls."

A security bug in an application is a software bug with security *implications*. The level of security in applications therefore relies inextricably on the quality of their engineering. In the paper "Tangible ROI through Secure Software Engineering," Kevin Soo Hoo and his coauthors measured the effort required to fix a security bug in the design phase of a software project compared to later phases such as implementation and testing. They found that the ROI on finding bugs in the design phase was 21%, 15% in the implementation phase, and 15% in the post-implementation testing phase. A long history of software-testing research supports the general principle that finding bugs earlier is more economically efficient.

Kevin Soo Hoo, Andrew Sudbury, and Andrew Jaquith, "Tangible ROI Through Secure Software Engineering," *Secure Business Quarterly*, vol. 1, issue 2001.

If the computers that records are stored on are insecure, how secure can the records be?

Another tip of the hat to Robert Morris. See the endnote for Chapter 2 in the section "What Does the Security Industry Sell?"

As we write this, Congress gives the average American federal agency a D grade for information security management.

U.S. House of Representatives, Committee on Oversight and Government Reform, "Seventh Report Card on Computer Security at Federal Departments and Agencies," April 12, 2007. From the time in 2006 when we wrote that to the release of the 2007 report, the average grade improved to a C–.

Facebook rose to prominence on college campuses, where it became an essential part of dating.

A colleague from an Ivy League university refers to Facebook as "fleshbook."

Non-Reasons to Spend on Security

The two-year pursuit came after he noticed a 79-cent error in accounting and soon after uncovered strong evidence of serious wrongdoing.

Clifford Stoll, *The Cuckoo's Egg*, Doubleday, 1989.

For several years, it seemed that spending on technologies to protect against fast-spreading internet worms would be an excellent reason to spend on security.

This text started life in the "Emerging Reasons to Spend" section. By the time we were done with the text, it no longer made sense there.

Without some unique way of using a particular technology, organizations should not think that spending on security products will enable them to sustain any advantage over their competitors.

For a ranging discussion of commoditization in IT, see Nicholas Carr, *Does IT Matter? Information Technology and the Corrosion of Competitive Advantage*, Harvard Business School Press, 2004.

Even with a unique technology, or way of using a technology, it may be challenging to explain the benefits effectively to prospective customers.

Some processes might be hard to replicate. For example, Microsoft uses static analysis technologies to analyze code, many of which are available to anyone who purchases the Visual Studio product. Those technologies are embedded in a process to make sure they are used effectively, and other companies may have a hard time getting that process right.

Emerging Reasons to Spend

For example, accounting and other financial documents could be "locked" so that only the accounting department and management could see them.

To be perfectly accurate, anyone can see them, but only the authorized people can make sense of the encrypted content.

Further, some DRM technologies have introduced security vulnerabilities into the computers DRM has been installed on or even removed from.

In particular, Sony shipped its customers insecure software from SunnComm and First4Internet DRM, and the uninstaller for the First4Internet system had additional problems.

The original problem was discovered by Mark Russinovich, "Sony, Rootkits and Digital Rights Management Gone Too Far," post to WinInternals blog, October 31, 2005, available at http://blogs.technet.com/markrussinovich/archive/2005/10/31/sony-rootkits-and-digital-rights-management-gone-too-far.aspx. Problems with the uninstaller were documented by Ed Felten and J. Alex Halderman, "Sony's Web-Based Uninstaller Opens a Big Security Hole; Sony to Recall Discs," post to Freedom to Tinker blog, November 15, 2005, www.freedom-to-tinker.com/?p=927. More data on the SunnComm issue is available in National Vulnerability Database, "Vulnerability Note VU#928689: SunnComm MediaMax privilege elevation vulnerability," last updated April 12, 2006, CVE-2005-4069.

The MediaMax problem was found by iSec Partners and was jointly announced by iSec, the Electronic Frontier Foundation, and SonyBMG, (now titled) "Update to Press Release: EFF Does Not Recommend Patch at This Time," December 6, 2005, www.eff.org/press/archives/2005/12/06. Felten documents that Halderman found that the installer left computers vulnerable even if users chose to decline the installation. Ed Felten, "MediaMax Bug Found; Patch Issued; Patch Suffers from Same Bug," blog post to Freedom to Tinker, December 7, 2005. Also documented in National Vulnerability Database, "Vulnerability Note VU#312073: First4Internet CodeSupport ActiveX control incorrectly marked 'safe for scripting,'" last updated December 7, 2005. CVE-2005-3650.

Consider the advertising of biotech firms involved in the bioengineering of crops and the "green" advertising of oil companies.

In 2001, the oil company that was once British Petroleum made the last of a slew of (confusing) name changes by renaming itself simply "BP" while adopting the slogan "Beyond Petroleum" to emphasize its "green credentials."

Even though what they are concerned about isn't real, it may be easier to behave as if it is real, and invest in "security theater."

This term is from Bruce Schneier, *Beyond Fear*, Springer, 2003.

How Much Should a Business Spend on Security?

These companies now focus their spending on their ability to recover from incidents, rather than trying to prevent them upfront.

Spending on business continuity planning or disaster recovery may provide tremendous security value.

Mean Time to Recover/Repair (MTTR) is a metric that can be used to measure the ability to respond to and contain incidents. The use of this metric is common in the operational IT world. We may see it become more widely adopted as a metric used by operational security teams as part of responding to incidents.

For example, ensuring that your spending covers an externally provided list such as COBIT or ISO 17799 may be a helpful part of a defense in a lawsuit.

COBIT is purported to be a leading edge list of "Control Objectives for Information and Related Technology" synergistically aligned to business objectives by the Information Systems Audit and Control Association. It presents learnings from a diverse set of contributing organizations.

"ISO/IEC 27002 part of a growing family of ISO/IEC ISMS standards, the 'ISO/IEC 27000 series' is an information security standard published by the International Organization for Standardization (ISO) and the International Electrotechnical Commission (IEC) as ISO/IEC 17799:2005 and subsequently renumbered ISO/IEC 27002:2005 in July 2007, bringing it into line with the other ISO/IEC 27000-series standards. It is entitled Information technology–Security techniques–Code of practice for information security management. The current standard is a revision of the version first published by ISO/IEC in 2000, which was a word-for-word copy of the British Standard (BS) 7799-1:1999." (From Wikipedia, ISO/IEC 27002, http://en.wikipedia.org/wiki/ISO_17799 visited February 10, 2008.)

Aren't you glad you looked?

Net present value (NPV) and economic value added (EVA) are two techniques that are far more sophisticated and useful than ROI.

G. Bennett Stewart III, *The Quest for Value*, 1991, HarperCollins. An excellent work on various economic valuation methods.

Those losses are typically calculated using annual loss expected (ALE), which is the probability of a loss event multiplied by the expected cost of the event.

ALE was first defined in National Bureau of Standards, *Guidelines for Automatic Data Processing Physical Security and Risk Management*, FIPS Pub 31, 1974, pp. 12–14.

The value of a brand could be calculated by asking what it would take to build an entirely new brand. They also believed that this would represent the upper limit on the possible cost of a breach (to have to build a whole new business from scratch).

We'd like to reinforce that this would be an absolute upper boundary, and that very few (single) events cause a company's brand to disappear. The Exxon Valdez disaster, the Tylenol scare, and even Union Carbide's Bhopal disaster didn't destroy those companies. The method derives from asset valuation methods. For example, see Benjamin Graham and David Dodd, *Security Analysis*, Third Edition, McGraw Hill, 2004.

Large numbers of customers have not yet pulled their business from companies that have suffered a breach, although the capital spent to recover from a breach has been significant in some cases.

"Following a data breach, organizations suffered an average increased customer churn rate of 2.67 percent, up from 2.01 percent in 2006. Four out of the 35 organizations suffered abnormal churn rates of more than 6 percent." Ponemon Institute, "2007 Consumer Survey on Data Security," June 25, 2007, p. 13. The TJX company has set aside $265 million to address its breach. See Evan Schuman, "TJX's Projected Breach Costs Increase to $216 million," StorefrontBacktalk blog, November 13, 2007, http://storefrontbacktalk.com/story/111307tjxloss. TJX is an outlier in most ways.

The TCO for a patch management solution within an enterprise is dominated by the need for appropriate testing of patches before they are deployed. The cost of the technological deployment system is relatively small in comparison.

This assumes that patches will be deployed by technology, rather than by people visiting each computer.

They have worked on problems within the economics of information security, including the question of how much a business should spend to protect a given information set. In their paper "The Economics of Information Security Investment," they present a mathematical model that incorporates vulnerability and potential loss.

Lawrence Gordon and Martin Loeb, "The Economics of Information Security Investment," ACM Transactions on Information and System Security (TISSEC), vol. 5, issue 4, November 2002. Also available in L. Jean Camp and Stephen Lewis (editors), *Economics of Information Security*, Kluwer Academic Publishers, 2004.

Specifically, a firm should not spend more on security measures than 37% of the expected loss.

Note that that paper just mentioned assumes that security investments are twice-differentiable continuous functions, a property we rarely see in a vendor's price list. It also assumes that security measures and losses are linkable spending. In other words, an organization could spend $37 to prevent the theft of its customer list and $74 to prevent the disclosure of its draft patent applications. Spending is more likely to "keep intruders out" than to keep them away from any particular item of data.

The Psychology of Spending

But even without such attempts, studies have shown that when people are presented with a number of descriptions of a scenario, the majority will remember the most alarming one.

W. Kip Viscusi, "Alarmist decisions with divergent risk information," *Economic Journal*, vol. 107, no. 445, 1997.

In reality, figures from the FBI and other law enforcement agencies show the number of child abductions by strangers is small—about 200 to 300 per year.

David Allender, "Child Abductions," in Robert Muller III, "FBI Law Enforcement Bulletin," vol. 76, no. 7, July 2007, www.fbi.gov/publications/leb/2007/july07leb.pdf.

In 2005, 11-year-old Brennan Hawkins got lost in the Utah mountains. For four days, he avoided searchers because he was afraid to talk to strangers.

Bruce Schneier, "Talking to strangers," blog post, June 23, 2005, www.schneier.com/blog/archives/2005/06/talking_to_stra.html.

Many people now prefer to drive rather than fly, or they choose to fly less often.

Joe Sharkey, "Business travel: On the road, flying less and enjoying it more," *New York Times*, September 9, 2003.

(And for the observant reader, this is yet another example of incentive failure, since the government isn't measured on how happy or frustrated airline travelers feel.)

Neither is the Transportation Safety Administration (TSA) measured on the number of driving fatalities. Many people now choose to drive rather than fly to avoid dealing with TSA "security measures." This is a negative externality, because driving is statistically more dangerous than flying. The "no fly" list maintained by the TSA contains the names of over a million people. Many people miss their flights because of the extra harassment that being (incorrectly) on that list causes. We shouldn't tolerate one part of government making bad decisions just because it is in their particular best interests to do so.

Presenting security numbers without context can create an emotional effect and lead to misdirected or inefficient spending.

Darrell Huff, *How to Lie with Statistics*, WW Norton & Company, 1993, and Andrew Jaquith, *Security Metrics: Replacing Fear, Uncertainty and Doubt*, Addison Wesley, 2007, p. 246.

On What to Spend

We would like to be able to provide detailed direction on what security technologies and services organizations should purchase, but alas, we cannot. The organizations at which the readers of this book are employed differ from each other.

One reviewer suggested that we should cover the work done by Geer, Jaquith, and Soo Hoo on pen testing and app vulnerability testing. He went so far as to suggest that the work Microsoft is doing with the Security Development Lifecycle is a good example. He claimed that that work validates investment in security analysis of software under development. (Adam works on the Security Development Lifecycle strategy team and is flattered.)

While we'd love to say positive things about pen testing, and while it can have a positive impact, it is challenging and expensive for most organizations to differentiate between charlatans and geniuses who offer to perform the work for you. This makes it hard for us to recommend it as broadly as our reviewer suggested.

When considering spending on a security product, a useful first question to ask is whether the core capabilities that the product would provide are already available within the organization's IT infrastructure.

We're setting aside Dan Geer's monoculture argument because the idea is centered around the risks of a monoculture and doesn't incorporate costs of managing a diverse environment.

In April 2004, the BBC reported the results of a study that showed that more than 70% of the respondents would reveal their computer password in exchange for chocolate.

See "Passwords revealed by sweet deal" on the BBC News web site at http://news.bbc.co.uk/2/hi/technology/3639679.stm.

A number of problems exist with both the expectation of the value that security policies will deliver and how they are traditionally employed.

See also Ross Anderson, *Security Engineering*, Wiley, 2001, p. 138.

Chapter 7, "Life in the New School"

People Are People

Some of the reasons people might not embrace the use of objective data to make better security decisions are more subtle.

Another reason, not related to people, is that we might not have a theoretical framework to help us, so we would just be measuring stuff. This would be like randomly walking around with a tape measure, noting the size of things. We might have objective data about the length of our driveway, the width of our car, and the size of our shoes.

In America, car accidents kill a far greater number of people than acts of terrorism, yet spending on antiterrorism measures dwarfs spending on road safety.

Here we're comparing Homeland Security spending to National Highway Traffic Safety Administration spending. There is other spending on safety, such as the grading of curves and placement of speed bumps or traffic lights. This money is rarely budgeted separately.

The spectacular, horrific nature of terrorism creates a strong emotional response.

We could say quite a bit on this topic, but, unusually for our endnotes, we will restrain ourselves.

Studies have shown that people find it difficult to think rationally about risks that carry heavy costs.

See generally Paul Slovic, *The Perception of Risk*, Earthscan Publications, 2000.

Perhaps this makes sense, to ensure that the organization will send appropriately senior representatives.

These senior people are more likely to be in a position to make decisions about sharing data, but they are less likely to be steeped in the operational details of what's happening.

Breach Data Is Not Actuarial Data

The *risks* to houses are also well known: floodplains are well mapped out, as are tornado-prone areas.

The U.K. insurance market is an interesting one. The industry has traditionally ignored flood risks there. See Computer Sciences Corporation, "CSC study finds flood risk will make insurance 'unaffordable' for many in UK," press release, November 5, 2007, www.csc.com/industries/insurance/news/11329.shtml.

In contrast to these topics, the technological landscape that affects the ease or difficulty of attacking or defending computer systems fluctuates as new technologies are introduced, as technologies are configured and reconfigured, and as the security of systems decays over time.

"One of the many problems to beset systems administrators who seek [to] secure their machines is a form of *entropy*. Over periods of time ranging from minutes to months, the *effective security* of a machine attached to a network will diminish." (Emphasis in original.)

From Alec Muffet, "WAN-hacking with AutoHack: Auditing security behind the firewall," 5th USENIX UNIX Security Symposium, 1995, www.usenix.org/publications/library/proceedings/security95/full_papers/muffett.ps.

The Human Computer Interface and Risk Compensation

People often think of security and usability as being at odds.

As long as security is perceived as being at odds with all other disciplines, the natural tendency of decision makers will continue to be to ignore or minimize it.

Some of these papers have been assembled into an excellent introductory book, *Security and Usability.*

Lorrie Faith Cranor and Simson Garfinkel, *Security and Usability: Designing Secure Systems That People Can Use*, O'Reilly, 2005.

This seems likely to be the case for as long as software is as complex as, say, a VCR.

Kent Sullivan pointed out that America's VCRs improved when on-screen programming came along, but not by very much. The real fix involved changing the blanking interval in television broadcasts to include time information. This raises a general point that user success is not an add-on, but rather a function of good system design.

Good security design involves putting the "right" security on the default path.

Sometimes users will need to make changes to get their jobs done. There is a complex trade-off between allowing them to make those changes easily and ensuring that they are aware of the security context, implications, and duration of their changes. Putting "too much" security or too much complexity in the path will cause users to feel annoyed or disempowered. If they must go through a security ritual too often, they'll become desensitized.

Third, even if security awareness training were shown to be effective, the "weakest link" principle applies. In other words, an attacker needs to convince only *one* employee to make the wrong choice.

The military and some banks apply two-person controls for high-value targets (or attempt to do so).

The Use and Abuse of Language

What is "secure" today is unlikely to be "secure" tomorrow.

Note that we didn't say *won't* be secure tomorrow. There are a small number of designs to which this doesn't apply. They are less common than we'd like.

In cryptography, a debate is raging over the use of the term "proven," for much the same reasons.

For example, Neal Koblitz, "The Uneasy Relationship Between Mathematics and Cryptography," Notices of the American Mathematical Society, September 2007, www.ams.org/notices/200708/tx070800972p.pdf.

Attempts to create strictly defined vocabulary within information security are likely doomed to failure as long as English remains a living language.

The malleability of a language is what makes it living. Languages that no one speaks are dead and, being dead, they are unchanging. Even when attempts to control language have official support, such as the *Académie Française*, they are forced to trail real usage.

Skills Shortages, Organizational Structure, and Collaboration

When an organization sends mixed messages about security, the cost is borne by the customers of that organization.

There's also a cost to the organization's security team. This might be of interest to security practitioners looking to identify and address externalities.

Chapter 8, "A Call to Action"

Embrace the New School

The goal of a university is not simply to educate students about fundamental concepts, but to teach them how to think about and solve the practical problems they will encounter in their work life.

One practical problem is how to write secure code. A good start might be improving how we train students to program. This is analogous to parents using proper grammar in front of their children. Since even well-trained programmers make mistakes, it may make sense to have a process in place to catch those errors.

Bibliography

Alessandro Acquisti, Allan Friedman, and Rahul Telang, "Is There a Cost to Privacy Breaches? An Event Study," Proceedings of the International Conference of Information Systems (ICIS), 2006.

John Adams, "Cars, cholera, and cows: the management of risk and uncertainty," Cato Policy Analysis No. 335, 1999.

Jill Aitoro, "Reports of federal security breaches double in four months," Government Executive.com, October 23, 2007, www.govexec.com/story_page.cfm?articleid=38348.

George Akerlof, "The Market for 'Lemons': Quality, Uncertainty and the Market Mechanism," *Quarterly Journal of Economics* 84 (3): 488–500, 1970.

David Allender, "Child Abductions," in Robert Muller III, "FBI Law Enforcement Bulletin," vol. 76, no. 7, July 2007, www.fbi.gov/publications/leb/2007/july07leb.pdf.

Ross Anderson, *Security Engineering*, Wiley, 2001, p. 138.

Ross Anderson, "Why information security is hard: an economic perspective," Applications Security conference, 2001, www.ftp.cl.cam.ac.uk/ftp/users/rja14/econ.pdf.

Asch, "Effects of group pressure upon the modification and distortion of judgements," pp. 151–162, D. Cartwright and A. Zander (editors), *Group Dynamics, Research and Theory* (Row, Peterson, Evanston, Illinois, 1953), cited in Simon Cole, *Suspect Identities: A History of Fingerprinting and Criminal Identification*, 2001, Harvard University Press.

M. Aschenbrenner and B. Biehl, "Improved safety through improved technical measures? Empirical studies regarding risk compensation processes in relation to anti-lock braking systems," "Challenges to accident prevention: the issue of risk compensation behavior," Styx Publications, 1994.

Association of Certified Fraud Examiners, "Report to the Nation on Occupational Fraud and Abuse," 2006, www.acfe.com/documents/2006-rttn.pdf.

Stefan Axelsson, "The base-rate fallacy and the difficulty of intrusion detection," ACM Transactions on Information and System Security (TISSEC), 3(3), pp. 186–205, ACM Press, ISSN: 1094-9224, 2000.

BBC News web site, "Passwords revealed by sweet deal," http://news.bbc.co.uk/2/hi/technology/3639679.stm.

Steve Beattie, Seth Arnold, Crispin Cowan, Perry Wagle, Chris Wright, and Adam Shostack, "Timing the Application of Security Patches for Optimal Uptime," USENIX 16th Systems Administration Conference (LISA 2002), Philadelphia, Pennsylvania, December 2002.

Steve Bellovin, "Re: CERT Reports and system breakins," in *Risks Digest* 15:28 (Peter Neumann, ed.), November 15, 1993, http://catless.ncl.ac.uk/Risks/15.28.html#subj8.

Thomas Blass, *The Man Who Shocked the World*, 2004, Basic Books.

John Boyd, "Organic Design for Command and Control," 1987. Available at www.d-n-i.net/boyd/organic_design.ppt.

California State Senate, "An act to amend, renumber, and add Section 1798.82 of, and to add Section 1798.29 to, the Civil Code, relating to personal information," September 25, 2002, http://info.sen.ca.gov/pub/01-02/bill/sen/sb_1351-1400/sb_1386_bill_20020926_chaptered.html.

L. Jean Camp, *Economics of Identity Theft*, 2007, Springer-Verlag.

L. Jean Camp and Stephen Lewis (editors), *Economics of Information Security*, Kluwer Academic Publishers, 2004.

Dawn Capeli and Michelle Keeney, "Insider Threat: Real Data on a Real Problem," CSI Conference, Washington D.C., November 2004, www.cert.org/archive/pdf/CSI-Presentation.pdf.

Carnegie-Mellon University press release, "DARPA established Computer Emergency Response Team," December 13, 1988, www.cert.org/about/1988press-rel.html.

Nicholas Carr, *Does IT Matter? Information Technology and the Corrosion of Competitive Advantage*, Harvard Business School Press, 2004.

CNN.com, "U.S. stuck on duct," http://money.cnn.com/2003/02/12/news/companies/ducttape/index.htm.

Simon Cole, *Suspect Identities: A History of Fingerprinting and Criminal Identification*, 2001, Harvard University Press.

Computer Sciences Corporation, "CSC study finds flood risk will make insurance 'unaffordable' for many in UK," press release, November 5, 2007, www.csc.com/industries/insurance/news/11329.shtml.

Robert Coram, *Boyd: The Fighter Pilot Who Changed the Art of War*, 2004, Back Bay Books.

Ian Cowie, "HMRC loses personal details of thousands," *Daily Telegraph*, November 3, 2007, www.telegraph.co.uk/money/main.jhtml;jsessionid=1FXKWDK0CVD2NQFIQMFCFGGAVCBQYIV0?xml=/money/2007/11/03/cnhmrc103.xml.

Lorrie Faith Cranor and Simson Garfinkel, *Security and Usability: Designing Secure Systems That People Can Use*, O'Reilly, 2005.

Robert Crease, *The Prism and the Pendulum: The Ten Most Beautiful Experiments in Science*, Random House, 2003.

Andrew Curry, "Giving Drivers the Benefit of the Doubt," *U.S. News & World Report*, March 18, 2007, www.usnews.com/usnews/news/articles/070318/26traffic.htm.

Eric Dash, "Weakness in the Data Chain," *New York Times*, June 30, 2005, www.nytimes.com/2005/06/30/technology/30cards.html (page 3).

Eric Dash and Tom Zeller, Jr., "MasterCard Says 40 Million Files Put at Risk," *New York Times*, June 18, 2005, www.nytimes.com/2005/06/18/business/18cards.html.

Mary Ann Davidson, "Unbreakable: Oracle's Commitment to Security," an Oracle white paper, February 2002, www.oracle.com/technology/deploy/security/pdf/unbreak3.pdf.

Bryn Dole, Steve Lodin, and Eugene Spafford, "Misplaced Trust: Kerberos 4 Session Keys," proceedings of the 1997 ISOC Conference.

Benjamin Edelman, "Adverse Selection in Online 'Trust' Certifications," a working draft as of October 15, 2006. Available at www.benedelman.org/publications/advsel-trust-draft.pdf.

Mark Eichin and Jon Rochlis, "With Microscope and Tweezers: An analysis of the Internet virus of November 1988," 1989 IEEE Symposium on Research in Security and Privacy, www.mit.edu/people/eichin/virus/main.html.

Carl Ellison, "Improvements on Conventional PKI Wisdom," First Annual PKI workshop, April 2002.

Federal Bureau of Investigation press release, "Over 1 million potential victims of botnet cyber crime," June 13, 2007, www.fbi.gov/pressrel/pressrel07/botnet061307.htm.

Federal Trade Commission, "2006 Identity Theft Survey Report," November 2007, www.ftc.gov/os/2007/11/SynovateFinalReportIDTheft2006.pdf.

Ed Felten, "MediaMax Bug Found; Patch Issued; Patch Suffers from Same Bug," blog post to Freedom to Tinker, December 7, 2005.

Ed Felten and J. Alex Halderman, "Sony's Web-Based Uninstaller Opens a Big Security Hole; Sony to Recall Discs," post to Freedom to Tinker blog, November 15, 2005, www.freedom-to-tinker.com/?p=927.

Charles Fishman, "They Write the Right Stuff," Fast Company, December 1996, http://fastcompany.com/magazine/06/writestuff.html.

S. Fosser, I. Saetermo, and F. Sagberg, "An investigation of behavioral adaptation to airbags and antilock brakes among taxi drivers," *Accident Analysis and Prevention*, vol. 29, no. 3, May 1997.

John Kenneth Galbraith, *The Economics of Innocent Fraud: Truth for Our Time*, 2004, Houghton Mifflin.

Gartner, Inc., "High-Profile Thefts Show Insiders Do the Most Damage," *Gartner FirstTake*, FT-18-9417, John Pescatore, November 26, 2002.

Dan Geer, "Shoes for Industry," keynote address, Shmoocon, 2006.

Barry Glassner, *The Culture of Fear: Why Americans Are Afraid of the Wrong Things,* 2000.

Irving Goffman, *The Presentation of Self in Everyday Life*, Anchor, 1959.

Lawrence Gordon and Martin Loeb, "The Economics of Information Security Investment," ACM Transactions on Information and System Security (TISSEC), vol. 5, issue 4, November 2002.

Benjamin Graham and David Dodd, *Security Analysis*, Third Edition, McGraw Hill, 2004.

Bill Gurstelle, "When Planes Fell from the Sky," December 22, 2006, Notes from the Technology Underground blog, http://nfttu.blogspot.com/2006/12/when-planes-fell-from-sky.html.

HarrisInteractive, "Many U.S. Adults Claim to Have Been Notified That Personal Information Has Been Improperly Disclosed," The Harris Poll #81, November 10, 2006, www.harrisinteractive.com/harris_poll/index.asp?PID=708.

Mayer Hillman, "Cycle helmets: the case for and against," Policy Studies Institute, 1993.

House of Lords, Science and Technology committee, "Personal Internet Security" report, July 24, 2007, www.publications.parliament.uk/pa/ld200607/ldselect/ldsctech/165/16502.htm.

Darrell Huff, *How to Lie with Statistics*, WW Norton & Company, 1993.

Information Technology Process Institute, "IT Controls Performance Study," www.itpi.org/home/performance_study.php, as described by Gene Kim, "Prioritizing Processes and Controls for Effective and Measurable Security," CERIAS Security Seminar, September 20, 2006, www.cerias.purdue.edu/video/secsem/secsem_20060920.mp4.

iSec, the Electronic Frontier Foundation, and SonyBMG, (now titled) "Update to Press Release: EFF Does Not Recommend Patch at This Time," December 6, 2005, www.eff.org/press/archives/2005/12/06.

Andrew Jaquith, *Security Metrics: Replacing Fear, Uncertainty and Doubt*, Addison Wesley, 2007.

Steven Johnson, *The Ghost Map*, Riverhead Books, 2006.

Barbara Kellerman, "When Should a Leader Apologize and When Not?," *Harvard Business Review*, April 2006, pp. 73–81.

Mark Klienman, "Microsoft helps FBI bust Chinese gang," *Daily Telegraph* online, July 25, 2007, www.telegraph.co.uk/money/main.jhtml?xml=/money/2007/07/24/bcnmicro124.xml.

Neal Koblitz, "The Uneasy Relationship Between Mathematics and Cryptography," Notices of the American Mathematical Society, September 2007, www.ams.org/notices/200708/tx070800972p.pdf.

Ufuk Koroglu and Bunyamin Demirkan, "Turkish Hacker Depletes 10,000 Bank Accounts," *Today's Zaman*, Istanbul, December 20, 2006, www.todayszaman.com/tz-web/detaylar.do?load=detay&link=39364.

Thomas Kuhn, *The Structure of Scientific Revolutions*, Second Edition, University of Chicago Press, 1970.

Abhiskek Kumar, Vern Paxson, and Nicholas Weaver, "Exploiting Underlying Structure for Detailed Reconstruction of an Internet-scale Event," proceedings ACM IMC, 2005.

Eric Lai, "Identity thieves hit customers at TD Ameritrade, E-Trade," *ComputerWorld* Online, October 24, 2006, www.computerworld.com/action/article.do?command=printArticleBasic&articleId=9004416.

Michael Lewis, *Moneyball: The Art of Winning an Unfair Game*, W.W. Norton & Company, Inc., 2003.

Bjorn Lomborg, *The Skeptical Environmentalist: Measuring the Real State of the World*, Cambridge University Press, 1998.

Ulrike Malmendier and Geoffrey Tate, "Superstar CEOs." Available at SSRN: http://ssrn.com/abstract=972725.

Andreas Marx, "The false positive disaster," Virus Bulletin, November 1, 2005.

S.A. Mathieson, "Gone phishing in Halifax," Elsevier Infosecurity, October 7, 2005, http://infosecurity-magazine.com/news/051007_halifax_e-mail.htm.

Geoffrey Moore, *Crossing the Chasm*, 1991, HarperCollins.

Geoffrey Moore, *Inside the Tornado*, 1995, HarperCollins.

Kunihiko Morishita, James Minamoto, and Nobuhito Sawasaki, "Notifications of data security breaches: Japan" at Bird & Bird, www.twobirds.com/english/publications/articles/Notifications_data_security_breaches_Japan.cfm.

Robert Morris, "If your software is full of bugs, why would you think it's secure?," keynote address, 4th USENIX Security Symposium, October 4–6, 1993, Santa Clara, California.

Ed Moyle, "Strange things are afoot with breach disclosure," Security Curve weblog, November 3, 2006, www.security-curve.com/blog/archives/000476.html.

Alec Muffet, "WAN-hacking with AutoHack: Auditing security behind the firewall," 5th USENIX UNIX Security Symposium, 1995, www.usenix.org/publications/library/proceedings/security95/full_papers/muffett.ps.

Vic Napier, "Risk Homeostasis: A Case Study of the Adoption of a Safety Innovation on the Level of Perceived Risk," 14th Annual Meeting of the American Society of Business and Behavioral Sciences, Las Vegas, Nevada, February 22, 2007, www.vicnapier.com/riskhomeostasis.htm.

Ryan Naraine, "Microsoft says recovery from malware becoming impossible, eWeek.com, April 4, 2006, www.eweek.com/article2/0,1895,1945808,00.asp.

National Bureau of Standards, *Guidelines for Automatic Data Processing Physical Security and Risk Management*, FIPS Pub 31, 1974, pp. 12–14.

National Research Council, "Trust in Cyberspace," 1999, as quoted in Steve Bellovin, "The State of Software Security," Information Security Law: Software Security and Vulnerability Reporting, Seton Hall University School of Law, November 2002, www.cs.columbia.edu/~smb/talks/vuln-legal.pdf.

National Vulnerability Database, "Vulnerability Note VU#312073: First4Internet CodeSupport ActiveX control incorrectly marked 'safe for scripting,'" last updated December 7, 2005. CVE-2005-3650.

National Vulnerability Database, "Vulnerability Note VU#928689: SunnComm MediaMax privilege elevation vulnerability," last updated April 12, 2006, CVE-2005-4069.

Helen Nissenbaum, "Privacy as Contextual Integrity," *Washington Law Review*, vol. 79, no. 1, February 4, 2004, pp. 119–158, http://crypto.stanford.edu/portia/papers/RevnissenbaumDTP31.pdf.

Office of the Privacy Commissioner of Canada, and Office of the Information and Privacy Commissioner of Alberta, "Report of an Investigation into the Security, Collection and Retention of Personal Information, TJX Companies Inc./Winners Merchant International L.P.," September 25, 2007, www.privcom.gc.ca/cf-dc/2007/TJX_rep_070925_e.asp.

Rob O'Neill, "It's campaign time on data-breach disclosure," *ComputerWorld*, June 11, 2007, http://computerworld.co.nz/news.nsf/scrt/23D66D5FDB5AC8C0CC2572F40000D29C.

Open Source Initiative, "The Open Source Definition," last edited July 7, 2006, www.opensource.org/docs/osd.

Frans Osinga, *Science, Strategy, and War: The Strategic Theory of John Boyd*, 2006, Routledge.

Scott Page, *The Difference: How the Power of Diversity Creates Better Groups, Firms, Schools, and Societies*, Princeton University Press, 2007.

Ponemon Institute, "2007 Consumer Survey on Data Security," June 25, 2007.

Karl Popper, *Conjectures and Refutations: The Growth of Scientific Knowledge*, Fifth Edition (revised), Routledge, 1989.

Kevin Poulson, "Breakable," SecurityFocus, visited January 1, 2008, www.securityfocus.com/news/309.

Kevin Poulsen, "Hacking Challenge Winners Allege $43,000 Contest Rip-Off," SecurityFocus, November 26, 2002, www.securityfocus.com/news/1717.

Thomas Ptacek and Timothy Newsham, "Insertion, Evasion, and Denial of Service: Eluding Network Intrusion Detection," 1998, Secure Networks, Inc. technical report.

Marcus Ranum, "How to really secure the Internet," Blackhat Briefings, 1997.

J. Reynolds, "The Helminthiasis of the Internet," RFC 1135, December 1989.

G. Rose, P. Hamilton, L. Cowell, M. Shipley, "A randomised control trial of anti-smoking advice; 10-year results," *Journal of Epidemiology and Community Health*, vol. 36, pp. 102–108, 1982.

David Rosenhan and Samuel Messick, "Affect and expectation," *Journal of Personality and Social Psychology*, vol. 3, pp. 38–44 (1966), as cited in Wikipedia, "Valence Effect," visited January 1, 2005, http://en.wikipedia.org/wiki/valence_effect.

Robin Rowland, "Spam, Spam, Spam: The Cyberspace Wars," CBC News Online, November 24, 2003, www.cbc.ca/news/background/spam/.

Mark Russinovich, "Sony, Rootkits and Digital Rights Management Gone Too Far," post to WinInternals blog, October 31, 2005, available at http://blogs.technet.com/markrussinovich/archive/2005/10/31/sony-rootkits-and-digital-rights-management-gone-too-far.aspx.

Julie J.C.H. Ryan and Theresa I. Jefferson, "The Use, Misuse and Abuse of Statistics in Information Security Research," Proceedings of the 2003 ASEM National Conference, St. Louis, Missouri.

Stuart Schecter, Rachna Dhamija, Andy Ozment, and Ian Fischer, "The Emperor's New Security Indicators: An evaluation of website authentication and the effect of role playing on usability studies," IEEE Symposium on Security and Privacy, May 2007, www.usablesecurity.org/emperor/.

Stuart Schecter and Michael Smith, "How Much Security Is Enough to Stop a Thief?" *Financial Cryptography*, 2003.

Alan Schiffman, "Instant Immortality," blog post to Recondite, July 2, 2004, http://webpages.charter.net/allanms/2004/07/instant-immortality.html.

Bruce Schneier, *Beyond Fear*, Springer, 2003.

Bruce Schneier, "Talking to strangers," blog post, June 23, 2005, www.schneier.com/blog/archives/2005/06/talking_to_stra.html.

Bruce Schneier, "Terrorists Don't Do Movie Plots," Wired Online "Security Matters" column, September 8, 2005.

Evan Schuman, "TJX Intruder Moved 80-GBytes of Data and No One Noticed," post to StorefrontBacktalk blog, October 25, 2007, http://storefrontbacktalk.com/story/102507tjxrevised-complaint.

Evan Schuman, "TJX's Projected Breach Costs Increase to $216 million," StorefrontBacktalk blog, November 13, 2007, http://storefrontbacktalk.com/story/111307tjxloss.

Howard Schurman and Stanley Presser, *Questions and Answers in Attitude Surveys: Experiments on Wording Form, Wording, and Context*, Academic Press, 1981.

Peter Seebach, "What you can do about phishing," IBM Developer Works, January 4, 2006, www.ibm.com/developerworks/web/library/wa-cranky60.html.

Carl Shapiro and Hal Varian, *Information Rules: A Strategic Guide to the Network Economy*, Harvard Business School Press, 1999.

Joe Sharkey, "Business travel: On the road, flying less and enjoying it more," *New York Times*, September 9, 2003.

Adam Shostack, "Breaches in SEC Reports," blog post on Emergentchaos.com, May 3, 2007, www.emergentchaos.com/archives/2007/05/breaches_in_sec_reports.html.

Adam Shostack, "Preserving the Internet Channel Against Phishers," www.homeport.org/~adam/phishing.html.

Adam Shostack and Chris Walsh, "Data About Data Breaches," slide 27, June 2007, presented at FIRST conference in Seville, Spain.

Brian Skyrms, *The Stag Hunt and the Evolution of Social Structure*, 2003, Cambridge University Press.

Paul Slovic, *The Perception of Risk*, Earthscan Publications, 2000.

The Social Security Administration, "Social Security Number Chronology," www.ssa.gov/history/ssn/ssnchron.html.

SonicWall, "SonicWall Phishing IQ Test, Phishing Facts," http://sonicwall.com/phishing/. Undated page, visited December 22, 2007.

Kevin Soo Hoo, Andrew Sudbury, and Andrew Jaquith, "Tangible ROI Through Secure Software Engineering," *Secure Business Quarterly*, vol. 1, issue 2001.

Michael Spence, "Job Market Signaling," *Quarterly Journal of Economics* 87 (3): 355–374, 1973.

J.G. Steiner, B. Clifford Neuman, and J.I. Schiller, "Kerberos: An Authentication Service for Open Network Systems," in Proceedings of the Winter 1988 USENIX Conference, February 1988.

G. Bennett Stewart III, *The Quest for Value*, 1991, HarperCollins.

Clifford Stoll, *The Cuckoo's Egg*, Doubleday, 1989.

Bob Sullivan, "Database giant gives access to fake firms," February 14, 2005, MSNBC, www.msnbc.msn.com/id/6969799/.

Peter Szor, *The Art of Computer Virus Research and Defense*, 2005, Symantec Press.

Edward Tufte, *Visual Explanations*, 1997, Graphics Press, pp. 27–37.

U.S. House of Representatives, Committee on Oversight and Government Reform, "Seventh Report Card on Computer Security at Federal Departments and Agencies," April 12, 2007.

Virginia State Attorney General, "FAQ Identity Theft," undated web page, visited December 22, 2007, www.oag.state.va.us/FAQs/FAQ_IDTheft.html.

W. Kip Viscusi, "Alarmist decisions with divergent risk information," *Economic Journal*, vol. 107, no. 445, 1997.

Chris Walsh, "A request," blog post January 3, 2007. Emergent Chaos blog, www.emergentchaos.com/archives/2007/01/a_request.html.

Kenneth Warner and John Slade, "Low tar, high toll," *American Journal of Public Health*, January 1992, vol. 82, no. 1.

Duncan Watts, *Six Degrees: The Science of a Connected Age*, Norton, 2003.

Dirk Weirich and Martina Angela Sasse, "Pretty Good Persuasion: A first step towards effective password security in the real world," 7th New Security Paradigms Workshop, pp. 137–143, 2001.

Dirk Weirich, Sacha Brostoff, and Martina Angela Sasse, "Transforming the 'Weakest Link': a Human/Computer Interaction Approach to Usable and Effective Security," *BT Technology Journal*, vol. 19, no. 3, pp. 122–131, 2001.

John Whiteside, "Expedia should consider the only definition of 'spam' that matters," The Opinionated Marketer blog, April 3, 2007, http://opinionatedmarketers.blogspot.com/2007/04/expedia-should-consider-only-definition.html.

Thomas Whiteside, *Computer Capers*, Mentor Executive Library, 1978, pp. 33–35.

Wikipedia, "Nash equilibrium," visited January 8, 2008, http://en.wikipedia.org/wiki/Nash_equilibrium.

Wikipedia, "Open source," visited January 5, 2008, http://en.wikipedia.org/wiki/Open_source.

Wikipedia, "Oracle Corporation," visited January 1, 2008, http://en.wikipedia.org/wiki/Oracle_Corporation.

Index

Symbols

80/20 rule, 29

A

ABS (antilock braking system) example (risk compensation), 96

academia, role in security industry, 24-25

access control for DRM (Digital Rights Management), 113

accidental security breaches, 64

actions, changing, 154-157

actuarial data, need for, 136-137

adoption of technologies, economics of, 84-88

adverse selection, 32

adware, 5

agency problems, 134

airline industry example (risk aversion), 123

ALE (annual loss expected), 119

altruistic approach to technology adoption, 85

analysis of objective data, 151-152

analysts, role in security industry, 23

Anderson, Ross, 82

annual loss expected (ALE), 119

antilock braking system (ABS) example (risk compensation), 96

anti-virus (AV) products, 7

applied mathematics, 79

assumptions, problems with, 133

attacks, number of, as evidence, 51

auditors
- in principal-agent relationships, 94
- role in security industry, 21

authentication, 6, 11

authoritarian approach to technology adoption, 86

authorization, 11

AV (anti-virus) products, 7

B

bank fraud, Y'nin case, 1

Beane, Billy, 39

Bellarmino, Roberto, 41

best practices, as marketing tactic, 36-38

bicycle helmets example (moral hazard), 98

Boyd, John, 25

brand, damage to, 106

breaches. *See* security breaches

bundling, 93

business partner requirements, role in security spending, 114

business processes
enabling, 106
law compliance for, 107-108
businesses, motivations for security spending, 106-108

C

CardSystems Solutions security breach, 35, 66
CERT (Computer Emergency Response Team), 56
certifications. *See* security certifications
Certified Information Systems Security Professional (CISSP), 31
change management, 116
checklists, as marketing tactic, 35-36
child abduction example (risk aversion), 123
ChoicePoint security breach, 62-63
cholera epidemic example, 61
CISSP (Certified Information Systems Security Professional), 31
Coakley, Martha, 10
collaboration, 144-145
company endorsements, as marketing tactic, 34
competitive advantage, role in security spending, 112
competitive disadvantage, role in security spending, 115
"complete" systems in security industry, 22
completist approach to security spending, 117
compliance spending, 107-108
computer crime. *See* online crime
Computer Emergency Response Team (CERT), 56
Computer Security Institute (CSI), 47
conferences, 24
configuration management, 116
contextual integrity, 102
Copernican astronomy example, 41
cost
of security breaches, determining, 120
of security spending, determining, 116-121
crackers, 20
credit fraud, ease of, 13
cross-disciplinary perspectives on information security, 81
cryptography, 80
CSI (Computer Security Institute), 47
***The Cuckoo's Egg* (Stoll), 110**

D

data breaches. *See* security breaches
deceptive business practices, non-disclosure of security breaches as, 69
Defcon, 26-27
deliberate security breaches, 64

design errors in security surveys, 48

digital forensics, 20

Digital Rights Management (DRM), 113

disclosing. ***See*** **publicizing**

diversity, 100, 152

DNS (Domain Name System), 85

DRM (Digital Rights Management), 113

E

economic value added (EVA), 119

economics
- agency problems, 134
- assumptions, problems with, 133
- of information security, 82-84, 152
  - *measuring software security, 88-91*
  - *principal-agent relationships, 93-94*
  - *stopping spam, 91-93*
  - *technology adoption, 84-88*

efficiency, role in security spending, 115

80/20 rule, 29

email
- problems with, 4-7
- spam, difficulty of stopping, 91-93

employee security awareness training, 129, 141

enabling business processes, 106

endorsements, as marketing tactic, 34

entrepreneurs, role in security industry, 21

equilibrium, 84-85

equipment, security breaches resulting from, 64

EVA (economic value added), 119

evaluations of software security, 89

evidence. ***See also*** **objective data**
- information-sharing efforts, 55-58
- instrumentation on internet, 54-55
- sources of, 41-46
- surveys, problems with, 46-49
- trade press, problems with, 50-51
- vulnerabilities, problems with, 52-54

experiments for testing hypotheses, 42

external measures approach to security spending, 118

externalities, 92, 137-138

F

failures of information security. ***See also*** **security breaches**
- email problems, 4-7
- identity theft, 11-13
- malware, 7-9
- security breaches, 9-10
- ubiquitous nature of failures, 14-15

fear
- as marketing tactic, 33-34
- risk aversion and, 122
- role in security spending, 111

feedback loops, 57

food inspection example (moral hazard), 98

framing questions for security spending, 126-127

free-riding, 84

G

Galileo, 41

Gordon, Lawrence, 121

governments, motivations for security spending, 108-109

groupthink, 26

guaranteed uptime, 44

H

hackers, 20
- role in security industry, 22
- underground hacker community, 26-27

Hawkins, Brennan, 123

heuristics in antivirus (AV) products, 8

high-security internet protocols, lack of adoption of, 85

Honeynet project, 55

hostile code. *See* malware

human nature. *See also* economics; psychology; sociology
- in information security, passwords example, 82
- in New School of Information Security, 132-136

hyperbolic discounting, 109

hypotheses, proving, 42-43

I–J

identification, 11

identity, separation of, 101-102

identity theft, 11-13. *See also* security breaches

incentives, 82, 152

individuals, motivations for security spending, 109

information security. *See also* security industry
- cross-disciplinary perspectives on, 81
- economics of, 82-84, 152
  - *measuring software security, 88-91*
  - *principal-agent relationships, 93-94*
  - *stopping spam, 91-93*
  - *technology adoption, 84-88*
- evidence. *See also* objective data
  - *information-sharing efforts, 55-58*
  - *instrumentation on internet, 54-55*
  - *sources of, 41-46*
  - *surveys, problems with, 46-49*
  - *trade press, problems with, 50-51*
  - *vulnerabilities, problems with, 52-54*
- failures of. *See also* security breaches
  - *email problems, 4-7*
  - *identity theft, 11-13*
  - *malware, 7-9*
  - *security breaches, 9-10*
  - *ubiquitous nature of failures, 14-15*
- human nature in, passwords example, 82

importance of, 1-4
mathematics and, 79-81
New School of, 15-16, 131-132, 147-149
actions, changing, 154-157
actuarial data, need for, 136-137
collaboration in, 144-145
externalities, strength of, 137-138
human behavior in, 132-136
objective data, analysis of, 151-152
objective data, need for, 149
objective data, sources of, 149-151
orientations, seeking new, 152
profiting from, 157-159
reactions, changing, 157
risk compensation in, 140-142
teaching, changing methods of, 153-154
terminology, abuse of, 142-143
usability in, 139-140
psychology and, 95-99
sociology and, 99-102

information sharing
as evidence source, 55-58
secrecy versus, 135-136

Information Sharing and Analysis Centers (ISACs), 56

insecure software, market domination of, 88-91

insiders, security breaches resulting from, 49, 65

instrumentation on internet, as evidence source, 54-55

insurance industry example, 137

interconnected nature of computers, 1-4

internal usage approach to technology adoption, 86

internet, open nature of, 14

internet Archive project, 14

internet worms. *See* worms

inventory management, 116

ISACs (Information Sharing and Analysis Centers), 56

IT vendors, role in security industry, 22-23

K–L

language. *See* terminology

law compliance for business processes, 107-108

law enforcement, role in security industry, 20

learning, changing methods of, 153-154

Lewis, Michael, 39

liability for insecure software, 90-91

locking screens example, 99

Loeb, Martin, 121

loss avoidance, 106

M

magazines, as marketing tactic, 34

malware, 7-9

marketing tactics of security industry, 33-38

mathematics, information security and, 79-81

measurements. ***See*** **security measurements**

measuring software security, 88-91

media (tapes, DVDs), security breaches resulting from, 64

military. ***See*** **U.S. military**

Moneyball **(Lewis), 39**

monoculture, 100-101, 152

Moore, Geoffrey, 87

moral hazard, 97-99

Morris Worm, 8

Morris, Robert Jr., 8

N

Nash Equilibrium, 84

negative externalities, 137

net present value (NPV), 119

network effect, 86

New School of Information Security, 15-16, 131-132, 147-149

- actions, changing, 154-157
- actuarial data, need for, 136-137
- collaboration in, 144-145
- externalities, strength of, 137-138
- human behavior in, 132-136
- objective data
  - *analysis of, 151-152*
  - *need for, 149*
  - *sources of, 149-151*
- orientations, seeking new, 152
- profiting from, 157-159
- reactions, changing, 157
- risk compensation in, 140-142
- teaching, changing methods of, 153-154
- terminology, abuse of, 142-143
- usability in, 139-140

Nissenbaum, Helen, 102

noninvestment in security, role in security spending, 111

nonprofit organizations, motivations for security spending, 109

notification laws, 62

- cost of, 71-74
- for security breaches, 68

NPV (net present value), 119

O

objective data. ***See also*** **evidence**

- analysis of, 151-152
- need for, 58-59, 149
- risk aversion and, 133
- security breaches as, 61-64
  - *criticisms of, 70-74*
  - *scientific evaluation of, 74-76*
  - *usage of, 76-77*
- sources of, 149-151

Observe, Orient, Decide, Act (OODA) concept, 25

Oluwatosin, Olatunji, 62

online crime, ease of, 1-4

OODA (Observe, Orient, Decide, Act) concept, 25

organizational structure, 144

organizations, security breach polls of, 65

orientations

- seeking new, 152
- within security industry, 25-27

outsourcing in principal-agent relationships, 94

P

Pareto Principle, 29

passwords example (human nature in information security), 82

patches, 95-96

PCI (Payment Card Industry) standards, 35

personal data storage, risks of, 67

personal information. *See* identity theft

perspectives. *See* orientations

pharming, 143

phishing, 6-7, 144

point-of-view. *See* orientations

police. *See* law enforcement

polls. *See* surveys

positive externalities, 138

pretexting, 143

principal-agent relationships, 93-94

prisoner's dilemma, 17-18

products
- marketing tactics for, 33-38
- sold by security industry, 27-32

profiting from New School of Information Security, 157-159

project valuation techniques for security spending, 119-121

"proof by unclaimed reward," as marketing tactic, 34

protocols, lack of adoption of, 85

proving hypotheses, 42-43

psychology
- information security and, 95-99
- objective data and, 133
- of security spending, 122-126

publicizing security breaches, 62-64, 157
- cost of, 71-74
- reasons for, 68-70
- types of organizations publicized, 66

Q–R

questions for security surveys, writing, 46

reactions, changing, 157

reporting. *See* publicizing

reputation, damage to, 106

respondents to security surveys, 46-47

return on investment (ROI), 119

reverse valence effect, 46

risk aversion
- objective data and, 133
- security spending and, 122-126

risk compensation, 96-97, 140-142

rock stars, 94

ROI (return on investment), 119

S

Sarbanes-Oxley Act (SOX), 107

SB1386 (security breach notification law), 62

Schechter, Stuart, 85

scientific evaluation of security breach data, 74-76

scientific evidence. ***See*** **evidence**

screen locking example, 99

seal programs, 32

seat belt example (risk compensation), 97

secrecy, information sharing versus, 135-136

Secure Shell (SSH) example (technology adoption cycle), 88

security breaches, 9-10. ***See also*** **identity theft**
- of CardSystems Solutions, 35, 66
- cost of, determining, 120
- data on, actuarial data versus, 136-137
- notification laws concerning, 62
- as objective data, 61-64
  - *criticisms of, 70-74*
  - *scientific evaluation of, 74-76*
  - *usage of, 76-77*
- publicizing, 62-64, 157
  - *cost of, 71-74*
  - *reasons for, 68-70*
  - *types of organizations publicized, 66*
- as source of objective data, 150
- types of, 64-67

security certifications
- for businesses, 32
- for individuals, 30-32

security industry
- challenges faced by, 147
- elements in, 19-25
- marketing tactics of, 33-38
- orientations within, 25-27
- prisoner's dilemma and, 17-18
- products and services sold by, 27-32

security measurements, difficulty of, 45-46

security patches, 95-96

security policies, problems with, 129-130

security products, purchasing, 154-155

security spending, 105
- cost of, determining, 116-121
- emerging reasons for, 112-116
- non-reasons for, 110-112
- psychology of, 122-126
- reasons for, 106-110
- on security products, 154-155
- what to purchase, 126-130

security surveys, problems with, 46-49

sensors on internet, as evidence source, 54-55

separation of identity, 101-102

service-level contracts, guaranteed uptime, 44

services sold by security industry, 27-32

sharing. ***See*** **information sharing**

signatures of viruses, 7

skills shortages, 144

skydiving example (risk compensation), 96

smoking example (risk compensation), 97

Snow, John, 61

social engineering attacks, 128, 143

social security numbers (SSNs), problems with, 12

sociology, information security and, 99-102
software products, role of security spending in, 114
software security, measuring, 88-91
SOX (Sarbanes-Oxley Act), 107
spam, 4-5, 91-93
speed of disclosure of security breaches, 68
spending. *See* security spending
SSH (Secure Shell) example (technology adoption cycle), 88
SSNs (social security numbers), problems with, 12
standards bodies, 24
stock market fraud, 2
Stoll, Clifford, 110
surveys
  problems with, 46-49
  about security breaches, 65

T

TCO (total cost of ownership), 121
teaching, changing methods of, 153-154
technology adoption, economics of, 84-88
telecommunications companies, uptime guarantees, 44
terminology, abuse of, 142-143
testing hypotheses, 42-43
theft prevention, 109
TJX, security breach affecting, 10
total cost of ownership (TCO), 121
trade press, stories in, 50-51
transaction costs, 89
trust creation, role in security spending, 113
TRUSTe seal program, 32
Turkish gangs, bank fraud case, 1

U

U.S. military, influence on security industry, 19-20
U.S. veterans, security breach affecting, 9
underground hacker community, 26-27
universities in New School of Information Security, 153-154
uptime guarantees, 44
usability, security and, 139-140

V

valence effect, 46
vendors. *See* IT vendors
venture capitalists, role in security industry, 21
veterans, security breach affecting, 9
viruses, 7-9
vocabulary in security surveys, 48

vulnerabilities, as evidence source, 52-54

vulnerability scanning, 125

W–Z

"wait and see" approach to security spending, 117

WEIS (Workshop on the Economics of Information Security), 152

wireless networks example, 111

worms, 8, 111

Y'nin, Ali (bank fraud case), 1

Preface

For more than a decade, surveys of Internet users, administrators, and developers have consistently ranked "security" as their top concern. Despite the advances in Internet security technology, the problem of criminal activity on the Internet has only become worse.

As Nicholas Negroponte, founder of the MIT Media Lab and the One Laptop Per Child association observed: *bits not atoms*. As the world goes digital, so does crime. Only the venue is new in Internet crime. Every one of the crimes described in this book is a new twist on an ancient story. Willie Horton robbed banks because, "That's where the money is." Today, the money is on the Internet, and so are the criminals trying to steal it.

People not bits: Internet crime is about people. Money is the means; technology is merely an end. Some Internet criminals are world-class technology experts, but rather fewer than you might expect. Most Internet criminals are experts in manipulating and exploiting the behavior of people rather than machines.

Internet crime is caused by the criminals, but certain limitations of the original design of the Internet and the Web have encouraged its growth. To change the behavior of people, we must change the environment in which they interact. Paradoxically, understanding the *problem* of Internet crime as a social process leads us to *solutions* that are primarily expressed as technical proposals.

If we are going to beat the Internet criminals, we are going to need both strategy and tactics. In the short term, we must respond tactically—foiling attacks in progress even if doing so costs more than accepting the loss. In the longer term, we must change the infrastructure of the Internet so that it is no longer a lawless frontier but do so in a way that does not compromise the privacy and liberties that have attracted people to the Internet in the first place.

We must pursue both courses. Unless we can bring Internet crime under short-term control through a tactical response, it will be too late for strategy. If we don't use the time bought by the tactical approach to advance a long-term strategy, we will eventually run out of tactical options.

The Internet has more than a billion users. It is a complex and expensive infrastructure. Changing the Internet is difficult, particularly when success requires many changes to be made at the same time and the people who must bear the cost are not always the ones who will see the benefit.

I am currently a participant in six different working groups tasked with changing a small part of the Internet. I have interactions with and occasionally appear at 20 more. Taken individually, none of the groups are likely to have a significant effect on the level of Internet crime. The best that can be hoped for is to move the problem from one place to another. Secure the e-mail system, and the criminals will start infiltrating Instant Messaging; secure Instant Messaging, and they will attack blogs or voice communications.

Taken together, the groups are working toward something that is much larger: a new Internet infrastructure that is a friendlier place for the honest person and a less advantageous environment for criminals.

The purpose of this book is to show how these pieces come together. In particular, it is an argument for a particular approach to Internet security based on *accountability*.

This book is arranged in four sections providing a rough narrative from problem to solution and from people issues to technology issues.

Section One: People Not Bits

Before we start to look at solutions, we need to understand both the problem we want to solve and the reasons it has not been solved before. What might surprise some readers is that technology only plays a minor role. *Money is the motive; people are the cause.* You don't need to be a technology expert to understand how these crimes work; the typical Internet criminal is not a technology expert.

The first two chapters deal with the problem. Chapter 1, "Motive," looks at the crimes themselves, every one a new twist on an ages-old scam, and Chapter 2, "Famous for Fifteen Mouse Clicks," looks at the criminals behind the scams. The common theme running through both chapters is that these crimes are due to the lack of accountability in the design of the Internet and the Web. To combat Internet crime, we must establish an accountable Web.

The next three chapters consider the problem of changing the Internet infrastructure to make it a less crime-friendly environment, and how to make the changes necessary to establish accountability. Chapter 3, "Learning from Mistakes," looks back at the reasons that the Internet is the way that it is. Chapter 4, "Making Change

Happen," looks forward and sets out a strategy for changing the Internet that is driven by pain and opportunity. Chapter 5, "Design for Deployment," describes an engineering approach based on that strategy: design for deployment.

Section Two: Stopping the Cycle

Having looked at the problem, we can begin to look at solutions to specific types of Internet crime, such as phishing and measures to limit the use of the criminal infrastructures that support them.

At this point, we are looking at measures that can be deployed in the short term with minimal changes to the existing Internet infrastructure. As a result, the measures tend to offer tactical rather than strategic advantage. Although tactical measures are valuable in the short run, we must accept that the respite they offer is temporary and use the time that they provide to deploy strategic changes to the Internet infrastructure that bring lasting benefits that the criminals find much harder to circumvent and make a profit from their activities.

Chapter 6, "Spam Whack-a-Mole," looks at previous efforts to control spam and the reasons that they have failed. Chapter 7, "Stopping Spam," describes more recent efforts to control spam by establishing an accountability infrastructure for e-mail use.

Chapter 8, "Stopping Phishing," examines the problem of phishing. Although phishing is not the only form of bank fraud on the Internet, it is currently the one that causes the most widespread concern.

Spam is one of the two principle engines of Internet crime. Chapter 9, "Stopping Botnets," looks at ways to disrupt the use of the other principle engine of Internet crime: networks of captured computers known as **botnets**.

Section Three: Tools of the Trade

Before looking at how to change the Internet infrastructure to make strategic changes, it is necessary to describe the technical tools available, in particular the use of cryptography.

Chapter 10, "Cryptography," presents a brief introduction to modern cryptography. Cryptography is a powerful tool but must be used with care. Security is a property of a system. A program can employ the most advanced cryptographic techniques known and still fail to control real risks and thus provide security in the real world.

Chapter 11, "Establishing Trust," describes mechanisms that are used to establish trust in the online world today and some of the recent developments in the state of the art that will help us to establish the infrastructure we need to meet our future needs.

Section Four: The Accountable Web

The final section of this book presents the actual technical architecture of the accountable Web. Each chapter focuses on a particular layer of security infrastructure, beginning with those where work is already well advanced.

Chapters 12, "Secure Transport," and 13, "Secure Messaging," describe work that is currently underway to create the next-generation transport and messaging layer security infrastructures. In particular, the design of Extended Validation certificates and Secure Internet Letterhead are examined.

Chapters 14, "Secure Identity," and 15, "Secure Names," address the issues of identity and naming. This area is currently hotly contested with OpenID, CardSpace, and SAML all competing for position. I believe that in the long run, all of these technologies will develop complementary niches within a common Identity 2.0 ecology.

Chapter 16, "Secure Networks," looks at the network layer and describes Default Deny Infrastructure, an architecture designed to meet the challenge of deperimeterization. Chapter 17, "Secure Platforms," describes some of the work currently underway to develop a secure operating system and the use of next-generation code signing.

Chapter 18, "Law," examines the use of the legal system to reduce Internet crime, ensuring that law enforcement and prosecutors have the tools they need to do their job. Chapter 19, "The dotCrime Manifesto," sets out a plan of action for stopping Internet crime.

A Note on Jargon

Most technologists (sometimes including me) use rather too much jargon. After 25 years in the technology business, I have come to the conclusion that the more jargon a person uses, the less he is likely to know what he is talking about.

While preparing to edit this book, I reread a book on a related topic that was also aimed at a general audience written some years ago. I was somewhat surprised to find it somewhat heavy going even though I had found it a light read at the time. The field has moved on in the years since the book was first published, and so has the language. Will anyone remember what a "Joe job" is in ten years' time? I hope not. I hope we have made both the attack and the jargon name for it obsolete.

To avoid this problem, I have adopted the following principles.

- Where a term has been used as a term of art for many years in the field, I use it. The term **social engineering** has been used in the security field to describe obtaining information from a person through some form of confidence trick.
- Where a jargon term is widely used in the establishment media, I use it. The term **phishing** is widely used to describe the theft of credentials through a social engineering attack.
- Where a term has been recently introduced and is either self-explanatory or readily remembered after explanation, I use that term after giving an explanation. The term **capture site** is used to refer to a Web site used to collect credentials stolen in a phishing attack.
- Where a term is used with different meanings inside and outside the field or is otherwise ambiguous, I avoid it. Even though the term **hacker** is commonly used to refer to computer criminals, it is often used in the field in the original sense of an expert trickster.
- Where a term is not widely used outside a specialist clique and is not self-explanatory without reference to other jargon terms, I avoid it. In particular, I make a point of avoiding the hacker jargon **leet speak**. The point of leet speak is that it allows cliques to show each other how clever they are through use of a private code.

Word games can be fun, but we won't beat the criminals if we allow them to choose the rules and the game. I was recently in a meeting where a speaker had a cute term for every Internet crime imaginable. The next morning they were all forgotten.

CHAPTER 1

Motive

Have you ever seen a bank robbery? Before the Web, the chance that you would have seen an actual bank robbery was quite small. Today, though, if you have e-mail, it is almost certain that you have been targeted by bank robbers.

By the last count, I receive more than 2,500 criminal e-mails a day. These criminals want my money; they want your money. How are we going to stop them?

The first step toward finding an answer is to understand how the crimes work. Knowing how Internet crimes work will do little to reduce the number of victims: it will only take a little longer for the criminals to find them. It is, however, the best way to make sure *you* do not become the victim.

Internet crime is real. It's organized. Internet criminals have stolen hundreds of millions of dollars and caused billions of dollars' worth of damage. The number of attacks and their sophistication is on the rise, and this trend is expected to continue for the next several years.

In the early years of the Web, Internet crime was mostly the actions of teenage vandals looking for a way to pass time. Attempting to make money from hacking was considered too risky, too likely to attract the attention of the authorities. Today it's all about the money.

One consequence of this change is that Internet crime has become much easier to predict. Only the most obsessive vandal would attempt the same crime in the same way, again and again for long enough for investigators to build a profile. The professional criminal does not become bored so easily and will keep doing what he is doing until the act no longer makes money or he is caught.

The Internet criminal changes his tactics frequently. The techniques that Internet criminals used to perform bank fraud three years ago simply do not work today. The techniques they are using today are not likely to be as profitable or as safe in three years' time. But the goal of the professional Internet criminal remains the same—to take money from other people—and so do the three basic strategies that he uses to achieve this goal: extortion, impersonation, and persuasion.

- **Extortion**—Criminals have operated extortion rackets for millennia. The Internet is a major engine of the global economy. Many companies cannot carry out their business when their Web site is down. A criminal who can make a site unreachable may find businesses willing to pay for protection.
- **Impersonation**—The money that the criminals are after is mostly stored in banks. Taking the money from the bank directly is far beyond the capabilities of most Internet criminals. Instead, they attack the system at its weakest link: the customer. The customer has access to his bank account through the Web. All the attacker needs to do is to cause the customer to divulge his account name and password.
- **Persuasion**—The most pervasive type of Internet crime is the confidence trick. The larger the pool of potential victims that the attacker can reach, the less credible the story needs to be. The Internet allows a criminal to reach an audience of more than a billion.

Internet crime is a mile wide and an inch deep. What appears at first glance to be something new invariably turns out to be a new way to perform an old scam.

The Tools of the Trade

The tools of the Internet criminal are chosen for effectiveness rather than sophistication. The Internet allows the criminal to contact a vast audience of potential victims, to communicate in ways that are difficult to trace, and to collaborate with other criminals. Criminals have always done such things but on a smaller scale. The Internet gives the criminal enterprise global reach and the whole world to hide in.

The Internet also gives the criminal a new capability: the ability to spy on the activities of people who are not in their immediate vicinity by taking control of their computer.

Of Bots and Botnets

Traditional criminals use stolen cars as getaway vehicles. Cyber criminals cover their tracks using stolen machines but do one better—the real owner continues to pay for gas.

Many Internet users believe that they are not at risk from Internet crime because they have nothing of value on their computer. But the computer itself has a value to the Internet criminal. The thief can steal the use of the machine without taking the physical machine, but the owner continues to provide the necessary space, power, and network connectivity.

In hacker jargon, there are many names for a machine that has been taken over. News reports often use the terms **bot** or **zombie**; within the field, the term **owned machine** is sometimes used.

Control of one bot gives the criminal a getaway vehicle. Running an Internet crime from your own house using the network connection you (or your parents) pay for is risky. Channeling communications through a bot allows the Internet criminal to lay a false trail.

The sophisticated criminal hides his activities through a constantly changing series of machines carefully chosen so that the trail passes through as many jurisdictions as possible.

Bots are also used to perform the crime itself. A bot can be used to attack other machines, to send spam, and to create other bots, forming a **botnet**. The more bots an Internet criminal controls, the more crime he can perform. Most worrying of all, perhaps, a bot can spy on the owner of the machine and watch as he logs in to his online bank or enters his credit card number.

Some years ago, taking over (**cracking**) machines was a bespoke industry. The attacker would select a machine and work on ways to break into it until something worked or he decided to give up and move to another target. Today it is easy to obtain hacking tools that probe thousands of machines at a time.

Botnet management has become a commodity, a low-skill, low-return Internet crime. Skilled professional criminals often prefer to "rent" the use of bots. A bot is priced on the black market according to the utility to the criminal: the speed of the Internet connection, the speed of the processor, and whether the network management is likely to shut it down quickly.

An attacker can gain control of a machine in much the same way that an army can capture a walled city: by direct assault or by subterfuge.

A direct assault requires the attacker to find an exploitable vulnerability in the defenses of the machine. Computers have no common sense; they just follow instructions. If a program is written properly, the only instructions that the computer will execute are the ones the programmer writes. If a program has a specific type of programming error, the computer might end up executing instructions that an attacker supplies.

A direct assault is unlikely to compromise a "securely" configured machine with every nonessential service turned off and every security fix installed. With a billion users and a billion-plus machines, there will never be a shortage of vulnerable targets.

Every machine that is connected to a network and has some form of processing capacity is a potential point of compromise: every router, every wireless gateway, every cable modem, every printer.

The vandals competed to crack the machine in the most ingenious ways they could. The professional Internet criminal is only interested in results and accordingly attacks the system at its weakest link: the user. Why bother working out how to bypass the computer defenses when the user can run any program you want? All you need to do is to persuade him to run it.

A program that has a hidden malicious purpose is called a **Trojan** after the Trojan horse of Greek legend. Mistaking the horse for a parting gift, the Trojans wheeled it into their city and left it unguarded while they went off for a feast. During the celebrations, the soldiers hidden inside the horse quietly slipped out and opened the city gates to let the waiting Greek army through.

Computer Trojans work in the same way. The user thinks that he is doing something harmless while the Trojan takes over his machine.

Five years ago, a Trojan attack could be neatly classified as a **virus, worm,** or **spyware.** But the changing tactics of the criminals have rendered the distinction obsolete. The terms **malware** and even **crimeware** have been introduced in an attempt to keep pace.

A true computer "virus" spreads from one infected machine to another as a biological virus does. Today the analogy is obsolete. Instead of waiting for their creations to spread gradually from one machine to another, the criminals pump out Trojan-bearing e-mails from a botnet.

Equally obsolete are the tools based on the assumption that the criminals will continue to respect these distinctions.

By the time the "virus" has been detected and analyzed, and "antivirus" signatures have been distributed, the attack will already have reached tens or hundreds of millions of machines, and the attacker will be busy creating his next attack.

When spyware first began to appear as a significant concern for computer owners, it was mostly ignored by the suppliers of "antivirus" software. It took a new group of vendors offering antispyware solutions for the antivirus vendors to realize that their customers expected to be protected from all forms of harm regardless of cause.

PREFACE

You may or may not have an inkling of what insecure software is, how it impacts your life, or why you should be concerned. That is OK. This book attempts to introduce you to the full scope and consequence of software's impact on modern society without baffling the reader with jargon only experts understand or minutia only experts care about. The prerequisite for this book is merely a hint of curiosity.

Although we interact with software on a daily basis, carry it on our mobile phones, drive with it in our cars, fly with it in our planes, and use it in our home and business computers, software itself remains essentially shrouded—a ghost in the machine; a mystery that functions but only part of the time. And therein lies our problem.

Software is the stuff of modern infrastructure. Not only is software infused into a growing number of commercial products we purchase and services we use, but government increasingly uses software to manage the details of our lives, to allocate benefits and public services we enjoy as citizens, and to administer and defend the state as a whole. How and when we touch software and how and when it touches us is less our choice every day. The quality of this software matters greatly; the level of protection this software affords us from harm and exploitation matters even more.

As a case in point, in mid-2007 the country of Estonia, dubbed "the most wired nation in Europe" because of its pervasive use of computer networks for a wide array of private and public activities, had a significant portion of its national infrastructure crippled for more than two weeks by cyber attacks launched from hundreds of thousands of individual computers that had been previously hijacked by Russian hackers. Estonia was so overwhelmed by the attacks that Estonian leaders literally severed the country's connection to the Internet and with it the country's economic and communications lifeline to the rest of the world. As one Estonian official lamented, "We are back to the stone age...." The reason for the cyber attack? The Russian government objected to Estonia's removal of a Soviet-era war memorial from the center of its capital, Tallinn, to a military cemetery.

The hundreds of thousands of individual computers that took part in the attack belonged to innocents: businesses, governments, and home users located around the world unaware their computers were used as weapons against another nation and another people. Such widespread hijacking was made possible in large part because of insecure software—software that contains manufacturing defects allowing, among other things, hackers to hijack and remotely control computer systems. Traditional defensive measures employed by software buyers such as firewalls, anti-virus, and software patches did little to help Estonia and nothing to correct software manufacturing practices that enabled the attacks in the first place.

During the same year, an experienced "security researcher" (a euphemism for a hacker) from IBM's Internet Security Systems was able to remotely break into and hijack computer systems controlling a nuclear power plant in the United States. The plant's owners claimed their computer systems could not be accessed from the Internet. The owners were mistaken. As the security researcher later stated after completing the exercise, "It turned out to be the easiest penetration test I'd ever done. By the first day, we had penetrated the network. Within a week, we were controlling a nuclear power plant. I thought, 'Gosh, this is a big problem.'"

Indeed it is.

According to IDC, a global market intelligence firm, 75 percent of computers having access to the Internet have been infected and are actively being used without the owner's knowledge to conduct cyber attacks, distribute unwanted email (spam), and support criminal and terrorist activities. To solely blame hackers or hundreds of thousands of innocent computer users, or misinformed—and some might say "sloppy"—power plant owners for the deplorable state of cyber security is shortsighted and distracts from the deeper issue. The proverbial butterfly that flaps its wings in Brazil causing a storm somewhere far away is no match for the consequences brought about by seemingly innocuous foibles of software manufacturers. As one analyst commented regarding insecure software as it related to hijacking of the nuclear reactor's computer systems, "These are simple bugs [mistakes in software], but very dangerous ones."

The story of Estonia, the nuclear reactor, and thousands of similar news stories merely hint at the underlying problem of modern infrastructure. The "big problem" is insecure software and insecure software is *everywhere*. From our iPhones (which had a critical weakness in its software discovered merely two weeks after its release) to our laptops, from the XBOX to public utilities, from home computers to financial systems, insecure software is interconnected and woven more tightly into the fabric of civilization with each passing day and with it, as former U.S. Secretary of Defense William Cohen observed, an unprecedented level of vulnerability. Insecure software is making us fragile, vulnerable, and weak. It is difficult to overstate the seriousness of the situation.

The threat of global warming might be on everyone's lips, and the polar ice caps might indeed melt but not for a time. What is happening *right now* because of world-wide interconnection of insecure software gives social problems once limited by geography a new destructive range. Cyber criminals, terrorists, and even nation states are currently preying on millions upon millions of computer systems (and their owners) and using the proceeds to underwrite further crime, economic espionage, warfare, and terror. We are only now beginning to realize the enormity of the storm set upon us by the tiny fluttering of software manufacturing mistakes and the economic and social costs such mistakes impose. In 2007, "bad" software cost the United States roughly $180 billion; this amount represents nearly 40 percent of the U.S. military defense budget for the same year ($439 billion) or nearly 55 percent *more* than the estimated cost to the U.S. economy of Hurricane Katrina ($100 billion), the costliest storm to hit the United States since Hurricane Andrew.[1] Disturbingly, $180 billion may be an exceptionally low estimate.

Since the 1960s, individuals both within and outside the software community have worked hard to improve the quality, reliability, and security of software. Smart people have been looking out for you. For this, they should be commended. But the results of their efforts are mixed.

After 40 years of collaborative effort with software manufacturers to improve software quality, reliability, and security, Carnegie Mellon's Software Engineering Institute (SEI)—an important contributor to software research and improvement—declared in the year 2000 that software was getting worse, not better. Such an announcement by SEI is tantamount to the U.S. Food and Drug Administration warning that food quality in the twenty-first century is poorer now than when Upton Sinclair wrote *The Jungle* in 1906.[2] Unlike progress in a vast majority of areas related to consumer protection and national security, progress against "bad" software has been fitful at best.

While technical complications in software manufacturing might be in part to blame for the sorry state of software, this book argues that even if effective technical solutions were widely available, market incentives do not work for, but *work against* better, more secure software. This has worrisome consequences for us all.

Incentives matter. Human beings are notoriously complex and fickle creatures who will do whatever it takes to make themselves better off. There is nothing intrinsically wrong with this behavior. Acting in one's best interests is what normal, rational human beings do. However, the complications arise because society is a morass of competing, misaligned, and conflicting incentives that lead to all manner of situations where one individual's behavior may adversely affect another. Nowhere is this more easily observed than how individuals conduct their everyday lives within free market economies. As such, *Geekonomics* is the story of software told through the lens of humanity and economics, rather than the lens of technology.

To see and to understand insecure software merely as a technical phenomenon to be solved by other technical phenomena is to be distracted from the larger issue. Software is a human creation and it need not be mysterious or magical. It also need not make us fragile, vulnerable, and weak. To understand software and its implications for society requires an understanding of how humans behave, not necessarily how software behaves. More specifically, this book looks at the array of incentives that compel people to manufacture, buy, and exploit insecure software. In short, incentives matter for any human endeavor and without understanding the incentives that drive people toward or away from a particular behavior, all the potential technical solutions that *might* help address the problem of insecure software will sit idle, or worse, never be created at all. After 40 years of effort with debatable improvement, this much is evident.

As with any complex issue, and especially with a complex issue such as software manufacturing, there are few "right" answers regarding how to fix the problem. However, there are ways of approaching complex issues more fruitful than others that are worth investigating. Protecting economic and national security from the effects of insecure software is as much an economic issue as it is a technological issue. We know software is as notoriously complex and fickle as the humans that create it, if not more so. But as a human creation, we need not understand insecure software in its entirety; we need merely to get humans to stop creating the stuff. And this is where incentives come in.

At base, economics teaches us, at least in part, how to get incentives right. Of course, economists are not always right when it comes to forecasting the expected effects of a particular incentive, but economics allows us to approach complex issues from a scientific perspective and make reasonable, better-informed decisions. By using and analyzing data—even imperfect data—economics allows us to view the world as it is, look back as it was, and to anticipate how it might be. Incentives help navigate the path to a desired future. The desired future of this author is a stable, secure, global infrastructure that propels humanity beyond its wildest dreams.

There are three primary themes in *Geekonomics*:

- First, software is becoming the foundation of modern civilization; software constitutes or will control the products, services, and infrastructure people will rely on for a wide variety of daily activities from the vital to the trivial.
- Second, software is not sufficiently engineered at this time to fulfill the role of "foundation." The information infrastructure is the only part of national infrastructure that is destructively tested while in use; that is, software is shipped containing both known and unknown weaknesses that software buyers are made aware of and must fix only *after* installation (or after losing control of your nuclear power plant). The consequences are already becoming apparent and augur ill for us all.
- Third, important economic, legal, and regulatory incentives that could improve software quality, reliability, and security are not only missing, but the market incentives that do exist are perverted, ineffectual, or distorted. Change the incentives and the story and effects of insecure software change also.

Because of the complexity of software itself and the complexity of manufacturing software, no single discipline, even one as powerful as economics, is sufficient for holistically addressing the topic at hand. As such, this book also contains a splash of psychology, physics, engineering, philosophy, and criminology that are mostly framed within the context of incentives. This book does not contain the complete story of insecure software, only those parts that a single author can realistically include in a book meant to inform, entertain, and enlighten.

I *like* software. I really do. Though the tone of my writing is often forceful and urgent regarding insecure software in general and software manufacturers in particular, I truly appreciate all the things I can do with software that I could not possibly do as quickly, efficiently, or cheaply without it. Writing this book was infinitely easier using a word processor than with a traditional typewriter (I haven't owned one of those for 20 years). But everything has a cost and not all costs are readily apparent at the time of acquisition. I had no less than three separate storage locations (laptop hard drive, USB key, network storage) for this book's manuscript just in case something should happen, which it inevitably did. My word processor application (which will remain nameless) crashed or froze roughly 40 times in the course of writing this book. Without software this book might not have been written as quickly compared to older methods. That is not in question. Without reliable backups, however, this book would not have been written at all.

Ironically, in writing this book I attempted to avoid providing a litany of software disasters in hopes of escaping claims that I might be promoting "fear, uncertainty, and doubt," a claim that so often pollutes and plagues discussions regarding software security; yet, many of my non-expert reviewers (the non-expert is this book's target audience) thought I was being unfair to software manufacturers because I did not provide the necessary probative evidence to establish why software manufacturers are partly to blame for threatening the foundation of civilization. "What was needed?" I asked. A litany of software disasters would be helpful, came the reply. And so my hope is that the litany of disasters provided in this book are seen as necessary to provide context and perspective for those unfamiliar with the subject and impact of insecure software, rather than the primary focus of the book.

CHAPTER 1

The Foundation of Civilization

"The value of a thing sometimes lies not in what one attains with it, but in what one pays for it—what it costs us."

—Frederick Nietzsche

For the city of London, 1854 was a dreadful year. An outbreak of cholera, the third in 20 years, claimed over ten thousand lives. Six previous city Commissions failed to adequately address London's growing sewage problem, leaving the entire metropolitan area—more than one million people—subject to the vagaries of overflowing cesspools, ill-constructed sewers, contaminated groundwater, and a dangerously polluted Thames River. Considering London was one of the most populated cities at the time and depended heavily on the Thames River, inaction had unfortunate consequences. Sadly, thousands of deaths could not properly motivate Parliament to overcome numerous bureaucratic and political obstacles required to address the crisis.

It was not until an inordinately hot summer in 1858 that the stench of the Thames so overwhelmed all those in close proximity to the river—particularly members of Parliament, many of whom still believed cholera to be an airborne rather than a waterborne pathogen—that resistance finally subsided. The "Great Stink" served as impetus to the largest civic works project London had ever seen.[1]

For the next ten years, Joseph Bazalgette, Chief Engineer of the Metropolitan Board of Works, constructed London's newer and larger sewer network against imposing odds. Despite Parliament's hard-won support and a remarkable design by Bazalgette himself, building a new sewer network in an active and sprawling city raised significant technical and engineering challenges.

Most obvious among these challenges was excavating sewer lines while minimizing disruption to local businesses and the city's necessary daily activities. Less obvious, but no less important, was selecting contracting methods and building materials for such an enormous project. Modern public works projects such as the California Aqueduct, the U.S. Interstate highway system, or China's Three Gorges Dam elicit images of enormous quantities of coordination and concrete. Initially, Bazalgette enjoyed neither.

Selecting suitable building materials was an especially important engineering decision, one that Bazalgette did not take lightly. Building materials needed to bear considerable strain from overhead traffic and buildings as well as survive prolonged exposure to and immersion in water. Traditionally, engineers at the time would have selected Roman cement, a common and inexpensive material used since the fourteenth century, to construct the extensive underground brickworks required for the new sewer system. Roman cement gets its name from Romans who used it in a vast majority of infrastructure for both the Republic and Empire. The "recipe" for Roman cement was lost during the Dark Ages only to be rediscovered during the Renaissance. This bit of history aside, Bazalgette chose to avoid Roman cement for laying the sewer's brickwork and instead opted in favor of a newer, stronger, but more expensive type of cement called Portland cement.

Portland cement was invented in the kitchen of a British bricklayer named Joseph Aspdin in 1824. What Aspdin discovered during his experimentation that the Romans did not (or were not aware of) was that by first heating some of the ingredients of cement—finely ground limestone and clay—the silica in the clay bonded with the calcium in the limestone, creating a far more durable concrete, one that chemically interacted with any aggregates such as stone or sand added to the cement mixture. Roman cement, in comparison, does not chemically interact with aggregates and therefore simply holds them in suspension. This makes Roman cement weaker in comparison to Portland cement but only in relative, not absolute terms. Many substantial Roman structures including roadways, buildings, and seaports survived nearly 2,000 years to the present.

It is the chemical reaction discovered by Aspdin that gives Portland cement its amazing durability and strength over Roman cement. This chemical reaction also gives Portland cement the interesting characteristic of gaining in strength with both age and immersion in water.[2] If traditional cement sets in one day, Portland cement will be more than four times as hard after a week and over eight times as hard in five years.[3] In choosing a material for such a massive and important project as the London sewer, Portland cement might have rightly appeared to Bazalgette as the obvious choice. There was only one problem: Portland cement is unreliable if the production process varies even slightly.

Portland cement might have rightly appeared to Bazalgette as the obvious choice. There was only one problem: Portland cement is unreliable if the production process varies even slightly.

The strength and therefore the reliability of Portland cement is significantly diminished by what would appear to the average observer as minuscule, almost trivial changes in mixture ratios, kiln temperature, or grinding process. In the mid-nineteenth century, quality control processes were largely nonexistent, and where they did exist were inconsistently employed—based more on personal opinion rather than objective criteria. The "state of the art" in nineteenth century quality control meant that while Portland cement was promising, it was a risky choice on the part of Bazalgette. To mitigate any inconsistencies in producing Portland cement for the sewer project, Bazalgette created rigorous, objective, and some would say draconian testing procedures to ensure each batch of Portland cement afforded the necessary resiliency and strength. His reputation as an engineer and the success of the project depended on it.

Bazalgette enforced the following regimen: Delivered cement sat at the construction site for at least three weeks to acclimate to local environmental conditions. After the elapsed time, samples were taken from every tenth sack and made into molds that were immediately dropped into water where the concrete would remain for seven days. Afterward, samples were tested for strength. If any sample failed to bear weight of at least five hundred pounds (more than twice that of Roman cement), the entire delivery was rejected.[4] By 1865, more than 11,587 tests were conducted on 70,000 tons of cement for the southern section of the sewerage alone.[5] Bazalgette's testing methodology proved so thorough, the Metropolitan Board who oversaw the project eventually agreed to Bazalgette's request to construct sewers entirely from concrete. This not only decreased the time required to construct the sewerage, but eliminated the considerable associated cost of the brickworks themselves.[6]

Once completed, Bazalgette's sewer system saved hundreds of thousands of lives by preventing future cholera and typhoid epidemics.[7] The sewer system also made the Thames one of the cleanest metropolitan rivers in the world and changed the face of river-side London forever. By 1872, the Registrar-General's Annual Report stated that the annual death rate in London was far below any other major European, American, or Indian city, and at 3.3 million people (almost three times the population from the time Bazalgette started his project), London was by far the largest city in the world. This state of affairs was unprecedented for the time. By 1896 cholera was so rare in London, the Registrar-General classified cholera as an "exotic disease." Bazalgette's sewer network, as well as the original cement used in its construction, remains in use to this day. Given that Portland cement increases with strength over time, it is likely London's sewer system will outlive even some of Rome's longest standing architectural accomplishments such as the aqueducts and the Pantheon.

Software and Cement

While Bazalgette's design of the sewer network was certainly important, in hindsight the selection and qualification of Portland cement was arguably the most critical aspect to the project's success. Had Bazalgette not enforced strict quality control on production of Portland cement, the outcome of the "Great Stink of London" might have been far different. Due to Bazalgette's efforts and the resounding success of the London sewer system, Portland cement progressed in a few short years from "promising but risky" to the industry standard used in just about every major construction project from that time onward.

Portland cement's popularity then, is due not just to its physical properties, but in large part to Bazalgette's strict and rigorous quality tests, which drastically reduced potential uncertainties associated with Portland cement's production. At present, more than 20 separate tests are used to ensure the quality of Portland cement, significantly more than Bazalgette himself employed. World production of Portland cement exceeded two billion metric tons in 2005, with China accounting for nearly half of that production followed closely by India and the United States.[8] This works out to roughly 2.5 tons of cement for every person on the planet. Without Portland cement, much of modern civilization as we know it, see it, live on it, and drive on it would fail to exist.

Cement is everywhere in modern civilization. Mixed with aggregates such as sand and stone, it forms concrete that comprises roadways, bridges, tunnels, building foundations, walls, floors, airports, docks, dams, aqueducts, pipes, and the list goes on. Cement is—quite literally—the foundation of modern civilization, creating the infrastructure that supports billions of lives around the globe. One cannot live in modern civilization without touching, seeing, or relying on cement in one way or another. Our very lives depend on cement, yet cement has proven so reliable due to strict quality controls that it has to a large extent disappeared from our field of concerns—even though we are surrounded by it. Such is the legacy of Bazalgette's commitment to quality: We can live our lives without thinking twice about what is beneath our feet, or more importantly, what may be above our head.

Civilization depends on infrastructure, and infrastructure depends, at least in part, on durable, reliable cement. Due to its versatility, cost-effectiveness, and broad availability, cement has provided options in construction that could not otherwise be attained with stone, wood, or steel alone. But since the 1950s, a new material has been slowly and unrelentingly injected into modern infrastructure, one that is far more versatile, cost-effective, and widely available than cement could ever hope to be. It also just so happens to be invisible and unvisualizable. In fact, it is not a material at all. It is software.

Like cement, software is everywhere in modern civilization. Software is in your mobile phone, on your home computer, in cars, airplanes, hospitals, businesses, public utilities, financial systems, and national defense systems. Software is an increasingly critical component in the operation of infrastructures, cutting across almost every aspect of global, national, social, and economic function. One cannot live in modern civilization without touching, being touched by, or depending on software in one way or another.

> *Like cement, software is everywhere in modern civilization.*

Software helps deliver oil to our cities, electricity to our homes, water to our crops, products to our markets, money to our banks, and information to our minds. It allows us to share pictures, music, thoughts, and ideas with people we might meet infrequently in person but will intimately know from a distance. Everything is becoming "smarter" because software is being injected into just about *every thing*. Software has accelerated economic growth through the increased facilities of managing labor and capital with unprecedented capacity. Hundreds of thousands of people if not millions owe their livelihoods to software. With its aid, we have discovered new medicines, new oil fields, and new planets and it has given us new ways of visualizing old problems, thereby finding solutions we might never have had the capacity, time, or ability to discover without it. With software we are able to build bridges once thought impossible, create buildings once thought unrealistic, and explore regions of earth, space, and self once thought unreachable.

Software has also given us the Internet, a massive world-wide network connecting all to all. In fact, connectedness in the twenty-first century is primarily a manifestation of software. Software handles the protocols necessary for communication, operates telecommunications equipment, bundles data for transmission, and routes messages to far-flung destinations as well as giving function and feature to a dizzying array of devices. Software helps connect everything to everything else with the network—the Internet—merely a by-product of its function. Without software, the network would be just a bunch of cables, just as a human cell without DNA would be just a bunch of amino acids and proteins.

Software is *everywhere*; it is everywhere because software is the closest thing we have to a universal tool. It exhibits a radical malleability that allows us to do with it what we will. Software itself is nothing more than a set of commands that tells a computer processor (a microchip) what to do. Connect a microchip to a toy, and the toy becomes "smart;" connect a microchip to a car's fuel injector, and the car becomes more fuel efficient; connect it to a phone, and the phone becomes indispensable in life's everyday affairs. Connect a microchip to just about anything, and just about anything is possible because the software makes it so. Software is the ghost in the machine, the DNA of technology; it is what gives *things* the appearance of intelligence when none can possibly exist.

The only aspect of software more impressive than software itself is the people that create software. Computer programmers, also known as software developers or software engineers, write the instructions that tell computers what to do. Software developers are in large part a collection of extremely talented and gifted individuals whose capacity to envision and implement algorithms of extraordinary complexity and elegance gives us search engines, operating systems, word processors, instant messaging, mobile networks, satellite navigation, smart cars, advanced medical imaging; the list goes on. As such, software is a human creation, and as a human creation it is subject to the strengths and foibles of humanity. This is where the similarities of cement and software become most interesting.

Software, like cement before it, is becoming the foundation of civilization. Our very lives are becoming more dependent on and subject to software. As such, the properties of software matter greatly: quality, reliability, security, each by themselves accomplish very little, but their absence faults everything else. Like Portland cement, software can be unreliable if production processes vary even slightly. Whereas variations in kiln temperatures, mixture ratios, or grinding processes can detrimentally affect the strength and durability of Portland cement after it has been poured, there are a host of similar, seemingly trivial variations in producing software that can detrimentally affect its "strength" when "poured" into microchips. It is up to humans to get the production process right.

Unlike Portland cement, for more than 50 years software of all types and function has been continuously released into the stream of commerce plagued by design and implementation defects that were largely detectable and preventable by manufacturers, but were not. This has and does result in catastrophic accidents, significant financial losses, and even death. The trepidation over insufficient software manufacturing practices extends back to the late 1960s when the North American Treaty Organization (NATO) convened a panel of 50 experts to address the "software crisis." While the panel did not provide any direct solutions, the concept of a "software engineer" was developed as a means to more closely align software manufacturing with the engineering discipline rather than artistic creativity. The intent, as far as we can tell, was to remove the "rule of thumb" in the production of software and all the inconsistencies such approximation introduces. After 50 years, defining what actually constitutes the principles and practice of software engineering has not progressed far. What is clear, however, is that the unfortunate history of software blunders sullies the reputation of software in general and distorts the genius of software developers in particular.

What is clear, however, is that the unfortunate history of software blunders sullies the reputation of software in general and distorts the genius of software developers in particular.

Perhaps most frustrating is the inconsistent use of quality control measures by such a wide range of software manufacturers for such an extended period of time. Software is infinitely more complex than cement to be sure, but complexity does not entirely account for systemic, reoccurring software manufacturing defects. Quality control measures—even in the absence of a clear definition for software engineering—have been and are available specifically to address problems with software production.

Software has its own modern-day equivalent of Joseph Bazalgette: his name is Watts Humphrey. Humphrey is a fellow and research scientist at Carnegie Mellon University's Software Engineering Institute (SEI) and is often called the "father of software quality" having developed numerous methodologies since the 1980s for designing quality and reliability into software products. In 2005, President George W. Bush awarded Mr. Humphrey the National Medal of Technology, the highest honor for innovation in the United States. The only problem in this story is that a significant portion of software manufacturers around the world still largely ignore or only superficially implement Humphrey's guidance. As a result, the Software Engineering Institute noted at the beginning of the twenty-first century that software was getting worse, not better. Such a proclamation augurs ill for civilization's newest foundation.

But if software quality were the only issue, perhaps we could discount the problem of low-quality software simply on the basis of "growing pains." After all, at 50 years old, some might argue software is still a relatively new phenomenon and that such failures in quality are understandable and even tolerable for such a young technology. When civil engineering was 50 years old, for instance, the brick had not even been invented yet.[9]

Yet when civil engineering was 50 years old, the profession was not building and connecting global infrastructure. Software's newness has not precluded it from being injected into nearly every aspect of modern civilization. That software connects everything to everything else magnifies even the smallest foibles in software production. This introduces a critical aspect of software vastly different from weaknesses in traditional building materials: once interconnected, even the smallest piece of insecure software may have global consequences. New or not, software needs to be worthy of its place.

Weaknesses or defects in software can not only result in a given software application failing for one reason or another (including no reason), but software defects can potentially be exploited by hackers, who, discovering or knowing the weakness exists, may use it to surreptitiously access and control a system from a continent away, stealing sensitive personal information such as credit cards or social security numbers or absconding with trade secrets or intellectual property. Such weaknesses could also be used to hijack computer systems and then turn those systems against their owners or against other nations and other peoples. In the end, insecure software is *right now* resulting in economic and social costs that are now well into billions of dollars per year with no sign of abatement. The trend is disturbing.

Understanding why this situation persists and seems to be only getting worse has important implications for modern civilization. In other words, new or not, society inevitably demands any technology used in the foundation of civilization, whether cement or software, should be given the time and attention foundations deserve. Bazalgette and his legacy expected no less; nor should we.

In the Shadow of Utility

The litany of documented software failures is extensive and tragic.[10] It does not take much effort to find examples of software failures resulting in loss of life, limb, money, time, or property. The trend only promises to become worse as software becomes more critical to almost every aspect of modern life; yet, software manufacturers enjoy an astonishing amount of insulation from government oversight, legal liability, consumer retaliation, and indeed, as some critics have observed, engineering skill. A proven record of significant, costly, and deadly failures with no significant decline in use by its victims is baffling. On top of—in fact, despite—these shortcomings, victims (consumers, corporations, and governments included) lavishly spend on acquiring and defending a clearly defective product. Why?

Software manufacturers enjoy an astonishing amount of insulation from government oversight, legal liability, consumer retaliation, and indeed, as some critics have observed, engineering skill.

Why do software manufacturers continue to produce and consumers continue to purchase unreliable and insecure software?

Why do software users willingly and repeatedly accept licensing terms that absolve software manufacturers of most forms of liability for any design or implementation defects that might result in injury, harm, or damages?

Why do governments make so few demands on software manufacturers while placing onerous compliance requirements on software buyers, who are least qualified to address the problems associated with software manufacturing?

Why should software not be subject to the same public policy concerns applied to other critical elements of national infrastructure?

Why do chickens cross the road?

Each of these questions is answered in part by this simple response: *to maximize utility*. We all do things that might appear perfectly acceptable in our own eyes that might appear perfectly crazy to someone else. A chicken crossing the road in the presence of drivers who may be willing to flatten the poor thing simply to interrupt the monotony of driving might appear rather crazy to an outside observer. In fact, from an economist's perspective, this is perfectly rational behavior on the part of the chicken so long as the chicken believes it will be better off for the crossing. Jumping out of an airplane with a parachute might seem perfectly crazy to observers, unless the skydiver believes they are better off for the jumping. Likewise, software buyers continuing to accept software licensing terms that put them at a distinct disadvantage legally, financially, or personally should the software fail might appear perfectly baffling, unless buyers believe they will be better off for the accepting.

Economists use the notion of *utility* to help explain why people behave the way they do. The concept of utility is a little like the concept of "happiness" only more general. I explain the concept of utility in more detail in Chapter 2, "Six Billion Crash Test Dummies," but sufficed to say, utility centers around the notion that most of us want to make our lives better, and that many of our life decisions are probably based on this desire. Software inarguably makes our life better, but like crossing the road or jumping out of an airplane or owning a swimming pool, everything has a cost.

It is not always the utility we get out of something or some activity that matters most, but how much it potentially costs us. Costs are not always obvious to the individual at "time of purchase" so to speak, and can be hidden or otherwise obscured. In general, cost can be measured in private terms, what it directly costs an individual to behave in a certain way, or measured in social costs, what it costs society for an individual to undertake a certain activity. The balance of private and social costs is the focus of many public policy efforts.

The private cost of smoking, for instance, is relatively low monetarily from an individual's view point, but can impose substantial social costs due to the prolonged medical services associated with caring for long-term chronic smokers. Imposing a cigarette tax is but one way to raise the private cost of an activity in order to deter the behavior, which thereby potentially reduces the social cost by reducing the total number of smokers in the population and how much they smoke.

People's evaluation of utility versus cost can lead to some fairly interesting situations. As a case in point, in the United States swimming pools kill or injure more children under the age of 14 than firearms. At 16 percent, accidental drowning was the second leading cause of injury-related death of children aged 14 and under in 2004 (car accidents ranked first); compare this with only 1 percent of children that died due to accidental discharge of firearms.[11] In fact, injury-related death due to accidental discharge of firearms ranks at the bottom of all other causes of death and injury among children including choking (17 percent), fire and burns (10 percent), and bicycle accidents, poisoning, and falls (each at 2 percent).

There are plenty of people, and parents in particular, who might forbid children playing at the home of a neighbor who possesses one or more firearms, but the likelihood of a child drowning at a neighborhood pool party is far higher than a child being injured or killed by the firearm of a neighbor. Yet few parents espouse an anti-swimming pool sentiment or join anti-swimming pool action groups as they would for firearms, even though statistics would certainly warrant such behavior. The rather simplistic answer to this incongruency is that a larger portion of the population sees the intrinsic utility of a swimming pool over and above the utility of possessing a hand gun. Yet a swimming pool incurs a much higher cost to both families and society than do firearms. Even things with obvious utility like a swimming pool can have a dark shadow.

Played out against this background of people's desire for utility (and not always recognizing the real cost), is the story of software. The questions at the start of this section really touch on the issues of self-interest and, more importantly, the incentives we have as individuals to undertake certain activities and the utility we derive. Understanding incentives also gives us a possible foundation to address the issues of why software manufacturing seems to be in the state it is in. If it is up to humans to get the production processes for Portland cement and software correct, then it is just as important, if not more so, to understand why humans behave as they do. Incentives are a good place to start.

As such, *Geekonomics* is not so much the story of software told through the lens of technology, but through the lens of humanity, specifically the incentives for manufacturing, buying, and exploiting insecure software. Economics is simply one way of understanding why humans behave as they do. But if economics is generally described as "the dismal science," then software engineering is economics' freakish, serotonin-deprived cousin. Economics is positively cheery and approachable in comparison. To date, the discussion regarding software has been largely dominated by technology experts whose explanations largely serve to alienate the very people that are touched most by software. *Us*.

Yet the congress of these two disciplines tells an important and consequential story affecting both the reader's everyday life and the welfare of the global community. The issue of insecure software is at least as much about economics as it is about technology. And so I discuss both in this book. This book is not intended to be a comprehensive economics text, a litany of software failures (although this is sometimes inevitable), a diatribe as to how the world is coming apart at the seams, or a prophecy that civilization's ultimate demise will occur because of "bad" software. Prophesizing disaster is cliché. Bad things happen all the time, and forecasting tragic events does not require an exceptional amount of talent, intelligence, or foresight. If anything, the world tolerates disaster and somehow still makes progress. This does not mean valid threats to economic and national stability due to "bad" software are illusory or should be minimized. On the contrary, the story of insecure software has not been readily approachable and therefore not well understood. We cannot manage what we do not understand, including ourselves. Software is a ghost in the machine and, at times, frustratingly so. But as software is a human creation, it does not need to remain a frustrating ghost.

My intent in this book is to give this story—the story of insecure software—a suitable voice so that readers from any walk of life can understand the implications. I promise the reader that there is not a single graph in this book; nor is there a single snippet of code. This story should be accessible to more than the experts because it is we who create this story and are touched by it daily. The consequences are too great and far-reaching for the average person to remain unaware.

The first task of *Geekonomics*, then, is to address the questions presented at the beginning of this section as completely as possible within the confines of a single book. This means some aspects may be incomplete or not as complete as some readers might prefer. However, if anything, the story of software can be entertaining, and this book is intended to do that as well as inform and enlighten.

The second and more difficult task of *Geekonomics* is to analyze what the real cost of insecure software might be. Swimming pools can have a high cost, but how costly is insecure software, really? This is a challenging task considering that unlike statistics regarding accidental drowning, good data on which to base cost estimates regarding insecure software is notoriously lacking and inaccurate for three reasons. First, there is presumed to be a significant amount of underreporting given that many organizations might not realize they have been hacked or do not want to publicly share such information for fear of consumer retaliation or bad publicity. Second, actual costs tend to be distorted based on the incentives of those reporting their losses. For some victims, they may tend to inflate losses in an effort to increase their chances of recovering damages in court. Other groups of victims might deflate costs in an effort to quell any uprisings on the part of customers or shareholders. Law enforcement and cyber security companies can tend to inflate numbers in an effort to gain more funding or more clients, respectively. Whatever the incentives might be for reporting high or low, somewhere within these numbers is a hint to what is actually going on. Finally, the real cost of something might not be measured in money alone.

The third and final task of *Geekonomics* is to identify current incentives of market participants and what new incentives might be necessary to change status quo. One alternative is always choosing to do nothing; simply let things work themselves out on their own, or more accurately, let the market determine what should be done. This book argues against such action. Any intervention into a market carries with it the risk of shock, and doing nothing is certainly one way of avoiding such risk. But intervention is necessary when a condition is likely to degenerate if nothing is done. The magnitude of the risk is great enough and the signs of degeneration clear enough that new and different incentives are needed to motivate software manufacturers to produce and software buyers to demand safer, higher quality, and more secure software.

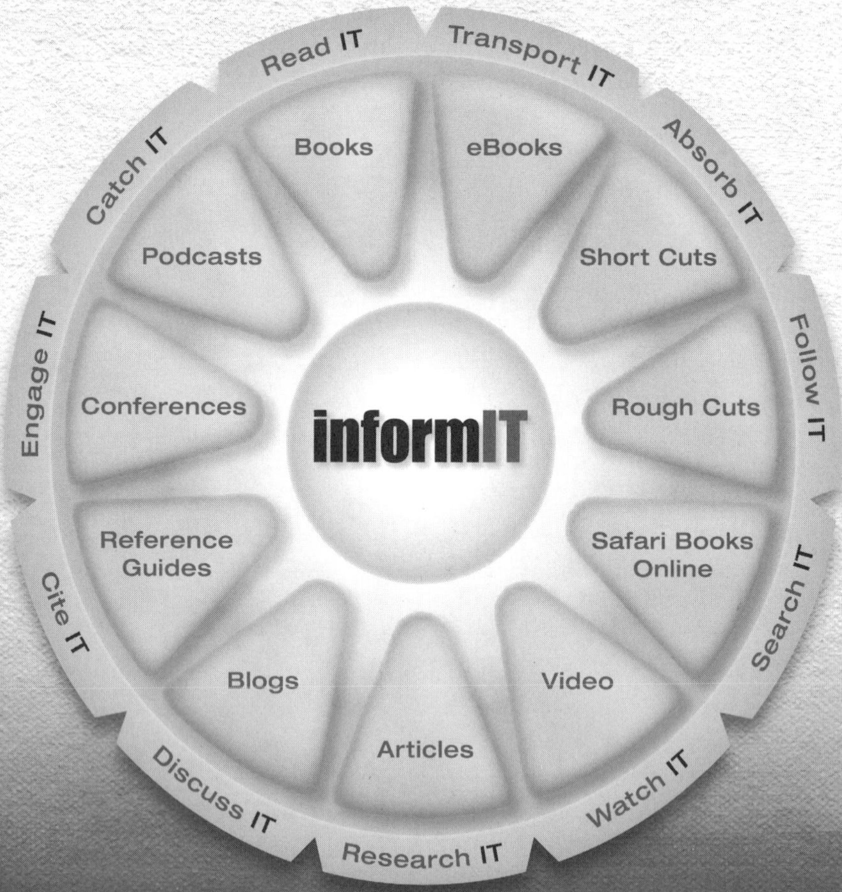